Catholic *[illegible]*
Room 204

S. M. Lucas, C.PP.S.

# Freedom, Bureaucracy, & Schooling

Prepared by the ASCD
1971 Yearbook Committee
VERNON F. HAUBRICH
Chairman and Editor

Association for Supervision and Curriculum Development, NEA
1201 Sixteenth Street, N.W.   Washington, D.C. 20036

Copyright © 1971 by the
Association for Supervision and Curriculum Development, NEA

*All rights reserved. No part of this publication may be reproduced or transmitted in any form or by any means, electronic or mechanical, including photocopy, recording, or any information storage and retrieval system, without permission in writing from the publisher.*

Price: $6.50
NEA Stock Number: 610-17508

The materials printed herein are the expressions of the writers and not a statement of policy of the Association unless set by resolution.

Library of Congress Catalog Card Number: 44-6213

# Contents

| | | |
|---|---|---|
| | Foreword<br>    John D. Greene | v |
| | Introduction<br>    Vernon F. Haubrich | vii |
| | *Part One* **Definitions and Limitations** | 1 |
| 1 | Freedom and Bureaucracy in the Schools<br>    Donald Arnstine | 3 |
| 2 | Schools as a "Guidable" System<br>    Amitai Etzioni | 29 |
| 3 | Law, Freedom, Equality—and Schooling<br>    Arthur E. Wise and Michael E. Manley-Casimir | 46 |
| 4 | Bureaucracy and Curriculum Theory<br>    Herbert M. Kliebard | 74 |
| | *Part Two* **The Elements of the System** | 95 |
| 5 | The Administrator Looks at His Practice<br>    Wilmer S. Cody | 99 |
| 6 | Educating the Teachers: Changing Problems<br>    Martin Haberman | 110 |
| 7 | Educating the Administrators<br>    Harvey Goldman | 127 |
| 8 | Teaching the Children: Does the System Help or Hinder?<br>    Larry Cuban | 147 |
| 9 | Supervisors and Coordinators: Power in the System<br>    Marilyn Gittell | 161 |

| | | |
|---|---|---|
| 10 | Who Gets Counseled and For What?<br>John W. M. Rothney | 174 |
| 11 | Crisis of the Modern University<br>Ernest Becker | 187 |
| 12 | Special Education: A Microcosm of Bureaucracy<br>Ann D. Clark | 220 |
| | *Part Three* Perspectives: A Look to the Future | 233 |
| 13 | The School as a Double Agent<br>James B. Macdonald | 235 |
| 14 | Alternatives and Innovations<br>Thomas A. Billings | 247 |
| 15 | Federal, Local, and In-Between<br>J. Myron Atkin | 259 |
| 16 | Does the Common School Have a Chance?<br>Vernon F. Haubrich | 269 |
| | Notes About the Authors | 281 |
| | ASCD 1971 Yearbook Committee Members | 285 |
| | ASCD Board of Directors | 286 |
| | Executive Council, 1970-71 | 286 |
| | Board Members Elected at Large | 287 |
| | Unit Representatives to the Board | 287 |
| | ASCD Review Council | 291 |
| | ASCD Headquarters Staff, 1971 | 293 |

# *Foreword*

THE "state of being" of schools and schooling is of much concern to the Association for Supervision and Curriculum Development. Evidence of this interest has been shown in myriad conferences, studies, seminars, and other kinds of professional meetings and services sponsored by the organization. This concern is also exhibited in many of the writings issued by ASCD. This yearbook is one in a distinguished line of professional works that have dealt with current and basic areas of interest to all persons in school work.

We in education find ourselves in a time of pivotal change. The institution of the public schools seems, however unbelievably, to be in a state of precarious balance. Forces are at work, both within and outside the "system," to affect this balance one way or the other. In either case, the change will be drastic and, in terms of the lives that will be touched, it is likely to be irreversible.

Our ancestors dreamed a great dream. They conceptualized and began to create, at first falteringly, then with growing confidence, a "common school." In this new and pragmatic creation, all the children of all the people would be welcome and would find rich and personal fulfillment for their lives as individuals and as citizens of a great democracy.

This dream has grown miraculously and almost frighteningly—in size. The enterprise of schooling has become a tremendous one, with all the complexities of a great and expansive undertaking. In many ways the history of this growth has paralleled and even accompanied the surging development of the gigantic technological and industrial enterprises of our time.

Perhaps in too many ways, as is indicated in the text of this volume, the institution of the "common school" has imitated other technological units of today. Perhaps the school has taken on the form, the impersonality, the ruthlessness, the centralization, the worship of efficiency, and other characteristics of commercial and competitive enterprises. In so doing, has the school lost some of the humanitarian and idealistic motivations that sparked its growth and won it unparalleled public allegiance in earlier times?

The writers of this volume have consulted their own experience and here communicate truth as they see it. Their indictment of many current practices of a bureaucracy-bound tradition of schooling is a searing one. Many of the traditional practices in the preparation of teachers and administrators, in the conduct of classroom, school, or system, in the vision and the reality of higher education, and in various other facets of schooling are laid bare with a merciless scalpel.

Yet, even in this examination of the shortcomings of bureaucracy, there is an element of hope. There is no condemnation of the enterprise of schooling simply for its largeness; for this largeness may actually be essential in society's fulfillment of its commitment to the meeting of the infinite variety of individual needs. There is, however, in these pages a reminder to educator and to citizen alike that we must be ever alert to our traditions and to the manner in which our public institutions exemplify these ideals in the volatile present. The schools are a public trust; they will not serve the public well unless the public holds their conduct in continuing, critical, and yet cordial scrutiny. This has been the intent of the writers of this volume.

We express appreciation to Vernon F. Haubrich, who served as chairman of the committee responsible for this yearbook and also as its editor. We also thank the members of the committee and the writers of the several chapters. Without such a generous gift of professional time and thought, an analysis such as that presented here would not be available to us.

We also acknowledge the contribution of the Publications Committee and of the Executive Committee in the original conceptualization of the ideas expressed in this volume.

We express appreciation to the editing and production staff of ASCD for its part in making this yearbook available: Robert R. Leeper, Editor and Associate Secretary, helped shape the original ideas, edited the final manuscript, and was in charge of production. Nancy Olson, Mary Albert O'Neill, Lana Pipes, Barbara L. Nash, and Teola T. Jones guided the many intricate details of the technical production of the volume.

*December 1970*     JOHN D. GREENE, *President, 1970-71*
*Association for Supervision
and Curriculum Development*

# *Introduction*

SCHOOLS are big business in American society. Indications are that the system of schooling (elementary, secondary, higher) is the largest "industry" in the country. Corporations; federal, state, and local governments; labor unions; professional associations; special, intern groups; the legal profession; the medical profession; and other service, productive, and political agencies and institutions have increasing financial and curricular interests in the school. As a partial consequence, school systems have become larger and larger. The growing importance of schools as credentialing agents has combined with size and bureaucracy to create immense problems for teachers and learners.

At one time, the major groups interested in the school were those more or less directly involved in teaching, learning, curriculum, or administration. The schooling process was basically supplementary to other educative agencies such as home, church, neighborhood, job, or apprenticeship. At some time in contemporary history (and I am deliberately vague about this) school became an important instrument in realizing state and national goals, became interconnected with industry, and became, in a word, bureaucratic.

It may be that the transition to an urban society required more organizational structure than anyone realized; it may be that our 20th century status as a world power demanded exploitation and efficiency in schools; it may be that the corporate structure required certain regulations which found their way into schools. Whatever the reason, we confront both a society and a school system which have become bureaucratized and standardized and which seem to grow ever more so.

Today's educator should consider three aspects of the growing problem of size, complexity, and bureaucracy. First, there is the importance of defining the limits of the inquiry and then of analyzing explicitly the concepts involved. Philosophical, organizational, and legal aspects of the problem are critical to an understanding of school organization.

Second, it is important to examine the specific organizational structures within the system of education. These include the university which educates teachers, counselors, administrators, and other educational personnel, and the problems faced by the various groupings in the educational arena.

Third, it is important for educators to examine the future of the common school in America. A perspective should include some of the constraints and limits as well as some of the hopes and promises that the common school has held for so many.

The system of schooling in America has been closely tied to ideals of intellectual curiosity, individualism, self-improvement, and social mobility. The central question is whether these ideals can survive new patterns of organization, administration, and training.

VERNON F. HAUBRICH
*Chairman and Editor*
*ASCD 1971 Yearbook Committee*

### ACKNOWLEDGMENTS

Those who have assisted in the production of this yearbook include the Yearbook Committee members and Robert R. Leeper, who aided in the conceptualization, criticism, and final outline of the yearbook; Mrs. Sheila McVey, who worked as my assistant during the first year of the project; Timothy Drescher, who gave assistance during the last four months with final editing changes; and, finally, Miss Barbara Below, who managed to type, retype, and aid in the speedy production of the final draft.

Many of my colleagues at the University of Wisconsin, Madison, and elsewhere gave advice, made suggestions, and read individual chapters for criticism. It goes without saying, however, that the final responsibility for the work lies with the editor and that criticism should be so directed. I trust that members of ASCD, members of the teaching profession, administrators, and all persons concerned with children and youth will find this yearbook an aid in their work.—V. F. H.

# Part One

## *Definitions and Limitations*

FOUR major works constitute the first section of the Yearbook. In Chapter 1, Donald Arnstine sets the issue of freedom in a political context and indicates the necessity of adequately considering the *conditions* of schooling in relationship to freedom to learn, to teach, and to develop. After noting the impact of bureaucratic organization, Arnstine makes his critical point: "a nation that provides no settings in which growing children and youth can democratically participate in the formation and carrying out of significant purposes cannot remain a democratic nation." Strong words which educators will wish to consider.

The second chapter is written by Amitai Etzioni, who is a sociologist and teacher at Columbia University. Etzioni attempts to bring to the teacher a view of system and organization and leads us to consider certain crucial aspects of the system of education. The schools "are a weak institution . . . [and] prosper only at the tolerance of the taxpayers." Unless educators take careful note of the necessity to continually build a consensus which supports their work, disaster can strike through the default of bond issues, the recall of school boards, and the firing of teachers. The schools must "rapidly and broadly increase their legitimation . . . or else financial shortage, riots, and alienation of citizens, parents, and students will severely constrict their very ability to function."

The third chapter by Arthur E. Wise and Michael E. Manley-Casimir is a look at the new relationships which the law has prescribed for students, teachers, and administrators. Two problems concern the authors: first, the "extent to which public school students are protected by the First Amendment rights to freedom of expression and press while in school," and second, "whether the provision of unequal educational opportunity within a state constitutes a denial by that state of the equal protection clause of the Fourteenth Amendment."

The changing relationships which these new factors imply and the new relationships of schools and their clientele constitute the remainder of this fascinating account.

In the fourth chapter, Herbert M. Kliebard uses the concept of industrial and organizational bureaucracy and applies it systematically to the development of curriculum theory and practice. Kliebard provides a historical review of critical stages in the development of mechanistic and corporate metaphors in the world of the educator. The activity analysis movement, the rise of input-output designs, behavioral objectives, and finally the rise of accountability in school operations are painstakingly described by Kliebard. In a careful manner, he shows parallels from industry which then are adapted by schools into "standardized units of production and work." Kliebard fears an increasing dehumanization of teachers, students, and administrators. His chapter should give pause to those who have so willingly moved to incorporate uncritically all of industry's techniques as regular classroom and school procedures.—V. F. H.

# 1

## *Freedom and Bureaucracy in the Schools*

### Donald Arnstine

Children and adults in schools are related to one another in many different ways: as partners, antagonists, subordinates, and authorities. These relationships can be found whenever education is undertaken in groups; they are essentially *political* relationships. Yet teaching and learning are the processes which normally engage the attention of most students of education; for this reason, political relationships are often minimized or ignored altogether. When this happens, questions of freedom become difficult to answer, for freedom is first and foremost a political, and not an educational concept. Educators interested in freedom have made little use of the analyses of freedom readily available in Western philosophy; they have isolated the pedagogical from the political dimension of education, studied the former, and forgot about the latter. We can learn from this mistake by asking why the separation was made in the first place.

It has traditionally been assumed that the concept of freedom operates in a political context. In a world in which no other people existed, a man could be neither free nor unfree. He could only be *conceived* as more or less free in relation to *others,* and the sort of relation in question was always one of action and consequences. Thus questions of freedom had to do with how and by whom one's actions were to be governed—in short, with government.

Yet education is not a process which can easily be conceived as composed of adults whose actions and interactions require some form of government. First, most parties to the educational process are children of varying ages and levels of maturity, who cannot be considered in the eyes of the government as "equal" in status to adults. Second, students are not expected to "act" at all, in the normal sense of that term. They are instead supposed to study and learn. Studying and learning are thought by many people to be rather peculiar sorts of actions—inner and covert, and without observable consequences for anyone else's studying and learning. Thus the concept of "government" would not apply to shadowy (and, of course, misconceived) actions like these, since they allegedly have no effect on others.[1]

Yet even though the key actions promoted by schools—studying and learning—appear to require no government, other actions do call for some kind of control. Teachers must show up for work and be paid, children must be scheduled throughout the day, discipline must be kept, and so forth. The control of all these diverse matters, which has grown into the bureaucracy discussed hereafter, is in the hands of people who are very seldom involved in the basic school activities of teaching and learning.

However odd this may sound when stated so bluntly, I believe it helps in understanding why political considerations have so seldom been thought relevant to the schools' focal concerns of studying and learning. In the absence of a political context, freedom becomes not simply a condition that is hard to get; it is one that is virtually impossible to conceive.

At this point many educational thinkers are likely to object and claim that not political freedom, but *intellectual* freedom is their main concern. By intellectual freedom, they usually mean the freedom to think, to learn, to develop interests, to follow an argument wherever it leads, to make choices, and so on. Now these are worthy ideals at which to aim, but it makes as much sense to expect to achieve them in a school *independent* of conditions of social and political freedom as it does to go fishing without a line. In the past when political freedom was extended to many, intellectual freedom was widely found. And whenever political freedom was absent, little evidence of intellectual freedom has been found. The record on this point is consistent all the way from Periclean Athens through Hitler's Germany to Richard Nixon's troubled America.

The reason for the close association between political and intellectual freedom is easy enough to understand, if not always easy

---

[1] Whether for this or some other reason, students and teachers are altogether left out of consideration when political relations are discussed by Vincent Ostrom in his essay, "Education and Politics," in: Nelson B. Henry, editor. *Social Forces Influencing American Education.* Sixtieth Yearbook of the National Society for the Study of Education, Part II. Chicago: University of Chicago Press, 1961. pp. 8-45.

for parents and teachers to act upon. Choices and decisions are made by people who intend to act in some way. If people are not free to act, but instead are arbitrarily restrained, then choices and decisions become equally constrained. The longer action is restrained in this way, the less likely it is that people will even *think* about choices or decisions. From this point it is but a short step to the cessation of thinking altogether. People who cannot act freely may busy themselves doing efficiently the tasks they have been assigned, and they may also engage in fantasies over the entertainments they have been given. In this way entire societies can acquire the mentality of slaves—and at the very same time enjoy the world's highest standard of living!

Thus it is possible to *think about* intellectual freedom apart from political freedom, but it is never possible to *get* the former without the latter. That is probably why so much educational thought about intellectual freedom dissolves into fantasy. But it is equally unrealistic to turn these separations the other way around: to believe that anything sensible could be said about intellectual freedom in an educational setting by *simply* considering the nature of political freedom.

Many excellent analyses of freedom in Western philosophy have shed very little light on its role in education. The present discussion will avoid any further attempt to analyze the abstract concept of freedom, or to define freedom, apart from the operation of the schools. Instead, the concept of freedom will initially be employed in a largely unrefined, everyday sense. We will enlist the aid of the social sciences in seeking freedom in educational settings, and in trying to understand why it is so hard to find. The philosophical task will consist in trying to keep this inquiry on the right track, and in attempting to gain meaning and significance from the results of this search, in suggesting what could be done about it, and who could do it.

This is to suggest that philosophy is not limited to finding the meanings of concepts. When it is seriously undertaken, philosophy may also suggest what kinds of actions would make sense in the light of the meanings that have been discovered:

> . . . obviously it is to mathematics, physics, chemistry, biology, anthropology, history, etc. that we must go, not to philosophy, to find out the facts of the world. It is for the sciences to say what generalizations are tenable about the world and what they specifically are. But when we ask what *sort* of permanent disposition of action toward the

world the scientific disclosures exact of us we are raising a philosophic question.[2]

Efforts to think about freedom and education can be fruitless when the two are discussed independently of each other. To become more sensitive to the dead ends that result from keeping separate considerations of politics, education, and even metaphysics, we will in the next section examine two representative English philosophers who discuss both freedom and education: John Locke and Bertrand Russell.

## Two Views of Freedom and Education

John Locke may not be the most vehement of the proponents of political liberty, but he is one of the best known, and is fairly representative of Anglo-American philosophical thought in the political realm. Locke took freedom to be one of nature's "givens," yet he seemed quite unable to find any role for freedom to play in his scheme of education.

Freedom, for Locke, had a firmer status than that of a mere moral or political right. It was the natural estate of man, predating social organization:

> To understand political power aright, and derive it from its original, we must consider what estate all men are naturally in, and that is, a state of perfect freedom to order their actions, and dispose of their persons and possessions as they think fit, within the bounds of the law of nature, without asking leave or depending upon the will of any other man.[3]

But Locke claimed that the law of nature, like most other laws, was not self-enforcing. Thus men unite into commonwealths so that more specific laws can be codified and made known, impartial judges can be established, and power to enforce the laws can be marshaled. Given these purposes for which men unite and create governments and laws, the one thing government must not do is infringe upon the very laws it creates and maintains. If it does, then the people have a right to rid themselves of the government:

> Whensoever, therefore, the legislative shall transgress this fundamental rule of society, and . . . endeavor to grasp themselves, or put into the hands of any other, an absolute power over the lives, liberties, and

---

[2] John Dewey. *Democracy and Education.* New York: The Macmillan Company, 1916. Copyright renewed in 1944 by John Dewey. p. 379.

[3] John Locke. *Two Treatises of Government.* Edited by Peter Laslett. New York: Cambridge University Press, 1960. Chapter 2.

estates of the people; by this breach of trust they forfeit the power the people had put into their hands for quite contrary ends, and it devolves to the people, who have a right to resume their original liberty, and by the establishment of a new legislative . . . to provide for their own safety and security, which is the end for which they are in society.[4]

For Locke, then, freedom is man's natural endowment, laws are made to safeguard it, and no people have an obligation to retain a government which fails to uphold or which violates those laws. Since a society maintains itself from generation to generation through its processes of education, and since Locke thought freedom to be so important in such a society, he could be expected to find a significant role for freedom in his system of education. But any such expectation must go unfulfilled. For Locke, like Rousseau who wrote later, eschewed the sort of educational setting to which freedom would even be relevant:

I am sure, he who is able to be at the charge of a tutor at home, may there give his son a more genteel carriage, more manly thoughts . . . with a greater proficiency in learning into the bargain . . . than any at school can do.[5]

In choosing tutoring (today we call it "individualized instruction") as the ideal educational setting, Locke denied the possibility of cultivating freedom by removing the student from a social setting. In the absence of other people to whom one's actions might be related, one is outside the only sort of context that could be called political. The relationship of a tutor to his pupil is an extension of the father-son relationship: whatever virtues may be found in it, they are not political ones. The roles of tutor and pupil, father and son, are shaped by very important social inequalities; they cannot form a government together.[6] Lest there be any doubt regarding this point, Locke expands on it by specifying the sort of person who would make a suitable tutor:

Seek out somebody that may know how discreetly to frame his manners . . . and gently correct and weed out any bad inclinations, and

---

[4] *Ibid.*, Chapter 10.

[5] John Locke. *Some Thoughts Concerning Education.* In: J. W. Adamson, editor. *The Educational Writings of John Locke.* New York: Longmans, Green, and Company, 1912. p. 52.

[6] See: Herbert W. Schneider. "High and Higher Education." In: Donald Arnstine, editor. *Philosophy of Education 1969.* Edwardsville, Illinois: The Philosophy of Education Society, 1969. p. 68.

settle him in good habits. This is the main point; and this being provided for, learning may be had into the bargain. . . .[7]

Of course, the tutor is expected to produce a very particular sort of English gentleman, regardless of the material (the child) given him. If possible, the tutor should enable his pupil to *like* the training he is given:

> The right way to teach them . . . is to give them a liking and inclination to what you propose to them to be learned, and that will engage their industry and application.[8]

But if the pupil does not like it, then:

> . . . stubbornness and obstinant disobedience must be mastered with force and blows. . . .[9]

Throughout his discussion of education, Locke never has occasion to mention any role for freedom. What is more significant, there never *could* be any role for freedom to play. The educational setting, for Locke, is a paternalistic one to which the very concept of government is irrelevant; the pupil is not "free" to become anything other than the sort of mannerly and industrious Protestant gentleman that Locke had in mind.

Two and a half centuries later, Western philosophical thought on education was augmented by Bertrand Russell, who also maintained and enriched the Western tradition of political freedom and humane social values:

> All institutions, if they are not to hamper individual growth, must be based as far as possible upon voluntary combination, rather than the force of the law or the traditional authority of the holders of power.[10]

But far more deliberately than Locke, Russell tried to carry these values into his consideration of education. Thus he saw that the teaching of government, freedom, and justice required that children be educated in groups,[11] where they could interact with and cooperate with one another.[12] He saw this as necessary for a demo-

---

[7] Locke, *Some Thoughts Concerning Education, op. cit.*, p. 15.

[8] *Ibid.*, p. 56.

[9] *Ibid.*, p. 61.

[10] Bertrand Russell. *Why Men Fight*. New York: The Century Company, 1929. p. 31.

[11] Bertrand Russell. *Education and the Good Life*. New York: Boni and Liveright, Inc., 1926. p. 149.

[12] *Ibid.*, p. 81.

cratic education, and he directly criticized Locke (and Rousseau) for recommending tutors—a practice which, he claimed, would be more fitting for an aristocracy.[13] Yet for all his concern with groups, Russell never discussed how they were to be organized or how decisions were to be made within them. Groups can as easily stifle freedom as promote it. Their mere existence offers no assurance that freedom will be learned.

Freedom in education was an ideal strongly held by Russell, who wrote that, "Instead of obedience and discipline, we ought to aim at preserving independence and impulse." [14]

> ... in view of the fact that no authority can be wholly trusted, we must aim at having as little authority as possible, and try to think out ways by which young people's natural desires and impulses can be utilized in education.[15]

There are grave dangers in gathering together a group of children "having as little authority as possible," for chaos and tyranny are at least as likely to occur as freedom is. It is just at this point—the practical implementation of freedom in educational settings—that Russell is silent, and his silence on what could be *done* to implement freedom in educational settings is as much a part of the Western tradition as is his very emphasis on freedom.

But Russell's ideal of freedom, puzzling as it is in an educational context, disappears altogether when confronted with his beliefs about learning and human behavior. Russell accepted Watsonian behaviorism as the "only valid method for the study of animal and child psychology." [16] He claimed that all human action is either instinctive or acquired by experience, and that the latter, which is "learnt," consists altogether in the acquisition of habits.[17] To make clear what he meant by habit acquisition, Russell referred to Thorndike's cats, who, through repeated trial and error, became in-

---

[13] *Ibid.*, pp. 16-17.

[14] Russell, *Why Men Fight, op. cit.*, p. 167.

[15] Bertrand Russell. "Freedom or Authority in Education." *Century Magazine* 109: 172-80; December 1924. Quoted in: Joe Park. *Bertrand Russell on Education.* Studies in Educational Theory of the John Dewey Society, Number 1. Columbus, Ohio: The Ohio State University Press, 1963. p. 175.

[16] Bertrand Russell. "The Training of Young Children." *Harper's Magazine* 155: 314; August 1927.

[17] Bertrand Russell. *The Analysis of Mind.* London: George Allen and Unwin, Ltd., 1921. pp. 51ff.

creasingly proficient at opening the latch on their cage. "It is by essentially similar processes," wrote Russell, "that we learn speaking, writing, mathematics, or the government of an empire."[18] It is Russell's belief that all (but "instinctive") human action is conditioned, and action which is conditioned is not chosen by the agent, but is instead the resultant of particular patterns of stimuli and reinforcements. However, this leaves us at a total loss in trying to understand what Russell could possibly mean by freedom in education. A voluntary or freely chosen action is by definition the contrary of a conditioned response. Since, for Russell, *all* that education could do would be to condition sets of complex habits in young people, there could be no room at all in schools for freedom or for free choices by students.

Any conception of education as conditioning necessarily conflicts with conceptions of freedom in education, since the actions of creatures who have been conditioned conform to norms and criteria chosen by *others*. With this point understood, we shall continue the inquiry into freedom by examining more closely the political context within which young people are educated.

## The Social Impact on Learning

It is axiomatic that people learn from their environment, but it is worth bearing in mind that it is the social dimension of the environment which has the most significant impact on learning. A jungle is an environment, but put a city-bred child into one, alone, and it is doubtful that he will learn enough to survive. Accompany the child with others who have had experience with jungles, and he may learn a great deal.

Since people in the schools are still people, there is no reason to suppose that learning in schools is not also strongly influenced by the social environment of learners. Yet much educational literature tends to deny this, for its overwhelming emphasis has traditionally been on the learning that is supposed to result from the content of study (the curriculum) and from the techniques of teaching.[19] The teacher, of course, has much to do (sometimes deliberately, and sometimes not) with the creation of a particular sort of social climate in his classroom, but what a child learns is not simply a function of

[18] *Ibid.*, p. 52.

[19] Robert Dreeben has also made this point and has indicated some documentary evidence for it. See: Robert Dreeben. *On What Is Learned in School*. Reading, Massachusetts: Addison-Wesley Publishing Company, Inc., 1968. pp. 42, 56-57.

what the teacher says or does. Learning in school is a function of the complex interactions and interrelations of *all* the varied people in the classroom (including the teacher).

This is why the issue of who is in the classroom is probably so much more important than what the curriculum is or what the teacher happens to be saying. The population of the class is dependent upon where the school district lines are drawn; whether the community or the school is racially, ethnically, or economically segregated; and whether or not vocational and academic tracking, or ability grouping, is practiced. These factors are educationally crucial because they determine who will be in the class together and thus what, in part, the social environment will be like.[20]

Yet the social environment, or climate, is not simply a function of who is physically proximate to whom. For at least equally if not more important is the particular structure of relations that exists between and among these people. These relations do not simply emerge as functions of the particular personalities of the people involved. The personalities of students and teacher and the peer culture of students do matter, for the social climate of every class is to some extent different from that of every other class.[21] But the real key to the social climate of the class is the constellation of forces—rules, customs, and pressures—according to which decisions in the class are made and actions are governed. These forces have their origin in the classroom and out of it as well—in administrators' offices, at the school board meeting, and within the mores of the wider culture. Together, they constitute what could be called the political structure of the school system.

Nearly everyone who ever attended school remembers that he was assigned lessons and told how to behave. The teacher was the

---

[20] In the Coleman report, one of the most comprehensive studies of schools ever undertaken, it was found that one of the factors most closely associated with achievement was independent of the curriculum, the teacher's training, the class size, or the extent of the library and other facilities; it was the social composition (degree of heterogeneity) of the classroom. See: U.S. Department of Health, Education, and Welfare. *Equality of Educational Opportunity.* Washington, D.C.: Superintendent of Documents, U.S. Government Printing Office, 1966.

[21] A dramatic example of the way in which informal social-political relations among group members have an impact on *achievement levels* of the individuals within the group can be found in Whyte's discussion of the relation between the bowling performances and the social status of gang members; see his *Street Corner Society.* This is summarized in: George C. Homans. *The Human Group.* New York: Harcourt, Brace & World, Inc., 1950. pp. 162-69.

immediate source of commands and sanctions, but few children realized that the teacher was a spokesman for a much wider and more pervasive set of norms. What the teacher has his pupils do must be compatible with the general climate, customs, and rules of the school. These rules and customs, in turn, depend very much on the school principal, whose own constraints are set by some higher administrator. And the chief administrator of a school district, the superintendent, is himself constrained by the rules, the values, and the opinions of influential laymen, most notably school board members.

Instruction and discipline in schools is thus under the control of a hierarchy of persons: teachers, department heads, principals, assistant superintendents, and the superintendent. Not only are these persons specialized in a variety of ways, but they are also appointed to their positions on the basis of technical qualifications: they were certified. Salaries are normally fixed for each type of position and they increase by standard increments. There is usually a regular system of promotion which depends heavily, although not exclusively, on seniority. These features of an organization—a hierarchy of offices filled by appointed people on fixed salaries, whose promotion depends largely on seniority—are just those mentioned by Max Weber as characteristic of the typical bureaucracy.[22]

To the above features, Peter Blau has added specialization, rules and regulations, and unemotional, impersonal relationships within the administrative hierarchy.[23] The structure of personnel within school systems illustrates the presence of these features as clearly and pervasively as any organization could. The multiplication of rules and regulations within schools has become almost legendary,[24] and such devices as nepotism rules (for example, a school principal is not normally permitted to hire his wife to teach in his building) are intended to reduce the emotional attachments within personnel relations.

Can bureaucracy be defended as a way of organizing schools? For many, the notion of bureaucracy is synonymous with evil; the

[22] See: Max Weber. "The Essentials of Bureaucratic Organization: An Ideal-Type Construction." In: Robert K. Merton *et al.*, editors. *Reader in Bureaucracy*. New York: The Free Press, 1952. pp. 21-22.

[23] Peter M. Blau. *Bureaucracy in Modern Society*. New York: Random House, Inc., 1956. pp. 18-19.

[24] See, for example: Bel Kaufman. *Up the Down Staircase*. Englewood Cliffs, New Jersey: Prentice-Hall, Inc., 1964.

term conjures up impersonal and bumbling officials bogged down in red tape. Some bureaucracies can indeed be so characterized, but that is a pathology of bureaucratic organization—what Robert Merton termed "over-organization"—the excessive development and dependence on routines which interfere with the purposes of the organization.[25] While this sometimes happens, it is never intended, for a bureaucracy is organized to do just the opposite: to make a complex organization work efficiently. Blau's definition of bureaucracy relates it to the purpose it serves:

> Bureaucracy . . . can be defined as organization that maximizes efficiency in administration, whatever its formal characteristics, or as an institutionalized method of organizing social conduct in the interest of administrative efficiency.[26]

Insofar as efficiency is an important criterion by which administrative systems must be measured, and bureaucracy is designed to maximize efficiency, bureaucracy can surely be defended. But the question remains, is this an appropriate way of organizing personnel *in schools?* For we are seeking freedom in education, and we need to find out whether bureaucracies are appropriate vehicles for the promotion and maintenance of freedom.

If the personnel structure of an organization is to be bureaucratic, then the goals of that organization must be clear and unambiguous. A bureaucracy may promote efficiency, but a group has to know where it is going if it is to try to be efficient about it. If a group's goals are *not* clear-cut and definite—if the members of the group are in fact permitted the freedom and even encouraged to change those goals—then questions of efficiency become secondary. Indeed, efforts to be efficient will even interfere with attempts to create better or more appropriate goals. Bureaucracy, then, appears to be a grave threat to freedom—not just when it has become bogged down in red tape, but *when it is working at its best.* Nowhere is this spelled out more clearly than in Blau's statement:

> If an association among men is established for the explicit purpose of producing jointly certain end products, whether it is manufacturing cars or winning wars, considerations of efficiency are of primary importance; hence bureaucratization will further the achievement of this objective. However . . . if an association is established for the purpose of deciding upon common goals and courses of action to implement them,

[25] Merton, *op. cit.*, p. 396.
[26] Blau, *op. cit.*, p. 60.

which is the function of democratic government (but not that of government agencies), the free expression of opinion must be safeguarded against other considerations, including that of efficiency. Since bureaucratization prevents the attainment of this objective, it must be avoided at all cost.[27]

"It must be avoided at all cost." That is strong language. Are we to conclude that bureaucracy is so antithetical to freedom that it must be abandoned as a mode of organizing school personnel? Assuming that freedom in education is desirable in a free society, it can only be concluded that bureaucratic school organization must be abandoned if two other matters can be demonstrated. First, it must be shown that the goals of education are not clear and fixed and behaviorally statable in unambiguous ways. Second, clear evidence must be found in schools of the personally and socially harmful effects of the absence of freedom, and a clear relation must be found between those effects and the bureaucracies in which school personnel are organized. The remainder of this section will try to show how these two claims about education and schools can be substantiated.

First, efficiency of means—the *raison d'être* of bureaucracy—demands that ends be clear, precise, and stable. Can educational ends, aims, or goals be stated in clear, unambiguous ways? When stated in such ways, will they remain stable? Is there, as programmers have so deeply wished, some agreed-upon list of "behavioral objectives"?

There are many such lists, but none exists that is universally agreed-upon. What is far more important, no such agreed-upon list ever *could* exist. A list of clearly stated behaviors for students to acquire would be virtually endless, and would give no indication of which behaviors to emphasize and which ones to treat as secondary. The *only* way of establishing such priorities in a list of precisely stated behavioral goals is to have a set of *more general goals*—and therefore non-behavioral and less precisely stated ones—which can serve to guide choices among the more specific ones.[28]

---

[27] *Ibid.*, pp. 22-23.

[28] Harry S. Broudy writes: "We cannot predict the particular acts by which the individual pupil will achieve or fail to achieve security, freedom from pain, and a sense of accomplishment, but perhaps we can predict the form such activities will have to take if the resulting life is to be judged good." See: Harry S. Broudy. *Building a Philosophy of Education.* Englewood Cliffs, New Jersey: Prentice-Hall, Inc., 1961. p. 38.

Since the question of freedom is at issue, it is more important to see how freedom is endangered by the notion of precise, behaviorally stated educational goals:

> ... unless looseness and flexibility in general educational objectives are retained, we shall be guilty of defining goals like "citizenship" as if only one set of behaviors satisfied our aims. This would be both foolish and dangerous, since a wide range of differing behavior patterns could all be indicated by a single objective such as "good citizenship." Some people manifest good citizenship by enlisting in the army, others by voting, and others by criticizing governmental policy. But "good citizenship" does not require all three behaviors. Only statements of educational objectives that are cast in general terms—and are defined in different ways in different contexts—allow teachers to modify more specific aims and methods in light of particular students and particular teaching situations.[29]

The point of this discussion is not to suggest that aims in education can be dispensed with altogether;[30] it is rather to emphasize as strongly as possible that aims in education are necessarily general, idiosyncratic, and alterable:

> ... it is well to remind ourselves that education as such has no aims. Only persons, parents, and teachers, etc., have aims, not an abstract idea like education. And consequently their purposes are indefinitely varied, differing with different children, changing as children grow and with the growth of experience on the part of the one who teaches.[31]

It is worth mentioning, too, that the recipients of school instruction—the children—have goals of their own which can be ignored only at the risk of undermining the entire educational process. But children grow and change, and thus the educational goals that emerge from the interaction of parents', teachers', and children's aims are themselves bound to keep changing.

The conclusion is thus inescapable that stable educational aims cannot *reasonably* be stated in clear and precise behavioral terms. Yet only when aims are stated clearly and behaviorally can they be

---

[29] Donald Arnstine. "The Language and Values of Programmed Instruction, Part II." *The Educational Forum* 28 (3): 340-41; March 1964. Used by permission of Kappa Delta Pi, An Honorary Society in Education.

[30] See: R. S. Peters. "Must an Educator Have an Aim?" In: R. S. Peters. *Authority, Responsibility, and Education.* New York: Paul S. Erikson, Inc., 1960. pp. 83-95.

[31] John Dewey, *op. cit.*, p. 125.

sought after *efficiently*.[32] As Blau pointed out, organizations with such aims are best suited to employ bureaucracies. We have seen that schools and school systems do not have aims statable in such ways. It follows, then, that a bureaucratic form of organization is inappropriate for institutions in which the purpose is teaching and learning.

Yet it has been objected that it is only a conjecture that bureaucracy limits freedom, and that people suffer as a result of such limitations. It is appropriate, then, for us to examine some of the ways in which bureaucracy does in fact limit freedom, and the undesirable impact that such limitations have on the people who make up and are served by those bureaucracies. What this implies for school systems, school personnel, parents, and pupils will also become evident.

When an institution is bureaucratically organized, a hierarchy of control has the effect of creating increasing amounts of apathy, passivity, and ineffectiveness. This is increasingly true the further one descends from the higher, directive positions to the lower, directed positions. This is normal in industry, where workers who have little control over their working environment become apathetic toward their work, dependent on superordinates, and foreshortened in their sense of time (a future is neither envisioned nor planned for).

In short, workers behave in immature ways when they are reduced to carrying out decisions made (but not necessarily explained or justified) by others.[33]

One should not expect people in schools to behave otherwise. Teachers will act immaturely in direct proportion to the extent that their behavior is directed from above. The immaturity of teachers (defined as before: apathy, passivity, ineffectiveness, and foreshortened time perspective) may be mitigated—and sometimes simply masked—by their advanced education and its residual benefits, and by a school administration which either distributes or effectively pretends to distribute decision-making power more widely. Yet the infrequency of teachers meetings, their sparse attendance, and the lack of action taken at them, all attest to powerlessness, apathy, and

---

[32] Or, if not stated behaviorally, then aims must be stated in concrete, observable units of production (for example, automobiles) in order that efficient means may be sought.

[33] See: Chris Argyris. *Personality and Organization*. New York: Harper & Brothers, 1957. pp. 60-66.

failure to plan for the future.[34] Students in schools have even less effective decision-making power—less freedom—than teachers.[35] If this were all there were to say about educational bureaucracies (which it is not), one could not avoid the conclusion that the organization of schools almost ensured that immature children would grow into immature adults.

In a bureaucratically organized school, teachers and pupils live in a state of social *anomie*—of social disintegration and alienation. The number of activities in which people effectively collaborate approaches zero (students are told to do their own work and are evaluated on that basis; teachers normally operate their own classroom, seeing other teachers only at lunch or at rest), and the group—whether of children in class or of teachers—has little control over its own members. These are just the criteria cited by Durkheim in characterizing *anomie*.[36] But in any case, whether one refers to social *anomie* or personal immaturity, the uncontrolled impact of bureaucracies on their members is a destructive one. If in industry the production of automobiles were held to be very important, one might be willing to tolerate the impact of efficient organization on the workers. Yet one wonders just *what* it is that schools are producing which, being so important, justifies the destructive effects of educational bureaucracies on teachers and pupils. Clearly, one thing such schools could not produce is a free citizenry.

Because of these harmful effects, bureaucracies establish mitigating procedures. In industry, aside from efforts to find competent leadership, rewards are given for outstanding performance, and subordinates are motivated to greater effort by being put into mutual competition for a limited number of more powerful positions.[37] The system of rewards, in which the workers are paid for their dissatisfaction, may not reduce apathy, but it keeps workers at their jobs. (This may be compared with the letter grades given to school chil-

---

[34] See: Myron Lieberman. *The Future of Public Education.* Chicago: University of Chicago Press, 1960. p. 192. Teachers as predominantly fearful and unwilling to assert or defend their opinions in school are described in a study by: Harmon Zeigler. *The Political Life of American Teachers.* Englewood Cliffs, New Jersey: Prentice-Hall, Inc., 1967.

[35] See: Carl Nordstrom, Edgar Z. Friedenberg, and Hilary A. Gold. *Society's Children: A Study of Ressentiment in Secondary School Education.* New York: Random House, Inc., 1967.

[36] Emile Durkheim. *Le Suicide.* Paris, France: Alcan, 1930. pp. 272-82.

[37] See: Argyris, *op. cit.,* pp. 61-63.

dren, ostensibly for achievement but often for compliance. But less emphasis is placed on rewards in school since children are required by law to attend.) Competition may provide motivation to greater effort—sometimes to surpass someone else, rather than to produce anything valuable—but it also tends to produce interpersonal conflict which may interfere with productivity.[38] People who are learning are no better off when pitted against one another.[39]

Under the conditions of bureaucratic organization in industry, employees faced with frustration, conflict, or boredom have a number of options for action. We shall see whether teachers and pupils in an educational bureaucracy have similar options. The worker in industry can leave and find another job—providing, of course, he is in good health, is not too old, has salable experience or skills, can afford an interim period without pay, and is not facing a contracting economy. Yet, while there are limitations on an adult worker's freedom to leave his job, the school pupil has virtually no freedom to quit at all until the legal leaving age is reached. Teachers who wish to leave their jobs face the same obstacles as any other worker, and another one as well. Teachers' salaries normally increase with years of experience, but there are many school systems which do not give full credit to an incoming teacher for all his previous years of experience. Thus, a move for an experienced teacher may mean a reduction in salary. Since experienced teachers are more likely to have families, the possibility of a salary reduction is a strong deterrent to leaving their jobs (it is also a powerful incentive to do what they are told).

The worker in industry can try to improve his situation by seeking a promotion. This is another option closed to schoolchildren. Normally, they *get* a promotion each year, but such a promotion neither distinguishes them from their peers nor improves their circumstances: they remain at the bottom of the educational hierarchy. Teachers can seek promotions but, except in cases of large schools where one may become a department head, this normally means becoming an administrator. Thus, promotion for a teacher does not improve his situation *as a teacher*—it simply means he leaves the field of teaching.

[38] See: M. Deutsch. "The Effects of Cooperation and Competition Upon Group Process." *Human Relations* 2: 129-52; 1949; and Stanley Levy and Lawrence Z. Freedman. "Psychoneurosis and Economic Life." *Social Problems* 4 (1): 55-67; July 1956.

[39] See: Douglas Williams. "Effects of Competition Upon Group Process." *Occupational Psychology* 30 (2): 85-93; April 1956.

Employees in a wide range of businesses and in industry often adapt to hierarchical control through a variety of defense mechanisms,[40] notable among which is a zealous and almost slavish adherence to rules and regulations. This formality, which also increases the amount of bureaucratic red tape and may interfere with the purposes of the organization, appears to increase as authority becomes more centralized and less understood at the lower echelons. Frederick Burin observes that as lower civil servants in Hitler's Germany became aware of how arbitrary were the norms that dictated their orders, they strove to preserve their sense of security by the more anxious observance of procedural rules.[41] This phenomenon is readily observable in schoolchildren, especially among girls whose enculturation results in tendencies to accept rather than reject authority. The strict and often zealous adherence to rules is so commonly seen in teachers as to have become stereotypical. While such people may be attracted to a career in teaching, it is also the case that educational bureaucracies help to create and strengthen such traits of personality.

Finally, the worker in industry adapts to his role within the bureaucracy by becoming apathetic; with his fellow workers he helps set standards of production lower than management's.[42] He goldbricks, and he focuses his concern on the material reward: his paycheck. Schoolchildren have options that are in a way similar to these, although they may not be as personally satisfying. The material reward—a high mark on the report card—has only symbolic value; unlike a paycheck, it has no market value.[43] Yet for many students, the symbolic value of the report card is enough to motivate them to work "for grades." Remarkably, educators voice disappointment at these students. Yet no employer was either surprised or disappointed over the fact that his employees worked for money.

[40] See: Argyris, *op. cit.*, p. 78.

[41] Frederick S. Burin. "Bureaucracy and National Socialism: A Reconsideration of Weberian Theory." In: Merton, *op. cit.*, p. 43.

[42] A classic example of this is found in the account of the Bank Wiring Observation Room of the Western Electric Company, in: F. J. Roethlisberger and William J. Dickson. *Management and the Worker.* Cambridge: Harvard University Press, 1946. pp. 379-548.

[43] A middle class child, of course, can eventually cash in his report card for college admission. Since youths from low-income homes normally cannot afford college, the report card lacks even this value for them. With so ineffective a reward system, it is little wonder that the educational bureaucracy has so much trouble controlling low-income students.

What *is* surprising is the fact that so many students *will* work for something as worthless as a report card.

In addition to working for their surrogate material rewards, students also show other similarities to industrial workers. Students, too, restrict quotas (unless reprisals prove too costly), and they, too, goldbrick when they can. Teachers engage in more sophisticated forms of these behaviors. Since nothing tangible is produced, quota-restriction is irrelevant to teaching, but goldbricking most typically appears in the teacher who teaches the same course, with the same lesson plans and the same materials,[44] year in and year out. Yet the material reward would seem not to function for teachers as it does for industrial and other workers. Many (and especially male) teachers could earn as good a salary by taking a job that called for less education and demanded less effort. The rewards that hold people within teaching careers, involving both consciously held ideals and unconscious attitudes, are far too complex to analyze or understand here.

When workers goldbrick, seem interested only in the money, or quit, and when schoolchildren loaf, seem interested only in "what the exam is going to be like," and often drop out of school, their superiors—managers or teachers—react in much the same way. The subordinates, be they workers or schoolchildren, are thought to be "naturally" lazy, apathetic, materialistic, careless, and wasteful.[45] Thus, people are accused by their superiors of being responsible for the very behavior that those superiors produced. There is a deep similarity between schoolchildren and black Americans,[46] both of whom are criticized for exhibiting patterns of behavior to which they are given no alternatives by those who (legally or economically) control them.

Since no bureaucratically organized institution, factory or school (or "school plant," in the jargon of the school administrators), can maintain itself in the face of extreme and continual noncooperation from the lower echelons, definite action must be taken. And since superordinates usually decide that the fault lies with their subordinates, actions are normally taken in order that they—the employees or the students—will change their attitudes.

[44] Very often it is the bureaucracy itself (to which these behaviors are responses) which selects the same materials each year.

[45] See: Argyris, *op. cit.*, p. 123.

[46] See: Gerald Farber. "The Student as Nigger." First appeared in the *Los Angeles Free Press* and was reprinted shortly thereafter in the *UCLA Daily Bruin* of April 4, 1967.

In industry, these actions have generally taken three forms.[47] The first two forms, stronger leadership and more careful evaluation and control, have their counterparts in schools when rules and regulations are increased in number and discipline is tightened (policemen regularly patrol the halls in many urban schools). The third common form of managerial action has been the institution of human relations programs. These are usually intended to inspire workers, or to make them feel that management is deeply concerned about their personal welfare. Such programs, often transparent to workers, can sometimes make matters worse:

> To emphasize to an assembly line worker that he should feel proud of the four bolts that he puts into the right rear end of a car may be viewed as an insult by the worker who is a "whole" human being.[48]

When teachers tell children, in a kindly way, that the work which seems so meaningless now will in fact be of great benefit in the future, the teachers are practicing a crude form of "human relations" (which itself is a form of selling). But in the hands of school administrators, who are increasingly required to take courses in it, "human relations" has become a sophisticated tool. Indeed, the techniques of "human relations" may be the last line of defense for administrators, who are under ever-increasing pressure from local parents, students, and their own more militant faculties. (It might be predicted that when this defense breaks down, the educational bureaucracy will undergo its most significant change since the popular establishment of public schools in the first half of the 19th century.)

Stronger leadership, tighter controls, and human relations programs very seldom change the attitudes of workers and students, unless the change is for the worse. In industry, increased absenteeism is often the result.[49] School absences show the same patterns. Since withdrawal from a situation signals the complete failure of parties to communicate with one another, the breakdown in relations between management and employee, administrator and teacher, or teacher and pupil is often attributed to a "failure of communication." This is, however, a serious mistake. For in treating a symptom as if it were a cause, this delays efforts to get at genuine causes and conditions.

[47] See: Argyris, *op. cit.*, pp. 130ff.
[48] *Ibid.*, p. 154.
[49] See: Peter Castle. "Accidents, Absence, and Withdrawal from the Work Situation." *Human Relations* 9 (12): 223-33; 1956.

The failure of people to communicate with each other does not *cause* low productivity or ineffective interaction; rather, it is ineffective interaction which eventually results in the cessation of communication. When, for example, unilateral decision making replaces conjoint action, people eventually stop saying meaningful things to one another. Whether it is a school staff or a union meeting, "where the leadership makes all significant decisions, meetings are dull, since only routine business is conducted, and there is no incentive for attendance." [50] Teachers are especially prone to believe that communication is a matter of verbalization and abstract understanding. But nothing could be further from the truth, and nothing could constitute a greater obstacle to understanding how bureaucracies work, how they expand the scope of their influence, and how they can be controlled:

> We often forget that the process called communication is, for most men, concerned with action and not with abstract understanding. One man has successfully communicated with another if the latter puts the former's suggestion into effect. In a large organization, communication gravitates to the channels through which this kind of result is achieved.[51]

The lack of freedom which is inherent in bureaucracy thus has a seriously debilitating effect on workers, and no less serious an effect on the people who teach and learn in the schools. Efforts to mitigate these effects which do not touch the organizational structure itself are only palliatives; attitudes and dispositions are not materially changed. The emphasis on greater rewards in industry (which is encouraged by unions) simply exacerbates the problem by drawing attention even further from the purpose or the interest of the work itself. Higher wages are no substitute for the freedom to participate in choosing the nature and conditions of one's work:

> Insofar as a man's livelihood is at the mercy of an irresponsible superior . . . who can compel his reluctant obedience . . . whose actions he is unable to modify or resist, save at the cost of grave personal injury to himself and his dependents . . . he may possess a profusion of more tangible blessings, from beer to motor-bicycles but he can hardly be said to be in possession of freedom.[52]

When freedom is absent, the nature of work becomes meaning-

---

[50] Blau, *op. cit.*, p. 111.
[51] Homans, *op. cit.*, p. 393.
[52] R. H. Tawney. *Equality.* London: George Allen & Unwin Ltd., 1929. p. 224.

less and the worker becomes apathetic—whether it is industrial labor or schoolwork. Peter Drucker has characterized such a situation in industry:

> For the great majority of automobile workers, the only meaning of the job is in the paycheck, not in anything connected with the work or the product. Work appears as something unnatural, a disagreeable, meaningless and stultifying condition of getting the paycheck, devoid of dignity as well as of importance. No wonder that this puts a premium on slovenly work, on slowdowns, and on other tricks to get the same paycheck with less work.[53]

Substitute "students" for "automobile workers," "study" for "work," and "grades and promotion" for "paycheck," and you have a fair characterization of much American education—whether in the city, where students openly rebel, or in the suburbs, where students are more compliant.[54]

## The Question of Efficiency

In a bureaucratic structure, considerations of efficiency outweigh all others. Efficiency takes precedence over freedom of expression, of dissent, and of the mutual formulation of common purposes. A bureaucracy may efficiently implement common purposes once they have been formed; it cannot form them. This inevitable opposition between freedom and bureaucracy poses the main issue in considering the organization of schools:

> Since Tocqueville's time . . . many formerly democratic organizations have become bureaucratized. We generally no longer govern our voluntary associations: we simply join them, pay our dues, and let experts run them. As a result, we have less and less opportunity for acquiring experiences that are essential for effective participation in democratic government.[55]

Americans believe that their children *should* be educated to participate in democratic government. They cannot learn how to do this in a family, which is not an organization of equals; and, as Blau

[53] Peter F. Drucker. *The Concept of the Corporation.* New York: The John Day Company, Inc., copyright © 1946 by Peter F. Drucker, used with permission of the publisher. p. 179.

[54] Even the popular press acknowledges that the malaise of American public school students extends beyond the inner city and deep into the more affluent schools of the suburbs. See: "What's Wrong with the High Schools?" *Newsweek* 75 (7): 65-69; February 16, 1970.

[55] Blau, *op. cit.*, p. 117.

observes, it is not likely to be learned in voluntary groups. Yet children certainly cannot gain practical experience in democratic participation in schools that are bureaucratically organized and controlled.[56] The conclusion seems clear: a nation that provides no settings in which growing children and youth can democratically participate in the formation and carrying out of significant purposes cannot remain a democratic nation. In the 1960's, this conclusion became clear to increasingly larger numbers of Americans, who paid for a war that few understood or wanted to fight, and who began to learn that the army and the police were governing them rather than protecting them.

If freedom is to flourish in schools, if teachers and pupils are to behave like self-directed, intelligent, and increasingly mature human beings, then the bureaucratic structure of school control must eventually disappear. Yet if bureaucracy is abandoned for the sake of freedom, then efficiency must be given up, too. Of course, this only means that efficiency must be given up as a *goal*—as something to aim at—not that it must be given up in practice. For all their current bureaucratic organization, nothing more *in*efficient could be imagined than American schools.[57]

Despite the practical inefficiency of schools, efficiency has been the overriding aim of school administrators ever since the growth of efficiency as the dominant consideration in business and industry. It may be recalled, for example, that accelerating bright students through the school grades got its impetus not from any considerations of the child's benefit, but from the belief that a child who spent less time in school was cheaper to educate.[58]

[56] Symptomatic of the denial of democratic participation in school affairs was a meeting of parents and staff of the DuVal Senior High School in Prince George's County, Maryland, following outbreaks of fighting in school during school hours. The PTA president invited members of the student government to attend this meeting, but when they arrived the principal, supported by most of the parents, insisted that they leave. "Having expelled the 'intruders,' the parents settled down to see if they could determine what the problem in the school was. . . ." The principal appeared to have found the answer: " 'You ask me what I want to restore discipline. Absolute authority. No appeals. No running to make telephone calls. No conferences. When I say something in the school, that's it. That's the authority I want.' Applause." See: Joan Biren. "Talking High School Blues." *Hard Times* 65: 3; February 16-23, 1970.

[57] See, for example: Peter Schrag. *Village School Downtown*. Boston: Beacon Press, 1967.

[58] See: Raymond Callahan. *Education and the Cult of Efficiency*. Chicago: University of Chicago Press, 1962.

Not only are those who hold positions of power in the educational bureaucracy enamored of efficiency, but they also tend—like all bureaucrats—to envision their major task as a maintenance operation. Far from being "impartial" officials, administrators in a school system are deeply committed to the maintenance of the system which maintains their own jobs.[59] Thus, with their ideals of efficiency and their concern with maintenance, it is not likely that school administrators, as presently trained and appointed, will ever constitute anything but an obstacle to the creation of freedom in education.

The administration of schools and school systems is legally responsible to school boards, but these bodies, at least as presently constituted in cities, are not likely to be effective in promoting freedom in education—even if they are composed of the most democratic-minded men and women. There are two important reasons for this. First, school boards must govern *through* their administrators, whose jobs will normally last much longer than the board members' tenure of office. Thus, professional administrators can always "wait out" the directives of school board members. Second, the school board lacks the administrators' expert knowledge, on which it must depend. Thus career school officials will in the long run get their way, while school board members come and go:

> Unless the electorate is given the opportunity to change the key experts as well as the politicians, elections will lose much of their significance.[60]

Thus, the roles and the mutual interrelations of school board members and school administrators pose a special problem for those concerned with freedom in education. A new school board will not change the character of the educational bureaucracy, and there is no way to make the vast and complex structure of school administrators simply disappear. (If there were, their disappearance would likely lead to chaos, which is not necessarily more desirable than bureaucracy.) It would appear, then, that if any significant change is due to appear in education, it is not to be sought from boards of education or from school administrators. If it comes at all, it can come only from those who are most directly involved in the processes

---

[59] See: J. D. Kingsley. "The Execution of Policy." In: Merton, *op. cit.*, p. 219.

[60] Seymour Martin Lipset. "Bureaucracy and Social Change." In: Merton, *op. cit.*, p. 232.

of education and most directly affected by those processes: the teachers, the students, and the local parents.

Teachers have already begun to organize for the purpose of exercising greater power. If a higher salary was the initial goal of many teacher groups, the power to get it has also shown teachers that they had the power to make decisions of educational (as well as financial) policy. Students, too, have begun to assert the legitimacy of their interests in the educational enterprise. The publication of student newspapers has made public the incompetence of some school personnel as well as the anti-educational influence of the school bureaucracy itself. Their use of the courts—even in such apparently trivial matters as the right to wear long hair—underlines their right to be considered young *people*—not simply as "software" being "processed" to fit a preestablished system. In the process of making their influence felt, teachers and students will not always be right.

Yet the very act of *making* decisions and having to live with the consequences will educate both groups, as well as the wider society.

That local parents have some right to participate in the determination of the policies that will guide the schooling of their children is already recognized in what has come to be called "community participation." But the granting of this right does not necessarily ensure participation: efforts of extraordinary complexity are made to exclude local people from the control of their schools. The history of the demise of community control in New York's Ocean Hill-Brownsville district is a monument to the inability of the educational bureaucracy to give up or share its power.[61] At the same time, this and other cases of "community participation" have shown how vulnerable local people are when, in the face of entrenched bureaucracies that oppose them, they cannot agree on very much among themselves.

The reason for the current ineffectiveness of local lay and parent groups in gaining educational power may be attributed to the fact that most of them (again, Ocean Hill-Brownsville serves as an example) do not represent *communities* at all. Homans has observed that, because a particular city, town, or district still has a name, a geographical boundary, and an identifiable population,

... we assume that it is a community and therefore judge that it is

---

[61] See: Joseph Featherstone. "Wiping Out the Demonstration Schools." *The New Republic* 162 (2): 10-11; January 10, 1970.

rotten. It would be wiser to see that it is no longer, except in the most trivial sense, a community at all.[62]

At the very least, community means a group of people creating and sharing common interests and purposes through some conjoint actions. It is probably true that few communities having geographic proximity survive in America at mid-century.[63] But it is also true—and perhaps of crucial importance—that *new* communities can be created. When a group of geographically neighboring people come together to decide on common problems and purposes—such as education—communities are born and grow.[64] It is thus misleading to suppose that preexistent "local communities" have a role to play in educational decisions. But the best hope for education—and society too—may lie in local participation in educational decisions, which will in turn help to create local communities where none existed before.

It has been the intention throughout this essay to show that no serious discussion of freedom in education could ever be limited to considerations of the curriculum of schools or the techniques of teaching. Freedom or its absence is directly a matter of the social and political structure of schools and school systems. Indeed, it is this structure which largely determines whatever particular impact on learners will be had by the curriculum and the techniques by which it is taught. It is for this reason that there is so much futility in the literature on educational change. Changes in the curriculum or in teaching techniques are not likely to make much of a difference in what children learn if the bureaucratic structure of schools remains unchanged. One could not teach children to appreciate gourmet cooking by serving a seven-course meal on a crowded school bus—no matter how well-prepared the meal. By the same token, "discovery" techniques of teaching and up-to-date texts will not result in better science education if they are employed within

---

[62] Homans, *op. cit.*, p. 367.

[63] This may be contrasted to communities *without* geographic proximity, for example, the AMA, the Democratic Party, the graduates of Wellesley College, the Friends of the Handel and Haydn Society, etc.

[64] This is what Horace Mann intended when he spoke of the community-creating role of the school board. Needless to say, he had smaller, face-to-face communities in mind than those served by school boards today. See: Lawrence A. Cremin. *The Republic and the School: Horace Mann on the Education of Free Men.* New York: Bureau of Publications, Teachers College, Columbia University, 1957. pp. 8, 19-20.

the same old bureaucratic structures that put severe restrictions on the choices of teachers and pupils.

The educational bureaucracy will never *give* freedom to teachers, parents, and pupils, for this would call for a voluntary release of power. Historically, no group in power has ever just given it away. When power was lost, it was actively taken by someone else. But if freedom is to appear in education, it cannot result from the efforts of any single group. Freedom is not a possession that can be given by one group to others; it is a condition that exists when all groups share in making decisions. This sharing of power will result in educational policies that are more tentative, and in practices that are more flexible and alterable. It will also result in the disappearance of the educational bureaucracy, and its replacement by more numerous, smaller, local centers of policy making.

Like the hole in a doughnut, freedom can never be created directly. It only appears when something else is achieved. That something else is *power:* the capacity to deliberately make decisions of educational policy and practice and to act on those decisions. Local parents, teachers groups, and school pupils have already taken the first tentative steps toward achieving that power. And as these groups have debated and acted, they have found—some of them for the first time—what it means to *think,* productively and effectively.

The genuine possibility of *doing* something encourages careful thought; action thus promotes thinking as well as creates power. When teachers, parents, and pupils can act, the resultant wide distribution of power will constitute the best guarantee of freedom in education. This freedom, which will accompany a reduction of the power of the present educational bureaucracy, is the only sort of freedom worth striving for in education. Other "freedoms" which can presumably be "given" by administrators to teachers, or by teachers to pupils, are superficial and illusory, and only distract attention from relationships of genuine political significance. But the consequential freedom that is sought in education is never found in the mere seeking; it can appear only when something else is deliberately aimed at:

> If attention is centered upon the conditions which have to be met in order to secure a situation favorable to effective thinking, freedom will take care of itself.[65]

[65] John Dewey, *op. cit.*, pp. 355-56.

# 2

# Schools as a "Guidable" System

## Amitai Etzioni

SCHOOLS again stand charged with curricular and structural rigidities, with inability to adjust to the rapidly changing needs of the contemporary society. Schools are depicted as attempting to perpetuate lower-middle class values, those closest to the hearts of teachers and small businessmen, to yesterday America. Schools are reported to be unresponsive to the needs of pupils from disadvantaged backgrounds as well as alienating to upper-middle class youths, who are no longer interested in hard work or adding to their affluence but seek a more hedonistic, reflective, cultural, or politically active life. Schools are said to be slow to introduce the innovations necessary to keep the country at the forefront in scientific creativity and technological developments. Some critics go so far as to suggest doing away with education in schools, preferring the spontaneity of the streets to contemporary "bureaucratic" education. Somewhat less extreme critics favor the establishment of a second range of school systems to circumvent the existing ones, which are viewed as hopelessly obsolescent, "immune" to innovation.

Without undertaking a study to determine to what extent American schools have ossified, I will briefly indicate the factors which make for rigidity and the conditions under which schools may "loosen up." In doing so, I shall focus on those factors which are relatively movable; other factors need to be studied before we will have a full explanation of the school world, but for policy makers and active citizens, the movable factors are of more interest. Such limitation is possible because the movable factors are *not* linked to the other factors so closely as to prevent far-reaching and encompassing changes without first unearthing, dismantling, and resettling the foundations. Actually, such reforms may be the best way to get at the "deeper" forces.

## Toward a Theory of "Societal Guidance"

In the attempt to relieve the sources of school system rigidities and to prescribe for increased transformability, we draw on a theory of societal guidance we have developed over the recent years.[1] The central question the theory attempts to answer is the following: under what conditions can a process be guided, a system be changed, in line with goals set by its members? We discuss the theory first abstractly, then apply it to school systems.

The social science literature offers two approaches to the subject.[2] The first is *voluntaristic*, in which the will (or commitment), brain power (or staff work), and skill (or political astuteness) of the leadership is expected to account for the difference between successful and unsuccessful social programs and institutions. (In the popular press, voluntaristic interpretations tend to focus on the President and his personal attributes to explain why America does or does not reduce crime, integrate the races, and so on.) Closely related are administrative theories which imply that if communication lines were set up properly, if labor were divided correctly, etc., the system could effectively accomplish its mission.

The second approach focuses on the forces which, for example, resist facts. This view implies that under most circumstances, it is not possible to anticipate or overcome all the numerous and intricate resistances to change; zigzagging and muddling through are a result of human nature, not the failing of this or that organization.

Our theory draws on both approaches. We ask about the qualities of the *controlling overlay* which attempts to direct and redirect the system, and the attributes of the *social underlay* which receives, rejects, or modifies the signals of the overlay, and emits some signals of its own to the overlay. Above all, we seek to understand the interplay between these two layers, which we see as determining the extent to which a system will move, ossify, or change.

To determine the elements necessary for an effective overlay, we draw on cybernetics. Cybernetics is the study of steering, of communication and control. Originally, it was mainly concerned with the ways in which groups of machines are guided to work jointly to realize goals that the cybernetic overlayer sets. Such an overlayer includes: (a) one or more centers transmitting signals to the units that carry out the work (there are some subunits in these

---

[1] Amitai Etzioni. *The Active Society: A Theory of Societal and Political Processes.* New York: The Free Press, 1968.

[2] *Ibid.*, Chapter 4.

centers which specialize in absorbing and analyzing incoming information and other subunits which specialize in making decisions); (b) communication lines leading from the centers to the working units, carrying specific instructions; and (c) feedback lines, carrying information and responses from the working units to the centers. Though many cybernetic models omit power lines, I consider these to be of major importance. If the steering units cannot back up their signals with rewards for those elements of the system that comply with the communications signals, and penalties for those who do not, many signals will be disregarded.

When all the elements described briefly here are available and function effectively, the result is an effective *control* system. Some engineers and managers maintain that a social system can be similarly directed. It is my position, however, that when a cybernetic model is applied to a social system, the model must take into account that, for both ethical and practical reasons, the working units cannot be coerced to follow "signals" unless these signals are responsive, at least in some measure, to the members' values and interests. In other words, the "downward" flow of control signals must be accompanied by "upward" and "lateral" (intermember) flows which shape what the members demand, desire, and are willing to do. Petitions to the government and doorbell ringing during elections are cases in point. In more technical language, these upward and lateral flows are referred to as *consensus building*.

The combination of control and consensus building—the mechanisms of societal cybernetics—is termed *societal guidance*.

## The Elements of Societal Guidance

The differences between active and passive social systems, between those more able and those less able to handle their problems, are best studied by examining one cybernetic factor at a time, although effective guidance requires that they be combined.

### Knowledge Units

When one examines the amount of funds, the size of the manpower force, and the capability of the experts assigned to collect and process knowledge in one specific area (for example, defense) in comparison with the resources devoted to other activities (for example, health), one can gain a rough idea how "knowledgeable" social action in the particular sector is likely to be. It becomes apparent, for instance, that one reason most societies score poorly in the management of domestic programs is that they spend much more on the knowledge required to handle nature. Thus, we know much more about the dark side of the moon than the inner side of our cities.

Whatever knowledge is "produced" must be communicated to the decision makers before it becomes useful to societal guidance. Even in corporations, research and development units face difficulties when they seek to gain the ear of top management. In less rational organizations, the distance between the experts and the decision makers is often enormous. It is not only that the knowledge available does not reach the decision makers, but that which they wish to know is not known to the knowledge makers.

## Decision Making

The decision-making strategies the guidance centers explicitly or implicitly follow obviously affect the quality of their efforts. Members of Anglo-Saxon societies are inclined to be pragmatic, to muddle through, making a few limited decisions at a time; they tend to oppose long-run planning. Such an approach is effective when the environment is relatively stable and the existing system is basically sound. But when fundamental changes are required, or when the system has ossified, the difficulties of such decision making mount.

Decision makers in totalitarian societies often err in the opposite direction. They tend to assume a greater capacity to control than they actually possess. Thus, they overplan and frequently launch major projects, or "Great Leaps," which they are forced to scale down and recast at great economic and human cost.

It would be tempting to state that the most effective decision-making strategy is a happy medium between muddling through or overplanning. But it seems more precise to suggest that the capacity to plan or to make encompassing and anticipatory decisions increases as the technology of communication, knowledge storing and retrieval, computation, and research improves. Since World War II, and especially during the past 15 years, the technology of communication has developed with great rapidity. Thus, the objective capacity to guide is on the rise; societies that were overplanning three decades ago now may find more of the tools their ambitious approach requires, and societies that muddle through are wasting more of their potential ability to guide than they did in earlier ages. This is not to say that totalistic planning can or will be carried out, but that more planning than was practicable in the past is becoming quite rewarding.

At the same time, each society seems to have roughly the decision-making apparatus suitable to its character. Decision-making strategies are not chosen merely on the basis of the technical capacity to guide; they partially reflect the political structure of the society. Democratic decision making tends toward muddling through because there is no effective central authority that can impose a set of central decisions, especially in domestic affairs. The decisions reached are the outcome of the pulling and pushing of a large variety of private and public interest groups. No consistent pattern is possible. Totalitarian decision making tends to follow a straight line, but it also tends to run roughshod over the feelings and interests of most of the citizens. Thus, the conditions under which a "middling" decision making may evolve—one that would be more encompassing and "deeper" than democratic decision making, and more humane than totalitarian decision making—lie not only in the availability of new technologies but also in a proper power constellation.

## Power

All communities (from the national to the local one) are compositions of groupings (economic, ethnic, regional, and so forth) that differ in the share they command of the totality of social resources and power. The distribution of resources and power in a community significantly affects its capacity to treat its problems and to change its ways. It is useful to consider the distribution of power in two respects: (a) between the members of a community and their government, and (b) *among* the members of the community.

The government may overpower a community. Such a situation arises when the state bureaucracies checkmate all other power centers in the society; an example of this is a take-over by a military junta. On the other hand, the government may be overpowered by the community or some grouping within it; such a situation arises in highly feudal societies and in tribal societies. When the government is overcentralized, societal guidance tends to be unresponsive to the needs and values of most of its members; when the government is overpowered, the major societal agencies for planning and acting are neutralized, or are directed to serve those member groupings which have amassed most of the power in the community.

Only a tense balance between society and the state—each one

guarding its autonomy—can result in relatively responsive and active guidance. Democracy itself requires such a power constellation. Sufficient government power is needed to prevent violent expression of the conflicts that inevitably arise among the members of the society, and to prevent the overpowering of some members by others. Autonomous "social" power must be held by groupings of members in order to sustain the political give-and-take, the capacity to change those who guide the state if they cease to be responsive to the plurality of its members.

Democracy, it follows, is most fully realized when the distribution of power among the members of a society most closely approximates equality. Since no social grouping has moral superiority, the only way to assure a society responsive to all the membership is to give each member as equal a share as feasible of the society's guidance mechanisms.

## Mobilization and Societal Change

The distribution of resources and power in all societies is inegalitarian; some members and groupings of members have much more power than others, and are thus able to slant societal efforts in directions that favor their interests. In order to be better equipped to treat its problems, our pluralistic society requires some reduction of power differences among its various groupings of members. One major way to achieve greater equality in the power structure is *mobilization of the underprivileged and weaker groupings.* It was through such mobilization that the working classes made their way into power in Western societies; Negro Americans are trying to mobilize now.

# The Limited Guidability of School Systems

In applying the preceding theory to the analysis of American school systems, we shall focus on three categories of factors—those pertaining to knowledge, decision making, and consensus building. Each category is *illustrated* in the school context; no attempts at exhaustive treatment are made.

## Knowledge Input

Kenneth Boulding distinguished between folk knowledge and scientific knowledge. "*Folk knowledge* is the process by which we acquire knowledge in the ordinary business of life, and in ordinary relationships in the family, among friends, and in the peer group, and so on."[3] *Scientific knowledge* entails the "constant revision of images of the world under the impact of refined observation and testing."[4] The introduction of new, highly efficient, and effective techniques in most areas of our life, from industry to medicine, involves the transition from heavy reliance on folk to scientific knowledge. One of the reasons contemporary schools are basically no different from the way they were in the beginning of the 19th century is that their management relies much more on folk than on scientific knowledge. Although we are unaware that there is scientific evidence to support our hunch, we would expect that those school systems which use more scientific knowledge are more efficient and more effective.

Most decision making in meetings of boards of education, offices of superintendents, or offices of school principals proceeds without the benefit of staff work or research which would characterize a similar decision in terms of magnitude in industry, the military, or the space agency. The point is not that the educational decision makers mix their knowledge with value judgment; this is natural, unavoidable, and basically desirable. The issues at hand—for example, should there be sex education in elementary schools?—are not just informational matters but also involve moral and political considerations. Therefore, it is to be expected that such issues will be colored by nonrational considerations.

Yet the same issues frequently also have an information content. To stay with the example at hand, the statements that teachers are qualified to teach sex education after X weeks of training; that the parents can provide better sex education than teachers; that teaching the course at all, or in a specific way, will lead to earlier sexual experimentation by the pupil, are all testable. On these issues, the educational decision makers are not ignorant, but they tend to draw on the folk knowledge they acquired in their own years of teaching, on discussion of the issues with teachers, and on personal observations. These are relevant, but they are inferior ways of knowing as compared to scientific knowledge. However, educational decision makers—it seems to us—are less inclined to draw upon scientific knowledge than are many other decision makers.

The most elementary reason for the less frequent use of scientific knowledge in the guidance of school systems as compared to

[3] Kenneth E. Boulding. *The Impact of Social Science.* New Brunswick, New Jersey: Rutgers University Press, 1966. p. 7.
[4] *Ibid.*

industry is that less education-relevant knowledge is produced. Hence, even the most open-minded, rational decision maker in education will frequently have to fall back on his folk knowledge because this is the only way of knowing he has. While some matters are by now rather carefully covered by research (for example, the efficacy of TV for instructional purposes as compared to preschool teaching), most relevant questions are not. Basically, we still do not know how to effectively help children from disadvantaged backgrounds to catch up and stay up; we do not know what the best way of teaching reading is; and, to stay with our example of sex education, most of the questions we have characterized above as researchable have not, as far as we can establish, actually been answered by research.

Investment in educational research is *much* smaller than in lunar visits, not to mention weapons or atomic energy. In 1969-70, the research budget of most programs of the U.S. Office of Education and other HEW agencies has been reduced.[5] Other sources of support for educational research are far from sufficient.

Unfortunately, much of the educational research that is conducted is low in quality. Educational research suffers from the low prestige in which teachers colleges and schools of education have been held in academia until recently, a factor which tended not to attract the best minds to research in education. Some improvement in the status of educational research can be expected as the increased concern with societal issues attracts more social scientists and economists to study education; some of the stigma is now being removed. As better research, and more of it, is carried out in this area, more and better minds are attracted to it.

Academicians tend to prefer basic rather than applied research and have helped to perpetuate the myth that the best way to gain knowledge is through individual work in the vineyards of basic research. While such preparation of the ground is needed, the link between basic and applied science is weak. Much of the basic research has no application, and much of the applied knowledge is not born out of basic research but is the result of applied work per se. Hence, in order to have applied psychology affect educational research needs, investment must be made in applied psychology as well as basic psychological research. In non-social science areas, this point has long been recognized. Medicine is not merely the teaching of biology and physiology, but also the teaching of the

---

[5] *The Chronicle of Higher Education,* January 19, 1970.

findings of medical research, traditions, skills; it has a core of knowledge of its own. Natural sciences also need systematic studies of technology and engineering. Studies of the relation of technology to basic sciences have taught us that information and stimulation are not all a one-way flow from science to technology (and hence to application), but a two-way flow, with at least as many findings flowing from technology to science as the other way around. In the social science area, which is the science that education draws on most, this is less fully realized. Attempts are being made to move directly from the findings of basic research to action programs.

Important for the growth of applied education is the establishment of educational laboratories whose missions include precisely the development of the applied and technological aspects of knowledge needed for improved educational programs. Hence, the *conception* of these laboratories seems to us to be fine and valid. The reason that these laboratories have answered only part of the need for applied research lies not in the concept, but in the way it was implemented. The difficulties encountered deserve a major study. Briefly, they lie in an untrained or poorly trained staff; fascination with esoteric, expensive technology, rather than with techniques for mass use; psychological reductionism, which leads to the search for causes and cures in the personality (or in interpersonal relations), while the leverages for change rest in the societal structure and processes; and, above all, disassociation of the laboratories from their "clientele."

These are only a few of the ineffectual communications links between the knowledge and the decision makers. Knowledge makers are not sufficiently "sensitized" to the constraints under which the decision makers operate, and the decision makers are not adequately "prepared" for the findings of research. Both sides act as if a good will and an open mind are all that is necessary. However, institutionalization of interaction is required. As a result, reports and recommendations of the knowledge makers are often ignored, because the "clients" (school boards, for instance) did not participate in "ordering" the product, nor did they prepare for its innovative implications.

Even given effective educational R and D centers and laboratories serving the various school systems, there would still be a need for a wider perspective in matters of educational policy. In other words, the knowledge makers should not overly concern themselves with the thousand smaller decisions—for example: Should we use instructional TV? What is the best classroom size for a given kind of student? What reading techniques are most effective? Should slum children be taught first in their English or in standard English? Instead, the knowledge makers should look to the long-range questions—for example: Should high school education be more humanistic or more technical in orientation in view of the changing needs of society? Is dropping out to be discouraged, or should avenues for ready return from a year or more of "leave" be provided for?

Recognizing the need to base longer-run policy on systematic input of knowledge, the U.S. Office of Education set up two institutes for policy research—one in Syracuse, New York, and the other in Stanford, California. Neither has so far fulfilled this function, as both were so remote from policy making that they focused on exploring Utopian futures, in abstract and general ways, with very little informational content, under the disguise of studying the year 2000. It might be of interest to note that the opposite imbalance seems to have occurred in the Institute for the Study of Poverty, set up by the U.S. Office of Economic Opportunity in Madison, Wisconsin. This one seems to have become too closely guided by the patron agency to allow for full-fledged autonomous critical research.[6] The Rand Corporation, in its work for the U.S. Air Force, provides a closer approximation of the kind of "think tank" needed by school systems, state departments of education, and the U.S. Office of Education.

The *knowledge absorbers of school systems* must be reorganized in order to be able to digest and use even that knowledge which is available now; as more powerful and relevant knowledge becomes available they must learn not only how to utilize it, but how to sort out the usable knowledge from the junk. Typically, research reports are handed in to boards of education or offices of superintendents. If the reports contain information which, even by implication, reflects poorly on the school—for instance, if the report suggests that the school reading program ought to be modified—the tendency is to suppress the report. (In one case, the superintendent offered to pay the full costs of the report on the condition that all copies would be burned.) When there is no direct threatening information, reports are frequently ignored. The basic issue is that exploring the consequences of new information, assessing innovations, deciding that they are to be used, then making the necessary adaptations and seeing to it that they are introduced, all require considerable effort.

[6] A systematic study of the Institute is under way, conducted by the National Academy of Science.

By and large, school systems and schools are long on organizational "bodies" and short on "heads"; they have insufficient staff in the headquarters, and little or no organization to deal with incoming knowledge or to help its utilization within the system. School systems should have research units of their own, not so much concerned with conducting research (although some "in-house" evaluation would be very helpful) as with dealing with the translation of findings into programs, and supervising their revisions as implementation is tried. All too often, schools act as if they subscribe to the rationalist model, according to which knowledge flies on its own wings; a new technique or procedure evolves and principals and teachers will pick it up as soon as its merits are explained to them—say, in a stenciled circular, over the intercom, or in a teacher's journal. However, long experience in and out of schools suggests that special organizations and efforts are needed, not only for the production of relevant knowledge, but to help its introduction into the system, from seminars for teachers on new techniques to verification that promised changes were actually made.

## Decision Making: Limited and Fragmented

A mistake wise administrators avoid is the assumption that they can manage the schools. Typically, most of the alternatives are closed off by forces beyond anyone's control, such as the nature of the building, for example, immovable walls, the failure of the last three bond votes, or the backlash mood of the public. Schools are probably less manageable than industrial corporations because they are more in the public eye; they deal in precious commodities (children, values); their achievements are difficult to measure; and their staff members have professional aspirations and hence tend to resist authority. Under what conditions school systems can be made significantly more guidable depends largely on new efforts at consensus building.

A central feature of the American school system, which distinguishes it from many other systems—for instance, the French and the Israeli—and which reduces its guidability while it increases the system's responsiveness to local needs and values, is its high *fragmentation*. It is common to refer in this context to decentralization, but this assumes there is a center which delegated its authority, in part, to subcenters. It is a key feature of the American education system that there is no center which can make any significant decisions for the nation's schools. The closest we come to decision-making centers are the state departments of education, but in most states much of the decision-making power does not reside in this department; it rests with thousands of school boards. This in turn means that the process of innovations consists of bargaining and persuasion, and not administrative decrees.

This is not to suggest that federalization of the guidance of education is desirable. Nationalization of education in America may well bring about an education system unresponsive to important local differences which the American people simply would not tolerate. Yet one must also realize the consequences of lack of centralization in assessing the speed with which the American schools can accommodate and the ways in which such accommodation can be brought about. It is by necessity slow and uneven. Thus, it is difficult to answer the question: can schools be recast to be more streamlined following a crisis, or in anticipation of a crisis? Some gain in guidability may be possible, but its significance will be hard to forecast. Actually, one may even argue that, in crises, schools "freeze" rather than innovate; this would seem to fit the situation in New York City.[7]

## Consensus Building

Schools are a weak institution; they are much less powerful than most corporations, from industries to armies. Schools prosper only at the tolerance of the taxpayers, and hence must take into account community pressures to keep up the legitimation of their efforts.[8] When they veer outside the fairly narrow band of alternate courses that the majority of the citizens of a community—its active elite and its politically conscious minorities—find tolerable without first gaining an "approval," the board of education is likely to be challenged in the next election; superintendents are made to resign; education becomes a major political issue in statewide elections (as in Cali-

[7] David Rogers. *110 Livingston Street: Politics and Bureaucracy in the New York City Schools.* New York: Random House, Inc., 1968.

[8] A typical illustration of the challenge to the legitimacy of the existing school system is the following statement in the Winter 1967 issue of the *Harvard Educational Review.* The authors are critical of the great society because "it accepts as given the premises that education is (a) formal schooling, operating as (b) a public monopoly, (c) modeled after the organizational structure and utilitarian values of corporate business." See: Fred M. Newmann and Donald W. Oliver. "Education and Community." *Harvard Educational Review* 37 (1): 73; Winter 1967.

fornia); school bonds are repeatedly defeated; and, ultimately, whole classes of people move their children out of public schools and cease to view them as "theirs." All this is rather well known; what is less clear is what conclusions follow.

Our theory suggests that public schools must either rapidly and broadly increase their legitimation, relying on old and new consensus-building mechanisms, or else financial shortage, riots, and alienation of citizens, parents, and students will severely constrict their very ability to function. Three different matters are involved: substance, procedure, and structure.

## Substance

Next to the family and the church, the schools are one of the most important normative agents of society in the transmission of moral and ideological values. No wonder there is continuous tension between those who formulate the curriculum for the school and various segments of the society whose values differ from those which guide the curriculum makers. In the past, such major value differences led to the establishment of parallel school systems; first the religious schools, especially Catholic ones, were formed, and recently secular private schools are proliferating, especially in the bigger cities. Further privatization of schooling would further undermine legitimation and tax base of the public system. The public system is unlikely to collapse, but it will be even more severely hobbled. Moreover, some of the challenges which the public schools have faced are also faced by the private—especially secular—schools. To identify the challenges is to determine what must be responded to.

One challenge is from the minorities, especially the black community. The black community seeks control of schools in its neighborhoods for a variety of reasons ranging from a desire to control the allocation of jobs, especially those of principals, to a desire to promote a distinct set of values, a black subculture. The public school as now constituted, even in areas in which all students are black, tends not to be an effective vehicle to communicate the black subculture; on the contrary, it is geared to transmit a lower-middle class white culture.

Many persons believe that it is necessary to respond to these demands by minority groups through denying their legitimacy. They would give three main reasons: (a) the black subculture is not rich enough to constitute a body deserving or requiring study; (b) the school should not make room for subcultures; it is to transmit only the dominant culture if national units are to be sustained; and (c) if one subculture is allowed in, all the others will make similar demands.

In reference to the first point, while this cannot be demonstrated here, there is, for example, a body of black literature, song, music, novels, and history which certainly provides adequate teaching material. Moreover, this body is rapidly growing; even if it was not big enough yesterday (when the "clients" were few), it is rapidly maturing. Second, while the school should transmit the prevailing culture, it enriches all students and helps those of a subculture to find their place in the school if it also transmits the values of the subcultures. True, unifying themes must be preserved; children cannot be allowed to learn that their subculture is superior to any other subculture or main theme. Finally, additional subcultures may indeed have to be accommodated; the Irish and the Italians may follow the blacks, Mexicans, and Orientals. This can be achieved without splintering the curriculum by (a) varying it according to the community (for example, in parts of Texas, most Mexican and black subcultures will have to be accommodated but not the Oriental one; the Oriental subculture in turn will have to be included in some parts of San Francisco); (b) general courses on the U.S.A. as a pluralistic, multi-ethnic society may provide part of the answer.

The specific curriculum reforms which are needed do not concern us here, nor can they be universal for all the parts of the country, from Montana to Harlem. It seems clear, however, (a) that greater attention to the pluralistic nature of the country should be provided in all schools, and (b) that where there is a demand, an opportunity to gain familiarity with one's subculture should be provided.

However, the student should be taught the subculture not as a substitute for the dominant culture but in such a way that he will better understand the main culture.

A second substantive revision concerns not the minority underclass variant, but the upper-middle class one. Man's schools are still most closely tied to the lower-middle class and upper working class values, reflecting most accurately the values to which the majority of teachers subscribe. These are the past-oriented values of the numerous small businessmen on the school boards; they are geared to the values of the industrializing society and seek to build up achievement motivation to produce hard working, orderly, saving students. These are the kinds of values now promoted in underdeveloped countries which seek to industrialize. But with a trillion dollar a year GNP, with the income per capita of the upper and middle classes soaring, there is a big and growing class of students who are oriented to the society which will take affluence for granted, and seek to explore ways to use it rather than further expand it. In this class, there is a growing interest in a life of reflection, cultural creativity, active participation in public affairs—and hedonism. The curricula of most schools have only begun to come to grips with these new demands. Thus, schools tend to alienate not only minority lower class students, but also the white sons and daughters of those who are well-off.

## Structure

It has been frequently pointed out that the school teaches not only in terms of what the teachers say, or what the curriculum offers, but in the way the whole system is set up. Robert Dreeben, in *On What Is Learned in School*, recently provided a careful analysis of the organizational properties of the school, depicting it as the transition belt from the warm family to the cold occupational world.[9] Viewed in this way, the school structure has changed little since schools were originally founded, or at least they have not changed since they began shaping persons to participate in the world of productivity in a response to the needs of industrial structures. Yet recently the productivity structure has changed by requiring even more persons with creative or professional skills, and thus it is necessary, for example, to train them differently, in different structures, with more independent study, greater flexibility in the size of teaching units, and in the time span of each unit. Some of what is being tried in this context is unavoidably gimmicky, innovating for innovation's sake, quick to gain popularity, soon to be forgotten. Other innovations deserve to be sustained, and out of these—slowly, to be sure—may emerge a new structure of instruction or, most likely, several alternative patterns of instruction, with the student being able to choose among them, perhaps even able to shift back and forth among them. Obviously, such a new school will emerge first in some parts of the country, while others will still sustain more traditional formats, either because they are more resistant to social change or because their clientele is still oriented to the productivity world.

[9] Robert Dreeben. *On What Is Learned in School*. Reading, Massachusetts: Addison-Wesley Publishing Company, 1968.

## Procedure

It is not surprising that superintendents, principals, and teachers tend to feel most comfortable when the decisions concerning curriculum and structure are left in their hands. They like to see themselves as professionals, and hence free from public scrutiny. They also have self-interests which are best served when the public mind is preoccupied with other matters. For instance, they pay no attention to the ways in which teachers gain their teaching qualifications—that is, by taking what are known as "Mickey Mouse" educational "method" courses. But with education becoming an ever more central societal ladder for upward mobility, both economically and socially, and with the concern over education being aroused in the general public by activist groups, it is hard to see how the public can be expected to be removed from the arena.

Next to being completely left alone, school systems (like other corporate bodies) prefer to consult the public in ways which allow the schools to help the public, especially the parents and taxpayers, to see things the schools' way. The PTA meeting has become a symbol of manipulated participation, of co-optation. In a different period than the one in front of us, and in parts of the country in which rapid social change has not yet reached, the professional claim for autonomy or the co-optation techniques may still work. But in schools at the forefront of change, new potency will have to be given to the old participatory mechanisms and new ones will have to be evolved, because unless the public will re-legitimate the schools, and unless the schools are willing to learn the reasons the public is withdrawing legitimacy, the school system—especially the public one—will be severely hampered in carrying out its mission.

To say that the school system must become more responsive to new demands of various publics is not to suggest a view of the school as a democracy, in which the teachers are elected and instructed by the parents, their students, or a town meeting. The result of such a mechanical application of democratic principles would be an education system which would be unacceptable not only to the teachers who value their professionalism, but also to the parents and students who value education. Herbert Kohl, who is quite favorable to radical experimentation, wrote in the October 1969 issue of *The New York Review of Books,* referring to a freedom school set up in Mississippi: "Many parents, however, wanted a stricter system that they thought would quickly prepare their children to read, do arithmetic, and follow rules, and they didn't care much for the liberal educational philosophy. . . ." Education, in fact, flows best down a status structure; when the teachers depend on their charges, it does not flow well. And there are many decisions for which professional knowledge is required.

At the same time, teaching is not medicine. Everyone has had a personal experience of good and bad teachers, and the criteria for telling them apart are not half as difficult to fathom as those of medicine. Schools are given to more public scrutiny than hospitals or law firms. Where the balance between professional autonomy and public accountability lies; how the public can be brought into genuine participation in helping reform schools without over-controlling—these are complex problems for which we cannot advance solutions here.[10] However, one observation seems safe: unless more and better consensus building—in matters of substance, structure, and procedure—is added to more informed and less fragmented decision making, the schools—especially the public ones—will be increasingly more out of step with a rapidly changing society and will suffer the battering that ossified institutions take in stormy days.

[10] For an elaboration, see: Amitai Etzioni, editor. *The Semi-Professions and New Organization.* New York: The Free Press, 1969.

# 3

# Law, Freedom, Equality— and Schooling

### Arthur E. Wise and Michael E. Manley-Casimir

"FREEDOM" and "equality" are the watchwords of the democratic ideology. Separately, each concept distinguishes a distinct strand in the evolution of the democratic tradition.[1] Together, they conjure images of the American ideal—the ideal which is formally enshrined in the Constitution of the United States. The Constitution, as amended and as modified by judicial interpretation, delineates the specific rights and privileges of the individual with respect to the state. The First Amendment, for example, clearly limits Congressional action in the area of individual rights and freedoms:

Congress shall make no law respecting an establishment of religion, or prohibiting the free exercise thereof; or abridging the freedom of speech, or of the press; or the right of the people peaceably to assemble, and to petition the Government for a redress of grievances.

The Fourteenth Amendment reaffirms the right of all citizens to the protection of the federal Constitution and prohibits any state from making or enforcing any law

. . . which shall abridge the privileges or immunities of citizens of the United States; nor shall any State deprive any person of life, liberty, or property, without due process of law; nor deny to any person within its jurisdiction the equal protection of the laws.

Yet in spite of the magnificence of these ideas, they are par-

[1] George H. Sabine. "The Two Democratic Traditions." *Philosophical Review* 61: 451-74; October 1952.

ticularly resistant to concrete formulation and implementation in day-to-day situations. Frequently, recourse to the courts is necessary for interpretation of the Constitutional provisions and for resolution of competing claims.

Profound and far-reaching questions have recently been raised concerning the application of the Constitution to education. These questions directly involve the ideas of freedom and equality contained in the First and Fourteenth Amendments to the Constitution. The overarching issue is whether public school students are protected by the Constitution and, if so, to what extent this protection covers them while in school. More specifically, the issue is one of discretionary justice.[2] In other words, are the discretionary judgments made by school officials in the organization and administration of the public schools consistent with the provisions of the Constitution, or are these decisions incompatible with the Constitution? In essence, this is the question that the courts are answering case by case.

This chapter is concerned with two main substantive questions. The first question is the extent to which public school students are protected by the First Amendment rights to freedom of expression and press while in school. The second question focuses on the current method of organizing education, especially in terms of the provision of financial resources, and asks whether the provision of unequal educational opportunity within a state constitutes a denial by that state of the equal protection clause of the Fourteenth Amendment. Relevant to both these questions is the applicability of the due process clauses of the Fifth and Fourteenth Amendments to students in school disciplinary proceedings. This is an important question that the courts have not yet faced squarely.

## Conceptual Framework

Golding provides an appropriate analytic framework for ordering these two controversial questions.[3] He suggests that the social ideal governing a community determines the system of rights enjoyed by the members of that community. The rights are derived from the social ideal. Thus, in the United States, the Constitution

[2] For a seminal analysis of the problems associated with discretionary justice see: Kenneth C. Davis. *Discretionary Justice*. Baton Rouge: Louisiana State University Press, 1969.

[3] M. P. Golding. "Towards a Theory of Human Rights." *The Monist* 52 (4): 521-49; October 1968. Used with permission of the author and publisher.

and the precedents of case law embody the system of rights enjoyed by the citizens. These rights received concrete formulation to facilitate the achievement of the democratic ideal as set forth by the Founding Fathers in their writings and such immortal documents as the Declaration of Independence.

There are two types of rights—option-rights and welfare-rights. The heart of option-rights is the idea that the individual possesses a limited sovereignty over property, things, and himself. The individual's personal sovereignty is limited by the sovereignty others can claim over him, by his duties toward others, and by his duty to himself. Otherwise the individual may act at his *option*. Golding succinctly defines option-rights in the following way:

> Option-rights are, in a sense, spheres of autonomy (although they should not be identified with such spheres, in my view). Such rights invoke the idea of freedom of the individual; and if we identify or connect, in an essential way, having rights with having option-rights, then the question of the extent of one's rights concerns the freedom that one is to have.[4]

Thus the notion of freedom is quintessentially involved with option-rights. Conceptualized as "spheres of autonomous action," option-rights include a limited sovereignty but take concrete shape in well defined and highly specific *freedoms*. Equality is also involved inasmuch as option-rights obtain to each full member of the community equally.

Welfare-rights complement option-rights. Just as freedom is the dominant conceptual emphasis in option-rights, so equality is the dominant emphasis in welfare-rights. Welfare-rights are essentially the rights of community members to an equitable share of the material goods and services of the community. As Golding notes:

> These are welfare-rights, and are rights to the goods of life or are derived from such rights. The great expansion of rights in modern times has taken place in respect of welfare-rights. Treitschke, I believe, has been credited with the statement that the greatest modern innovation is the idea that every person has a right to an education; and this would fall into the category of welfare-rights.[5]

The problematic issues derive from membership status in the community. Full members may legitimately claim all the option-rights and welfare-rights to which they are entitled by the terms of

[4] *Ibid.*, p. 546.
[5] *Ibid.*, p. 543.

the ideal. Yet to what extent do those who are less than full members enjoy the rights which the ideal imports? Traditionally, children and teen-agers were considered minors, that is, not full community members and consequently not entitled to the rights enjoyed by a full member. The conception of students as partial community members is reflected in the doctrine of *in loco parentis*.[6] This doctrine recognized that students were not full community members and conferred a wide latitude of discretionary power upon school officials to stand "in place of parents" to the child while the child was under the school's jurisdiction. However, recent court decisions affirming the option-rights of public school students suggest a changing conception of the membership status of students in contemporary American society.

Although, in theory, members of minority and other "unincorporated"[7] groups are entitled to full benefits of their welfare-rights, in actual practice there are wide discrepancies in the degree to which people have access to and actually enjoy the material goods and services of the society. Education, historically considered a privilege, has become a personal imperative. The life chances of the individual are largely determined by the level of his educational achievement. A high school diploma or a college degree facilitates access to the occupational structure. Occupational success usually confers economic security, social status, and a generally satisfying life style. These benefits, in large part, flow from educational achievement. Hence, barriers to equal educational opportunity that derive from the traditional organization and administration of public schools may constitute a denial of the welfare-rights of individuals and groups of citizens.

This chapter explores both the option-rights and welfare-rights of public school students. Option-rights are discussed in terms of the First Amendment rights to freedom of expression and freedom of press. Welfare-rights are analyzed in terms of the growing debate

---

[6] For the historical development of the doctrine of *in loco parentis* see: Kaye D. Moran. "An Historical Development of the Doctrine Loco Parentis with Court Interpretations in the United States." Unpublished Ph.D. dissertation, University of Kansas, 1967. Chapter 2.

[7] The term "unincorporated" is used by Westin to mean those who ". . . have been blocked in various ways from access to the mainstream of American political and social life." See: Alan F. Westin. "Responding to Rebels with a Cause." In: *The School and the Democratic Environment*, The Danforth and Ford Foundations. New York: Columbia University Press, 1970. p. 69.

over the applicability of the equal protection clause of the Fourteenth Amendment to the provision of public school education. The right to due process is discussed last because it is relevant to both option-rights and welfare-rights.

## Option-Rights of Public School Students

The Fourteenth Amendment, as now applied to the States, protects the citizen against the State itself and all of its creatures—Boards of Education not excepted. These have, of course, important, delicate, and highly discretionary functions, but none that they may not perform within the limits of the Bill of Rights. That they are educating the young for citizenship is reason for scrupulous protection of Constitutional freedoms of the individual, if we are not to strangle the free mind at its source and teach youth to discount important principles of our government as mere platitudes.

Such Boards are numerous and their territorial jurisdiction often small. But small and local authority may feel less sense of responsibility to the Constitution, and agencies of publicity may be less vigilant in calling it to account.[8]

In this now classic citation from *West Virginia* v. *Barnette* (the case in which the state requirement that children in public schools salute the flag was found to violate the First and Fourteenth Amendments), Mr. Justice Jackson asserted the general protection of the Constitution for school students. More recently, the courts have become involved with other aspects of students' rights. Three sets of cases illustrate the trend of extending constitutionally guaranteed option-rights to public school students. The first set concerns the First Amendment right to freedom of expression through the wearing of buttons and armbands. The second set involves the right to freedom of expression in matters of personal dress and grooming. The third set deals with the First Amendment right to freedom of press.

### *Freedom of Expression: Buttons and Armbands*

The cases in this group concern the student's right to freedom of expression as protected by the First and Fourteenth Amendments to the Constitution. *Burnside* v. *Byars*[9] came before Judge Gewin

[8] *West Virginia State Board of Education* v. *Barnette*, 319 U.S. 624 (1943), 637.
[9] *Burnside* v. *Byars*, 363 F.2d 744 (5th Cir. 1966).

of the Fifth Circuit Court of Appeals on July 21, 1966. The case involved the decision of a Mississippi high school principal forbidding students from wearing "freedom buttons" in school on the grounds that the buttons did not advance the educational program and would cause a commotion in the school. The buttons in question contained the words "One Man One Vote" around the edge and "SNCC" inscribed in the middle. Mrs. Burnside and two other appellants charged that the school regulation prohibiting the wearing of buttons on school property was unreasonable and abridged their children's right to freedom of speech under the First and Fourteenth Amendments. The appellees argued that the principal's rule was reasonable and necessary to the maintenance of proper discipline in the school.

The Court held that the wearing of "freedom buttons" as a way of silently communicating a matter of vital public concern is covered by the First Amendment right to freedom of speech and is thus protected against infringement by state officials. Judge Gewin noted that First Amendment rights can be abridged by state officials only if the protection of legitimate state interests requires such an abridgment. The Court acknowledged the need for reasonable school rules and regulations:

> The establishment of an educational program requires the formulation of rules and regulations necessary for the maintenance of an orderly program of classroom learning. In formulating regulations, including those pertaining to the discipline of school children, school officials have a wide latitude of discretion. But the school is always bound by the requirement that the rules and regulations must be reasonable. It is not for us to consider whether such rules are wise or expedient but merely whether they are a reasonable exercise of the power and discretion of the school authorities.[10]

Moreover the Court clarified the criterion of reasonableness:

> Regulations which are essential in maintaining order and discipline on school property are reasonable. Thus school rules which assign students to a particular class, forbid unnecessary discussion in the classroom and prohibit the exchange of conversation between students are reasonable even though these regulations infringe on such basic rights as freedom of speech and association, because they are necessary for the orderly presentation of classroom activities. Therefore, a reasonable regulation is one which measurably contributes to the maintenance of order and decorum within the educational system.[11]

[10] *Ibid.*, p. 748.
[11] *Ibid.*

Finally the Court concluded by emphasizing that:

... school officials cannot ignore expressions of feelings with which they do not wish to contend. They cannot infringe on their students' right to free and unrestricted expression as guaranteed to them under the First Amendment to the Constitution, where the exercise of rights in the school buildings and schoolrooms do not materially and substantially interfere with the requirements of appropriate discipline in the operation of the school.[12]

In passing, it is interesting to note that on the same day, the same Court heard *Blackwell* v. *Issaquena County Board of Education*.[13] This case also involved a school rule prohibiting the wearing of freedom buttons in school, but the Court reached a quite different decision here because the wearing of buttons created a major disturbance. In the Court's words:

There was an unusual degree of commotion, boisterous conduct, a collision with the rights of others, an undermining of authority, and a lack of order, discipline, and decorum.[14]

Hence the Court found the rule reasonable. Moreover, while responding to the point that the school rule denied the students' First Amendment right to freedom of expression, the Court noted:

The constitutional guarantee of freedom of speech "does not confer an absolute right to speak" and the law recognizes that there can be an abuse of such freedom.[15]

Perhaps the single, most important case dealing with the option-rights of high school students is that of *Tinker* v. *Des Moines Community School District*.[16] In this case, heard before the Supreme Court, two high school students (John Tinker and Christopher Eckhardt) and a junior high school student (Mary Tinker, John's sister) were suspended from their respective schools in Des Moines, Iowa, for wearing black armbands to school to protest the Vietnam war. Their action defied the prohibition of this activity by the school authorities.

[12] *Ibid.*, p. 749.
[13] *Blackwell* v. *Issaquena County Board of Education*, 363 F.2d 749 (5th Cir. 1966).
[14] *Ibid.*, p. 754.
[15] *Ibid.*, pp. 753-54.
[16] *Tinker* v. *Des Moines Community School District*, 393 U.S. 503, 89 S. Ct. 733 (1969).

Mr. Justice Fortas, in an eloquent opinion for the majority, stated that:

... the wearing of armbands in the circumstances of this case was entirely divorced from actually or potentially disruptive conduct by those participating in it. It was closely akin to "pure speech" which, we have repeatedly held, is entitled to comprehensive protection under the First Amendment.[17]

Moreover, teachers and students enjoy First Amendment rights while at school. "It can hardly be argued that either students or teachers shed their constitutional rights to freedom of speech or expression at the schoolhouse gate." [18] At the same time, the special circumstances of the school place legitimate constraints on the exercise of these rights. The problem in this case occurs where First Amendment rights of students conflict with school rules.

Mr. Justice Fortas' opinion is impressively phrased and worth citing in some detail:

The District Court concluded that the action of school authorities was reasonable because it was based upon their fear of a disturbance from the wearing of the armbands. But, in our system, undifferentiated fear or apprehension of disturbance is not enough to overcome the right to freedom of expression. Any departure from absolute regimentation may cause trouble. Any variation from the majority's opinion may inspire fear. Any word spoken, in class, in the lunchroom, or on the campus, that deviates from the views of another person may start an argument or cause a disturbance. But our Constitution says we must take this risk ... and our history says that it is this sort of hazardous freedom—this kind of openness—that is the basis of our national strength and of the independence and vigor of Americans who grow up and live in this relatively permissive, often disputatious, society.[19]

Here the Supreme Court is speaking of option-rights in virtually the same terms as Golding does:

... the hard practical problem concerns not whether option-rights exist, but rather the extent to which they should exist and the areas in which they should exist. To allow for option-rights (and freedom) in any way that is more than trivial is to take the *risk* that their possessors will do what is wrong, harmful, or foolish within the spheres of autonomy.[20]

---

[17] *Ibid.*, pp. 505-506.
[18] *Ibid.*, p. 506.
[19] *Ibid.*, pp. 508-509.
[20] Golding, *op. cit.*, p. 547.

The Court explicitly affirmed that students possess the option-rights guaranteed by the Constitution:

> In our system, state-operated schools may not be enclaves of totalitarianism. School officials do not possess absolute authority over their students. Students in school as well as out of school are "persons" under our Constitution. They are possessed of fundamental rights which the State must respect, just as they themselves must respect their obligations to the State. In our system, students may not be regarded as closed-circuit recipients of only that which the State chooses to communicate. They may not be confined to the expression of those sentiments that are officially approved. In the absence of a specific showing of constitutionally valid reasons to regulate their speech, students are entitled to freedom of expression of their views.[21]

The option-rights of students are not restricted to classroom hours:

> A student's rights, therefore, do not embrace merely the classroom hours. When he is in the cafeteria, or on the playing field, or on the campus during the authorized hours, he may express his opinions, even on controversial subjects like the conflict in Vietnam, if he does so without "materially and substantially interfer[ing] with the requirements of appropriate discipline in the operation of the school" and without colliding with the rights of others. . . . But conduct by the student, in class or out of it, which for any reason—whether it stems from time, place, or type of behavior—materially disrupts classwork or involves substantial disorder or invasion of the rights of others is, of course, not immunized by the constitutional guarantee of freedom of speech.[22]

Finally, the Court held that since the wearing of armbands caused discussion out of class but did not interfere with order and work in the classroom, action of the school authorities abridged the students' constitutional right of freedom of expression.

This single decision is certainly a landmark. The Supreme Court has delineated more precisely than before those aspects of school life over which the school authorities may exercise control and has placed beyond the pale of school regulation those spheres of student autonomy which are protected by the Constitution. Moreover, the decision affirms that students are "persons" under the Constitution and are entitled to the protections afforded by its clauses except where exercise of those option-rights "substantially disrupts or materially interferes" with school activities.

[21] 393 U.S. 503, 511.
[22] *Ibid.*, p. 512.

## Freedom of Expression: Personal Dress and Grooming

The cases in this set involve the issue of the school's prescription of student dress codes and more particularly the question of long hair. Federal district courts in several states have declared that students cannot be excluded from school merely on the basis of their hair length.[23] In the District Court of Western Wisconsin, Judge Doyle ruled that choice of hair style and length is an individual's personal choice and is a right guaranteed by the Constitution.[24] This decision was appealed to the Seventh Circuit Court of Appeals.

The case involved the right of Thomas Breen and James Anton, students at Williams Bay High School, to wear their hair longer than permitted by the school's Dress and Grooming Code. Circuit Judge Kerner, writing the majority opinion for the Seventh Circuit, observed that:

The right to wear one's hair at any length or in any desired manner is an ingredient of personal freedom protected by the United States Constitution.[25]

Moreover, he stated that although the justifications for a statute may differ depending upon whether adults or high school students are involved, "... the Constitution protects minor high school students as well as adults from arbitrary and unjustified governmental rules."[26] The Court concluded that the Williams Bay School Board had not shown that the distraction caused by long hair was sufficient to warrant state invasion of students' individual freedom. In the words of the Court: "To uphold arbitrary school rules which 'sharply implicate basic constitutional values' for the sake of some nebulous concept of school discipline is contrary to the principle that we are a government of laws which are passed pursuant to the United States Constitution."[27]

In addition, the Court rejected the doctrine of *in loco parentis* as a justification for the school's action.

Although schools need to stand in place of a parent, in regard to certain matters during the schools hours, the power must be shared with

---

[23] As examples, see: *Griffin* v. *Tatum*, 300 F. Supp. 60 (M.D. Alabama 1969); *Zachary* v. *Brown*, 299 F. Supp. 1360 (N.D. Alabama 1969); *Richards* v. *Thurston*, 304 F. Supp. 449 (N.D. Massachusetts 1969).

[24] *Breen* v. *Kahl*, 419 F.2d 1034 (7th Cir. 1969).

[25] *Ibid.*, p. 1036.

[26] *Ibid.*

[27] *Ibid.*, p. 1037.

the parents, especially over intimately personal matters such as dress and grooming. Since the students' parents agree with their children that their hair can be worn long and because it would be impossible to comply with the long hair regulation during school hours and follow the wishes of the students and their parents as to hair length outside of school, in the absence of any showing of disruption, the doctrine of "in loco parentis" has no applicability.[28]

The Wisconsin Superintendent of Public Instruction, William C. Kahl, requested the State Attorney General to appeal this decision to the Supreme Court. The Supreme Court considered the petition to hear the case but denied *certiorari*.[29]

The length of a student's hair may seem a trivial issue. However, it reflects a growing concern with the status of public school students in the society at large—a concern which is being manifested in the increasing number of judicial decisions upholding the option-rights of students. That the length of hair is important is attested by the attention given to the issue by the courts. In the Wisconsin case, the Court, by upholding the rights of students to wear their hair as they please, is extending the range of freedoms students possess. At the same time the decision both restricts the scope of discretionary power that school officials may exercise and seriously undermines the viability of *in loco parentis* as a justification for school control of student conduct.

## Freedom of Press

The case of *Scoville* v. *Board of Education of Joliet Township High School District 204* was heard in the federal District Court for North-Eastern Illinois on July 19, 1968.[30] Raymond Scoville and Arthur Breen, students at Joliet Central High School, published a "literary journal" entitled *Grass High* which urged students to refuse or destroy all "propaganda" published by the school administration.

In addition, the editorial severely criticized school attendance regulations as asinine, and attacked the senior dean as having a sick mind. However, the distribution of *Grass High* apparently created no disturbance or disruption of classes.

School officials instituted disciplinary proceedings against

[28] *Ibid.*
[29] *Breen* v. *Kahl, supra,* cert. den. 26 L. Ed. 2nd, 268.
[30] *Scoville* v. *Board of Education of Joliet Township High School District 204,* 286 F. Supp. 988 (N.D. Illinois 1968).

Scoville and Breen which culminated in their expulsion from school by the school board. Their parents then brought an action charging that the expulsion order violated their sons' constitutional rights to freedom of speech and free press. Judge Napoli found that although public school boards are not immune from First Amendment limitations, speech may be regulated where there is a "clear and present danger" from the act. In this case, the speech constituted a ". . . direct and substantial threat to the successful operation of the school."[31] Judge Napoli continued:

> Under most circumstances, responsible criticism of school administrative officials is no less protected by the First Amendment than responsible criticism of other state officials. . . . However, where speech takes the form of immediate incitement to disregard of legitimate administrative regulations necessary to orderly maintenance of a public high school system; and where the speech occurs, not on a street or in a public park, where the rights of free speech are virtually absolute, but rather on the very property dedicated to a special public use, the education of younger citizens; and where the speech is directed to an audience which, because of its immaturity, is more likely than an adult audience to react to the detriment of the school system, then it is the opinion of this Court that the interest of the state in maintaining the school system outweighs the protection afforded the speaker by the First Amendment.[32]

The significance of this opinion lies not in the final disposition of the case but in the reasoning contained therein. The Court clearly upheld the action of school authorities in regulating the right to free speech and free press when the exercise of these rights in a public school threatens the continued operation of the school. Of course, this is perfectly reasonable and a correct conclusion. But the Court implicitly acknowledges that responsible criticism may be directed at school administrators by high school students. In other words, the First Amendment right to free speech and free press is applicable to high school students provided these rights are exercised in a manner compatible with responsible adult behavior and with the special nature of the school as an institution for the education of younger citizens.

## Welfare-Rights of Public School Students

Today, education is perhaps the most important function of state and local governments. Compulsory school attendance laws and the great

[31] *Ibid.*, p. 992.
[32] *Ibid.*

expenditures for education both demonstrate our recognition of the importance of education to our democratic society. It is required in the performance of our most basic public responsibilities, even service in the armed forces. It is the very foundation of good citizenship. Today it is a principal instrument in awakening the child to cultural values, in preparing him for later professional training, and in helping him to adjust normally to his environment. In these days, it is doubtful that any child may reasonably be expected to succeed in life if he is denied the opportunity of an education. Such an opportunity, where the state has undertaken to provide it, is a right which must be made available to all on equal terms.[33]

In this statement in *Brown v. Board of Education* the Supreme Court made its strongest pronouncement on the issue of welfare-rights for public school students. Here, of course, the Court was establishing the proposition that segregation on the basis of race was a denial of equal protection. Even today, however, it is clear that the state is not required by the federal Constitution to provide public education. However, when the state chooses to provide education, it must do so in a way which does not discriminate on the basis of race. The equitable distribution of education *vis-à-vis* race continues to be a troublesome issue. Nonetheless, since education seems to be assuming the characteristic of a welfare-right, it seems appropriate to raise a more general question concerning the distribution of educational opportunity.

## Equality in Education

The question is whether the Equal Protection Clause of the Fourteenth Amendment to the Constitution of the United States compels a state to afford equal educational opportunity to all students attending the public schools within that state without regard to where they live or the wealth of their local communities.[34]

Within nearly every state there are wide disparities in the amounts of money spent for the education of children in the public schools. Some children receive the benefits of an education costing several times that received by others. For example, in 1967-68 per pupil expenditures in Michigan ranged from $1,038 to $412.

---

[33] 347 U.S. 483 (1954), pp. 492-93.

[34] Arthur E. Wise. "Is Denial of Equal Educational Opportunity Constitutional?" *Administrator's Notebook* 13 (6): 1-4; February 1965; Charles U. Daly, editor. *The Quality of Inequality: Urban and Suburban Public Schools.* Chicago: University of Chicago Center for Policy Study, 1968.

The importance of these differences has been underscored by a recent study of educational opportunity in the State of Michigan. Guthrie and his colleagues found substantial empirical support for the following propositions:

The quality of school services provided to a pupil is related to his socioeconomic status, and that relationship is such that lower quality school services are associated with a pupil's being from a lower socioeconomic status household.[35]

A relationship exists between the quality of school services provided to a pupil and his academic achievement, and that relationship is such that higher quality school services are associated with higher levels of achievement.[36]

The post-school performance of a pupil is related to his achievement in school, and that relationship is such that higher achievement is associated with "success" and lower achievement is associated with "lack of success."[37]

In summary, there is a chain of relationships among pupils' socioeconomic status, school expenditures, quality of available school services, pupils' achievement, and pupils' post-school performance. To be sure, each set of factors is not solely determined by the preceding set in the chain. Nonetheless, each set of factors is partially determined by the preceding set in the chain. It should be noted, however, that the findings of this study controvert the popular understandings of the implications of the Coleman Report.[38]

Variation in educational opportunity arises from the way states finance public education. In nearly all states, statutes place primary reliance for financing schools on the local property tax. The local school district is empowered to levy taxes on the local tax base. Within limitations, the local school district is free to raise as much in taxes as is politically feasible. Educational opportunity is, then, very largely a function of the local assessed valuation per pupil.

Indeed, it is generally true that poor school districts tax themselves at a higher rate than do rich school districts. However, these

---

[35] James W. Guthrie, George B. Kleindorfer, Henry M. Levin, and Robert T. Stout. *Schools and Inequality.* Washington, D.C.: The Urban Coalition, 1969. p. 49.

[36] *Ibid.,* p. 92.

[37] *Ibid.,* p. 147.

[38] James S. Coleman and others. *Equality of Educational Opportunity.* Washington, D.C.: Superintendent of Documents, U.S. Government Printing Office, 1969.

higher tax rates do not compensate for the deficiencies in the local tax base. Moreover, state aid equalization disbursements fail by design to compensate for the differences in local taxable capacity.[39] In short, the operation of school finance programs fails to provide even an approximation of equality in school support. And, it may be argued, the least is being provided where it is needed most. Equality of educational opportunity in the United States is a myth.

Equal protection of the laws is presumably guaranteed by the federal Constitution. Moreover, most state legislatures are charged by their own state constitutions with the responsibility for establishing and maintaining "a uniform system of public schools." The present system of public school resource allocation is manifestly inconsistent with these charges. It is clear that school finance structures have evolved without reference to equal protection standards. It is clear that state legislatures have developed school finance legislation without substantial reference to apparent state constitutional mandates. Because state legislatures have refused to confront the problem, the issue is ripe for judicial action.

The situation is directly comparable to that which led the Supreme Court to assume jurisdiction over legislative apportionment. For at least 50 years prior to reapportionment, state legislatures struggled with the periodic reapportionment which was mandated by their own constitutions. These attempts failed for a variety of political reasons. Similarly, for at least 50 years, state legislatures have struggled with the equalization of educational expenditures. To expect state legislators to vote for programs which do not yield direct benefits to their own constituents is unrealistic, as can be seen in the fact that few equalization programs are passed which fail to provide some revenue to even the wealthiest districts.

In effect, a state's school finance statutes embody a de facto classification of the students in the state on the basis of the school district where they happen to reside. This classification, explicitly on the basis of school districts and implicitly on the basis of local assessed valuation per pupil, largely determines the quality of educational opportunity the student is to receive.

The U.S. Constitution allows states to classify. Generally, however, the Supreme Court has ruled that a classification to be reasonable must be related to the purpose of the law. The question becomes: Is the classification of students according to the tax base

[39] See generally: J. Alan Thomas. *School Finance and Educational Opportunity in Michigan.* Lansing, Michigan: Michigan Department of Education, 1968.

where they live sufficiently related to the purpose of the law to be considered reasonable?

The logic of the case for equal educational opportunity is to be found in three lines of Supreme Court decisions. These cases enunciate general principles which, while not controlling in the present instance, at least indicate how the Court might approach the problem of inequality in education.[40]

The school desegregation cases, especially *Brown* v. *Board of Education* in 1954, began to define public education as a constitutional right which fell within the scope of the Equal Protection Clause. Of course, the Court was here attempting to establish the proposition that discrimination in education by the state may not be based on color. In a later attempt to avoid desegregation, officials of one county in Virginia closed the public schools and supported private, segregated schools. At the same time, public schools in all the other counties of the state were being maintained. In *Griffin* v. *County School Board,* the Court held:

> Whatever nonracial grounds might support a state's allowing a county to abandon public schools, the object must be a constitutional one, and grounds of race and opposition to desegregation do not qualify as constitutional.[41]

The state cannot permit differences among school districts when the basis for that difference is race.

The proposition that geography alone cannot form the basis for quantitative differences from one part of a state to another emerges from the reapportionment cases. Here the Court was establishing the principle that historical accidents associated with the boundary lines of local governmental units could not be used to dilute the value of some votes.

The concept of equal protection has been traditionally viewed as

[40] The argument is developed in: Arthur E. Wise. *Rich Schools, Poor Schools: The Promise of Equal Educational Opportunity.* Chicago: University of Chicago Press, 1969. Alternative formulations are also available. See: John E. Coons, William H. Clune, III, and Stephen D. Sugarman. "Educational Opportunity: A Workable Constitutional Test for State Financial Structures." *California Law Review,* April 1969, pp. 305-421; Harold W. Horowitz and Diana L. Neitring. "Equal Protection Aspects of Inequalities in Public Education and Public Assistance Programs from Place to Place Within a State." *UCLA Law Review,* April 1968, pp. 787-816; and David L. Kirp. "The Constitutional Dimensions of Equal Educational Opportunity." *Harvard Educational Review,* Fall 1968, pp. 635-68.

[41] 377 U.S. 218, 231 (1964).

requiring the uniform treatment of persons standing in the same relation to the governmental action questioned or challenged. With respect to the allocation of legislative representation, all voters, as citizens of a state, stand in the same relation regardless of where they live. Any suggested criteria for the differentiation of citizens are insufficient to justify any discrimination as to the weight of their votes, unless relevant to the permissible purposes of legislative apportionment. Since the achievement of fair and effective representation for all citizens is concededly the basic aim of legislative apportionment, we conclude that the Equal Protection Clause guarantees the opportunity for equal participation by all voters in the election of state legislators.[42]

By implication, there may be some criteria which justify differentiation among persons within a state; at least in the case of voting, geography is not one of these.

The third general proposition concerns the irrelevance of wealth to social justice and is based on cases in the area of the administration of one of a state's services—criminal justice. These cases confronted one kind of discrimination between the rich and the poor in the application of state laws. The landmark case was *Griffin* v. *Illinois*.[43] The Supreme Court held that an indigent defendant cannot be denied the same opportunity to appeal an adverse judgment that is available to others simply because he cannot afford the price of a transcript of the trial proceedings:

> It is true that a state is not required by the federal Constitution to provide appellate courts or a right to appellate review at all. . . . But that is not to say that a state that does grant appellate review can do so in a way that discriminates against some convicted defendants on account of their poverty.[44]

The Griffin rule has been extended to include a wide range of services which the state must make available to indigent defendants. It has become increasingly clear that governmental discrimination may not be based upon wealth, at least in the area of criminal justice.

The general propositions which have emerged from these three lines of cases create a climate within which one can question whether the absence of equal educational opportunity within a state constitutes a denial by that state of the equal protection of its laws. While it is not precisely clear what the outcome of such a challenge

---

[42] *Reynolds* v. *Sims*, 377 U.S. 533, 565-66 (1964).
[43] 351 U.S. 12 (1956).
[44] *Ibid.*, p. 18.

would be, one principle does seem to emerge—the amount of money spent on the education of a child should not depend upon his parents' economic circumstances or his location within the state. It might well depend upon *relevant* distinguishing characteristics of the child.

## Equality of Educational Opportunity

Welfare-rights in education may be more resistant to implementation than option-rights. What is an equitable allocation of educational resources? What is equality of educational opportunity? Equality of educational opportunity is a philosophical construct. A good definition of the term is one which could be supposed to reduce the high correlations among socioeconomic status, level of educational services, and student achievement. A good definition is one which is administratively feasible.

The standard which most clearly emerges from the three areas of constitutional adjudication reviewed is the *negative definition*. Equality of educational opportunity exists when a child's educational opportunity does not depend upon either his parents' economic circumstances or his location within the state. In other words, the allocation of educational resources to every student shall not depend upon either of these "arbitrary" factors. Although this definition has the virtue of being precise, its usefulness is limited. It is more useful for demonstrating that equality does not exist; it is less useful for specifying the conditions of equality.

A second standard represents an ideal standard of equal educational opportunity. The *full opportunity definition* is theoretically the ultimate interpretation of equal educational opportunity. It asserts that educational resources shall be allocated to every student until he reaches the limits imposed by his own capabilities. The fatal shortcoming of this definition is obvious—educational resources are limited. Expending resources on every individual until he can no longer profit from them is impossible. Thus, as a realistic standard for specifying the conditions of equality, the full opportunity definition is meaningless.

The majority of states currently employ some variation of what has been called the *foundation definition* of equal educational opportunity. Typically, the state foundation program stipulates a "satisfactory minimum offering," expressed in dollars, which shall be guaranteed to every student. When a local school system cannot supply that minimum offering at the state-mandated tax rate, the state makes up the deficiency. The degree of "equality" resulting from these programs is suggested by the findings of the Michigan Study.

While the foundation definition specifies a minimum in terms of educational resources, the *minimum attainment definition* specifies a minimum in terms of educational outcomes. The minimum attainment standard requires that educational resources be allocated to every student until he reaches a specified level of attainment. Obviously, this standard requires far greater expenditures for some students than for others. Thus, for example, when a student's reading achievement falls below the norm for his grade, additional resources would be provided.

The foundation and minimum attainment definitions are expressed in terms of minima; other definitions go beyond minima. The *leveling definition* of equal educational opportunity requires that resources be allocated in inverse proportion to students' ability. This standard is based on the assumption that students should, as nearly as possible, leave school with an equal chance of success. Since some students are more able than others and/or come from home backgrounds which facilitate their education, the schools should attempt to diminish these differences by concentrating on the less advantaged students. To be sure, there are limits to the extent to which schooling can result in equal attainment for all. Nevertheless, the allocation of resources in inverse proportion to students' ability would tend to result in equality of attainment.

While the leveling standard requires the allocation of educational resources in inverse proportion to students' ability, the *competition definition* requires their allocation in direct proportion. This standard assumes that students have different capacities to profit from instruction and that the more able a student is, the greater should be his access to educational resources. The equality demanded by this standard is equality in the competition for access to educational resources. The relevant basis for competition is ability and not wealth or geography.

The competition standard assumes that ability is a legitimate basis for a differential allocation of the amount of educational resources; the *equal dollars per pupil definition* assumes that ability is an illegitimate basis. The equal dollars per pupil definition requires that educational resources be allocated equally to all students. Which resources and how they are used, of course, vary with the "needs" of the individual.

An approximation to the equal dollars standard may be termed the *maximum variance ratio definition*. This standard requires that educational resources be allocated so that the maximum discrepancy in per pupil expenditures does not exceed a specified ratio. This approach would be similar to the approach employed in the reapportionment cases. Thus, the courts might require that the maximum variation in per pupil expenditure be no more than two to one or one-and-a-half to one. Variation can be justified as an accommodation to educational needs, price-level differences, or differences in the economies of scale.

Finally, a standard—closely related to the negative standard described earlier—which emerges from the three areas of constitutional adjudication reviewed is the *reasonable classification definition*. This standard requires that what is regarded as a "suitable" level of support for a student of specified characteristics is suitable for that student wherever he lives within the state. The definition requires a categorization of students on the basis of ability and interests. Thus, for example, if a six-hundred-dollar-a-year education is regarded suitable for college-bound students of average ability, then that amount should obtain throughout the state. Or, if a twelve-hundred-dollar-a-year education is suitable for disadvantaged students in the primary grades, then that is what should obtain statewide.

Recently, a number of court tests of the constitutionality of school finance legislation have been brought. The most important of these has been *McInnis* v. *Ogilvie* which was ruled upon by the U.S. Supreme Court on March 24, 1969.[45] The U.S. District Court for Northern Illinois had dismissed the complaint for failure to state a cause of action and for non-justiciability.[46] On appeal, the Supreme Court affirmed the lower court's decision *per curiam*—without opinion.

The meaning of this action is ambiguous. Practically, it has meant that several other cases have been dismissed on the strength of *McInnis*. Technically, the meaning of the Court's action is inscrutable since it gave no reason for its decision. Theoretically, it does suggest that plaintiffs be well prepared before again appealing to the Supreme Court.

We should not be surprised at the initial judicial response to educational inequality. To place the judgment in *McInnis* in perspective, we should note the lengthy judicial history of other egalitarian causes. The first crack in the *Plessy* v. *Ferguson* segregation

[45] 394 U.S. 322.
[46] 293 F. Supp. 327.

wall did not appear until 1938.[47] It took until 1954 for the Supreme Court to announce that the opportunity for an education, "where the state has undertaken to provide it, is a right which must be made available to all on equal terms." Indeed the pronouncement in *Brown* marked the beginning of the "egalitarian revolution in judicial doctrine."[48] To be sure, the enunciation of a judicial principle is only the beginning.

In 1946 the Supreme Court unequivocally denied that it could entertain jurisdiction over the process of legislative apportionment.[49] Sixteen years later, in connection with a complaint which presented "neither a novel electoral situation nor any legal theory which had not been urged unsuccessfully in the prior cases,"[50] the Court chose to interject itself vigorously into the problems of reapportionment.

We are put on notice by the Court's pronouncement in the Poll Tax Case:

> The Equal Protection Clause is not shackled to the political theory of a particular era. In determining what lines are unconstitutionally discriminatory, we have never been confined to historic notions of equality. . . . Notions of what constitutes equal treatment for purposes of the Equal Protection Clause do change.[51]

Legal reasoning has been defined as

> . . . reasoning by example. It is reasoning from case to case. It is a three-step process described by the doctrine of precedent in which a proposition descriptive of the first case is made into a rule of law and then applied to a next similar situation. The steps are these: similarity is seen between cases; next the rule of law inherent in the first case is announced; then the rule of law is made applicable to the second case.[52]

The key to understanding this process is the realization that "the determination of similarity or difference is the function of *each*

---

[47] *Missouri ex. rel. Gaines* v. *Canada*, 305 U.S. 337.

[48] Philip B. Kurland. "The Supreme Court, 1963 Term Foreword: 'Equal in Origin and Equal in Title to the Legislative and Executive Branches of the Government.'" *Harvard Law Review* 78: 144; November 1964.

[49] *Colegrove* v. *Green*, 328 U.S. 549.

[50] Phil C. Neal. "*Baker* v. *Carr:* Politics in Search of Law." In: Philip B. Kurland, editor. *The Supreme Court and the Constitution.* Chicago: University of Chicago Press, 1965.

[51] *Harper* v. *Virginia Board of Elections*, 383 U.S. 663 (1966), 669.

[52] Edward H. Levi. *An Introduction to Legal Reasoning.* Chicago: University of Chicago Press, 1948. pp. 1-2.

*judge.*"[53] Thus it becomes possible to characterize this effort as "an exercise in legal fantasizing" while at the same time observing "the overwhelming sense one gets of changes in the Court's attitudes toward specific issues and its willingness to find constitutional bases for legislation."[54]

It was possible at least in 1968 for Kurland to say:

> The logic of the case for equal educational opportunity is inexorable. It is a far stronger argument than most that carry the Supreme Court these days. If logic were the life of the law, the proposition that states must afford equal educational opportunity to all their students, given the premises, should be accepted as established. If, as is more likely, at least in the Supreme Court, that the personal desires of the Justices or their will "to do good" underlies their judgments, there is even more reason to expect the quick announcement of a principle of equal educational opportunity.[55]

The changing composition of the Supreme Court must make us pessimistic about Kurland's prediction for the near term; for the long term, logic may prevail.

## Procedural Due Process

The right to procedural due process as guaranteed by the Fifth and Fourteenth Amendments is neither an option-right nor a welfare-right per se. However, procedural due process is essential to the safeguarding of both kinds of rights. Due process is vital to the preservation of option-rights. As Justice Fortas observes:

> Procedure is the bone structure of a democratic society; and the quality of procedural standards which meet general acceptance—the quality of what is tolerable and permissible and acceptable conduct—determines the durability of the society.[56]

If education is considered a welfare-right, at least in the philosophical sense, then due process is quintessentially important. Abbott portrays the case well:

[53] *Ibid.,* p. 2.

[54] Carol Lopate. "Review of *Rich Schools, Poor Schools.*" *Teachers College Record* 71 (2): 52-54; December 1969.

[55] Philip B. Kurland. "Equal Educational Opportunity or the Limits of Constitutional Jurisprudence Undefined." In: Charles U. Daly, editor: *The Quality of Inequality: Urban and Suburban Public Schools.* Chicago: University of Chicago Center for Policy Study, 1968. pp. 52-53.

[56] Abe Fortas. *Concerning Dissent and Civil Disobedience.* New York: New American Library, Signet Edition, 1968. p. 120.

The problem can be put in greater perspective by considering the importance of fair procedure to the student involved. That he has much to fear from the arbitrary use of power may be as true on the secondary level as at a college or university. This is particularly so where misconduct may result in an expulsion or a lengthy suspension. The stigma of compulsory withdrawal is likely to follow even the high school student for many years after the incident has been settled in the mind of the institution concerned. Such a procedure almost always involves a permanent notation on the student's record which may have long-lasting effects on his entrance into college or the job market. And if the child is unable to return to school, the economics of a premature withdrawal are just as startling, but more tangible, evidence of the burden that he must shoulder.[57]

There is very little litigation that relates to procedural due process for students in school disciplinary proceedings. Nevertheless, the issue certainly warrants the attention of the Courts. *Dixon* v. *Alabama State Board of Education* involved the suspension of college students without notice or a hearing.[58] Although the extent to which due process for college students is applicable to high school students is problematic, several aspects of the case are instructive and appear to be directly relevant to the high school.

Circuit Judge Rives, writing the majority opinion for the Fifth Circuit Court of Appeals, held that due process entitled the students in question to notice and the opportunity for a hearing before being expelled.

Whenever a governmental body acts so as to injure an individual, the Constitution requires that the act be consonant with due process of law. The minimum procedural requirements necessary to satisfy due process depend upon the circumstances and the interests of the parties involved.[59]

The Court laid down the following guidelines on the nature of the notice and hearing required by due process. The notice should contain a statement of the specific charges. The nature of the hearing should vary depending on the particular circumstances, but both sides should have the opportunity to present a case. The hearing should not be a full-dress judicial hearing with the right to cross-examine witnesses, although the rudiments of an adversary pro-

---

[57] Michael Abbott. "Demonstrations, Dismissals, Due Process, and the High School: An Overview." *School Review* 77: 131; June 1969.

[58] *Dixon* v. *Alabama State Board of Education*, 294 F.2d 150 (5th Cir. 1961), cert. den. 368 U.S. 930 (1961).

[59] *Ibid.*, p. 155.

ceeding could be preserved. The student should be informed of the witnesses against him together with oral or written notification of the facts to which each witness testifies. Moreover, the student should be given the opportunity to defend himself against the charges and introduce either oral testimony or written affidavits on his behalf. The results and findings of the hearing should be presented in a report open to the student's inspection.

The extent of the applicability of due process to the high school student in school disciplinary proceedings is difficult to determine. One case that sheds some light on the general question is *In re Gault*.[60] The parents of Gerald Gault brought an action charging that their son had been denied various aspects of procedural due process in juvenile delinquency proceedings. The United States Supreme Court held that whether the proceedings are criminal or delinquency, where there is a possibility of commitment to a state institution like a reform school in which the juvenile's freedom is restricted, the child and his parents must receive adequate written notice of the specific issues and be advised of their right to be represented by counsel. If they are unable to afford counsel, then counsel should be appointed for them. Moreover, the Supreme Court asserted that the juvenile is protected by the Fifth Amendment privilege against self-incrimination.

The significance of this case lies in the Supreme Court's acknowledgment that in the adjudicatory treatment of juveniles the essentials of due process must be observed especially where the sanction is potentially severe. However, Justice Fortas, writing for the majority, implied an important distinction between the need for procedural protections in an adjudicatory proceeding and in the earlier stages of proceedings involving juveniles.

> The problems of pre-adjudication treatment of juveniles and of post-adjudication disposition are unique to the juvenile process; hence what we hold in this opinion with regard to the procedural requirements at the adjudicatory stage has no necessary applicability to other steps of the juvenile process.[61]

This distinction lies at the heart of the court's decision in *Madera v. Board of Education of the City of New York*.[62] In this case, the Seventh Circuit Court of Appeals upheld the Board of

[60] *In re Gault*, 387 U.S. 1 (1967), 87 S. Ct. 1428 (1967).
[61] 87 S. Ct. 1428, 1445.
[62] *Madera v. Board of Education of the City of New York*, 386 F.2d, (2d. Cir. 1967), cert. den. 390 U.S. 1028 (1968).

Education's policy prohibiting the appearance of counsel to represent the student and parents at a "Guidance Conference." The court reasoned that the guidance conference is neither a criminal nor a punitive proceeding; its purpose is to try to solve the behavioral difficulties of the particular student and to determine how the student may best be readmitted to the educational system. Since the guidance conference is clearly not an adjudication, the counsel provisions of the Sixth Amendment are not applicable.

Moreover, the court identified the issue as one of procedural due process unrestricted by the specific protections of the Fifth and Sixth Amendments. The fact that the guidance conference can *ultimately* lead to a loss of personal liberty for the child or to a suspension or to the withdrawal of his right to attend the public schools does not justify the full panoply of procedural safeguards at the guidance conference.

What constitutes due process under any given set of circumstances must depend upon the nature of the proceeding involved and the rights that may possibly be affected by that proceeding.[63]

The court relied upon the position taken in *Opp Cotton Mills* v. *Administrator:*

The demands of due process do not require a hearing, at the initial stage or at any particular point or at more than one point in an administrative proceeding so long as the requisite hearing is held before the final order becomes effective.[64]

Clearly the applicability of due process to public school students in school disciplinary proceedings has not yet been faced and urgently needs judicial attention. However, the cited cases illustrate some of the relevant considerations. The public school is an agency of the state government, thus the student enjoys the general protection to due process under the Fourteenth Amendment. As a citizen of the United States the student is also protected by the due process clause of the Sixth Amendment.

Paraphrasing Judge Rives' reasoning, when the school acts to expel a student, the act should be consonant with due process of law, although the precise procedural requirements depend upon the circumstances of the case. This position is consistent with the reasoning of *In re* Gault. Expulsion from school has important consequences for the student. Not only does expulsion constitute a severe

[63] *Ibid.*, p. 780.
[64] *Ibid.*, p. 785.

sanction by materially curtailing the freedom of the student, it significantly restricts his subsequent life-chances by denying him the opportunity to continue his education at that school, and may thereby limit his future employment opportunities.

The reasoning in the Madera opinion suggests that school discipline proceedings are not adjudications. The expulsion hearing is the nearest feature of school discipline to an adjudication but this is at most a quasi-judicial proceeding. A literal application of Madera to school discipline would certainly result in denying representation by counsel to students involved in major discipline offenses. Nevertheless the court implied that due process may well be required before a child is expelled or receives a temporary suspension from school, because the result of expulsion is "... the drastic and complete termination of the education experience in that particular institution." [65]

In fact, the Madera case has a limited and somewhat ambiguous significance. A strict construction of school discipline proceedings as nonadjudicatory hearings is hardly useful. The fact is that school discipline proceedings, whether adjudicatory or not, can result in substantial sanctions with potentially disastrous long-range consequences for the student. This is reason enough to guarantee due process. Hopefully, the courts will recognize the paramount importance of fair procedure to the high school student and insist on due process in discipline proceedings. In such a development, the guidelines laid down in the Dixon case provide a reasonable starting point.

An additional reason for insisting on the presence of due process in discipline proceedings derives from the school's role as an agency of democratization. Although it is often held that schools need not be democratically organized and administered to be effective in teaching the young how to be democratic citizens, there are cogent reasons for the proposition that, particularly in the school, the student should be treated in a manner compatible with the fundamental notions of liberty, equality, and justice to which the larger society is dedicated. Thus the school should respect both the option-rights and welfare-rights of students and provide appropriate procedural mechanisms to safeguard these rights. Nor is it necessary for school administrators to wait for the courts to decide that students should receive procedural due process in school. There is no reason except personal whim and hidebound tradition that prevents

[65] *Ibid.*, p. 784.

administrators from taking the initiative, displaying a modicum of creativity, and implementing a discipline system that incorporates the essentials of due process.

## Implications

Historically, the doctrine of *in loco parentis* conferred upon school officials a wide latitude of discretion in the day-to-day organization and administration of schools. Occasionally the decisions of school officials have been subject to judicial review, but for the most part the courts have been reluctant to intervene in educational matters. Nevertheless, where administrative actions have resulted in the abrogation of the provisions of the Constitution, the courts have been required to review the decisions. These cases have involved both the option-rights and the welfare-rights of public school students. Yet for both sets of cases the larger issue is the question of discretionary justice. The courts are in effect deciding whether administrative discretion was exercised in a fair and reasonable manner or in an arbitrary and capricious manner. The substantive issue is the degree to which decisions by school officials are compatible with the Constitution. Taken together, these questions involve the fundamental notion of the justice afforded to students by school officials in the day-to-day operation of the school.

Judicial affirmation of the option-rights of public school students reflects in part the society's willingness to extend adult status (that is, full membership in the community) in some areas to those traditionally viewed as minors. The concomitant effect of this trend is to restrict the scope of the discretionary power that school officials may exercise. Judicial decisions are redefining the boundaries of administrative authority and frequently assert that administrative authority must be exercised in a *reasonable* fashion.[66] School officials are being told that they must respect the constitutional rights of students; that they may not abrogate these rights for the sake of administrative convenience; and that they must be generally more circumspect and less arbitrary in their administrative decisions. The net effect is that school officials must become much more concerned that their decisions are compatible with the liberty enshrined in the constitutionally protected option-rights of students and with the justice that is essential to the preservation of these rights.

[66] For a detailed legal analysis of this position, see: Robert L. Ackerly. *The Reasonable Exercise of Authority.* Washington, D.C.: National Association of Secondary School Principals, 1969.

The single, most important implication of this trend involves the provision of procedural due process in school discipline proceedings. School administrators must deliberately seek to provide organizational mechanisms to protect the rights of students in school. In effect this means restricting administrative discretionary power voluntarily in the interests of improving the quality of justice dispensed by the school.

The tension between the full recognition of the option-rights of public school students and the need of the school to regulate student conduct constitutes one dimension of the dilemma that school administrators face. The other dimension is the conflict between the full realization of the welfare-rights of students and the present organization of schools in terms of equal educational opportunity.

# 4

# *Bureaucracy and Curriculum Theory*\*

### Herbert M. Kliebard

HISTORIANS of education agree that American education went through a kind of metamorphosis after the turn of this century, but the nature and effect of the changes are in some dispute. In the popular mind, the reforms that were wrought during that period—indeed the whole first half of the 20th century—have become associated with a broad and loosely defined "progressive education" movement. John Dewey is seen as the dominant force in American educational practice with an undisciplined child-centered pedagogy dubiously ascribed to him. Even a cursory examination of the work of educational reformers during this period, however, indicates that influential leaders differed widely in the doctrines they espoused and in the pedagogical reforms they advocated. Clearly, the educational ideas of a David Snedden or a Franklin Bobbitt differed enormously from those of a John Dewey or a Stanwood Cobb. There is no doubt that this was a period of ferment in education, with new ideas filling the void being created by the steadily declining theory of mental discipline.

The picture that emerges from the apparently frenetic educational activity during the first few decades of this century seems to be one of growing acceptance of a powerful and restrictive bureaucratic model for education which looked toward the management techniques of industry as its ideal of excellence and source of inspiration. The dominant metaphor for educational theory in the early

---

\* I am grateful to the Research Committee of the Graduate School, University of Wisconsin, for granting the summer research leave which made it possible for me to conduct the research reported here in part.

20th century was drawn not from the educational philosophy of John Dewey or even from romantic notions of childhood, but from corporate management. As Ellwood Cubberly explicated that model in 1916,

> Every manufacturing establishment that turns out a standard product or a series of products of any kind maintains a force of efficiency experts to study methods of procedure and to measure and test the output of its works. Such men ultimately bring the manufacturing establishment large returns, by introducing improvements in processes and procedure, and in training the workmen to produce larger and better output. Our schools are, in a sense, factories in which the raw products (children) are to be shaped and fashioned into products to meet the various demands of life. The specifications for manufacturing come from the demands of twentieth-century civilization, and it is the business of the school to build its pupils according to the specifications laid down. This demands good tools, specialized machinery, continuous measurement of production to see if it is according to specifications, the elimination of waste in manufacture, and a large variety in the output.[1]

Children, in other words, were to become the "standard products" which would be fashioned according to the design specifications set forth by the social world. The institution of schooling was simply that vast bureaucratic machinery which transforms the crude raw material of childhood into a socially useful product. A redesigned curriculum, stripped of the playful and wasteful, was to be the chief instrument in effecting the change.

## Scientific Management

The context for the bureaucratization of the school curriculum that was to take place in the 20th century was manifest in the general social and intellectual climate of American society at the turn of the century. The late 19th century saw the breakdown of a community-centered society and with it the ideal of the individual as the unit element in social life. The press of corporate expansion and urbanization made the individual merely a cog in a great machine. Whereas the individual retained a measure of recognition in a community-centered society, the vast new social and economic units robbed him of his identity. Responses to this fundamental change in American society ranged from the economic radicalism of Henry George to the utopian socialism of Edward Bellamy. But "the

[1] Ellwood P. Cubberly. *Public School Administration.* Boston: Houghton Mifflin Company, 1916. p. 338.

ideas that filtered through and eventually took the fort," according to Wiebe, "were the bureaucratic ones peculiarly suited to the fluidity and impersonality of an urban-industrial world."[2]

The particular response that captured the imagination of Americans at the turn of the century was a form of idealized bureaucracy known widely as scientific management. Its principal spokesman was Frederick W. Taylor, and its watchword was efficiency. Taylorism differs from classical conceptions of bureaucracy (for example, Weber) in its emphasis on sheer practical efficiency rather than analysis of complex lines of power and influence within organizations. Under Taylor's concept of scientific management, productivity is central, and the individual is simply an element in the production system. Basic to Taylor's conception of scientific management was the assumption that man is motivated by economic gain and would sacrifice much in the way of job satisfaction and physical ease in order to achieve such gain. Yet scientific principles had to be applied to the workman as well as to the work, and this involved careful study of the workman's "own special abilities and limitations" in an effort "to develop each individual man to his highest state of efficiency and prosperity"[3] (anticipating, in a way, the modern guidance movement in schools).

One of Taylor's proudest accomplishments was to inveigle a man he called Schmidt into increasing his handling of pig iron at a Bethlehem Steel plant from 12½ tons a day to 47 tons. Schmidt was selected after careful observation and study of 75 men, partly because he was observed to trot home in the evening about as fresh as when he trotted in to work in the morning and partly because inquiries revealed that he was "close with a dollar." Taylor even gives an extended verbatim account of his discussion with Schmidt:

"Schmidt, are you a high-priced man?"

"Vell, I don't know vat you mean."

"Oh, yes you do. What I want to know is whether you are a high-priced man or not."

"Vell, I don't know vat you mean."

"Oh, come now, you answer my questions. What I want to find out is whether you are a high-priced man or one of these cheap fellows here. What I want to find out is whether you want to earn $1.85 a day or

[2] Robert H. Wiebe. *The Search for Order 1877-1920.* New York: Hill and Wang, 1967. p. 145.

[3] Frederick Winslow Taylor. *The Principles of Scientific Management.* New York: Harper & Brothers, 1911. p. 43.

whether you are satisfied with $1.15, just the same as all those cheap fellows are getting."

"Did I vant $1.85 a day? Vas dot a high-priced man? Vell, yes, I vas a high-priced man."

"Oh, you're aggravating me. Of course you want $1.85 a day—everyone wants it! You know perfectly well that that has very little to do with your being a high-priced man. For goodness' sake answer my questions, and don't waste any more of my time. Now come over here. You see that pile of pig iron?" [4]

Using this economic motivation, Taylor proceeded to instruct Schmidt in the efficient performance of every stage of the operation. Schmidt's step must have been a little heavier as he trotted home that night.

Thus, the individual under Taylorism was not ignored; on the contrary, he was made the subject of intense investigation, but only within the context of increasing product output. Through time and motion studies, the worker's movements were broken down into minute operations and then standards of efficiency were developed for each of the operations. The rules of scientific management and psychological principles were then applied to the worker to bring him up to the appropriate level of efficiency. As Mouzelis summarizes the individual's role under Taylorism, "The organisation member was conceived as an instrument of production which can be handled as easily as any other tool (provided that one knows the laws of scientific management)." [5] The essence of scientific management was the fragmentation and analysis of work and its reordering into the most efficient arrangement possible.

One of the attractions of Taylorism was that it carried with it an ethical dimension which bore a superficial resemblance to some of the tried and true virtues of the 19th century. Taylor's first professional paper, for example, delivered in 1895 at a meeting of the American Society of Mechanical Engineers, made the case for a "piece-rate system" partly on moral grounds. The minimum time for each operation would be computed and the worker would be paid for his performance relative to that fixed performance level. In this way, the workman's interest would coincide with that of his employer and "soldiering" (loafing on the job) would be eliminated. Once the work load was broken down into elementary operations, an

---

[4] *Ibid.*, pp. 44-45.

[5] Nicos P. Mouzelis. *Organisation and Bureaucracy: An Analysis of Modern Theories.* Chicago: Aldine Publishing Company, 1967. p. 85.

"honest day's work" could be scientifically computed.[6] "If a man won't do what is right," Taylor argued, *"make him."* [7] Since scientific rate-fixing could be used to outline the dimensions of virtuous activity, industry could be rewarded and sloth punished.

The appeal of Taylor's doctrine of scientific efficiency was not limited to an elite corps of business leaders. The rising cost of living in the early 20th century was a matter of great concern to the broad American middle class, and scientific management promised lower prices through increased efficiency. The wide publicity given the Eastern Rate Case of 1910-11 also drew much popular attention to the cause of efficiency. Railroads were asking an increase in freight rates, and, arguing against their position, Louis Brandeis claimed that scientific management could save the railroads a million dollars a day. In support of his contention, he brought forward a series of witnesses in the form of efficiency experts. As Haber summarized the effect of their testimony, "The Eastern Rate Case was transformed into a morality play for up-to-date middle-class reformers" [8] which eventually culminated in an orgy of efficiency affecting millions of Americans. The effect on the schools was not long in coming.

## Bureaucratic Efficiency in School Management and Curriculum Theory

The bureaucratic model for curriculum design had a rather unremarkable birth. School administrators simply reacted to the influence of the scientific management movement in industry by interpolating those methods to the management of schools. Managers of schools patterned themselves after their counterparts in industry and took pride in adapting the vocabulary and techniques of industry to school administration.[9] Cost accounting and maximum

---

[6] Cited in: Samuel Haber. *Efficiency and Uplift: Scientific Management in the Progressive Era 1890-1920.* Chicago: University of Chicago Press, 1964. pp. 1-3.

[7] Frank Barkley Copley. *Frederick Winslow Taylor: Father of Scientific Management.* New York: Harper & Brothers, 1923. Quoted in: Haber, *ibid.*, pp. 2-3.

[8] Haber, *op. cit.*, p. 54.

[9] The administration aspect of the bureaucratization of the schools has been ably interpreted by: Raymond E. Callahan. *Education and the Cult of Efficiency: A Study of the Social Forces That Have Shaped the Administration of the Public Schools.* Chicago: University of Chicago Press, 1962.

utilization of school plants were among their paramount concerns. The period, in fact, may be regarded as one in which the "transition of the superintendent of schools from an educator to a business manager" took place.[10]

The efficiency movement, however, was to affect more than just the administration of schools. Its most profound effect was on curriculum theory itself. Among the early prophets of the new efficiency in school administration was the man who later was to become the preeminent force in curriculum reform, and, indeed, the man who gave shape and direction to the curriculum field, John Franklin Bobbitt.

Bobbitt's early work essentially followed the main line of adapting business techniques for use in schools. In 1912, for example, Bobbitt took as his model of efficiency the operation of the Gary, Indiana, schools. "The first principle of scientific management," he announced, "is to use all the plant all the available time."[11] Although the typical school plant operates at 50 percent efficiency, the "educational engineer" in Gary set as his task the development of a plan to operate at 100 percent efficiency during school hours. Although a relatively high level of efficiency of school plant operation was achieved by creating regular and special periods of activity, perfect efficiency was thwarted by the fact that the school plant was used only five days a week. "That an expensive plant should lie idle during all of Saturday and Sunday while 'street and alley time' is undoing the good work of the schools," Bobbitt complained, "is a further thorn in the flesh of the clear-sighted educational engineer."[12] He also mourned the closing of the school plant during the summer, "a loss of some 16 percent, no small item in the calculations of the efficiency engineer."[13]

Bobbitt's second principle of scientific management, "to reduce the number of workers to a minimum by keeping each at the maximum of his working efficiency,"[14] reflected the need for division of labor and job specialization in the school. His third principle simply involved the elimination of waste. Here, Bobbitt commented on

[10] *Ibid.*, p. 148.
[11] John Franklin Bobbitt. "The Elimination of Waste in Education." *The Elementary School Teacher* 12 (6): 260; February 1912.
[12] *Ibid.*, p. 263.
[13] *Ibid.*, p. 264.
[14] *Ibid.*

the wasteful concomitants of "ill-health and lowered vitality" and commended Superintendent Wirt's efforts to provide appropriate recreational facilities for the students in the Gary schools.

Bobbitt's fourth principle of general scientific management made the leap from the areas of simple plant and worker efficiency into the realm of educational theory itself:

> Work up the raw material into that finished product for which it is best adapted. Applied to education this means: Educate the individual according to his capabilities. This requires that the materials of the curriculum be sufficiently various to meet the needs of every class of individuals in the community; and the course of training and study be sufficiently flexible that the individual can be given just the things he needs.[15]

This extrapolation of the principles of scientific management to the area of curriculum made the child the object on which the bureaucratic machinery of the school operates. He became the raw material from which the school-factory must fashion a product drawn to the specifications of social convention. What was at first simply a direct application of general management principles to the management of schools became the central metaphor on which modern curriculum theory rests.

"Educate the individual according to his capabilities" has an innocent and plausible ring; but what this meant in practice was that dubious judgments about the innate capacities of children became the basis for differentiating the curriculum along the lines of probable destination for the child. Dominated by the criterion of social utility, these judgments became self-fulfilling prophecies in the sense that they predetermined which slots in the social order would be filled by which "class of individuals." Just as Taylor decided that "one of the first requirements for a man who is fit to handle pig iron as a regular occupation is that he shall be so stupid and phlegmatic that he more nearly resembles in his mental makeup the ox than any other type," [16] so it was the schools that now were to determine (scientifically, of course) what biographical, psychological, or social factors in human beings fit them to be the hewers of wood and the drawers of water in our society. Although still in undeveloped form, this conception of the work of the school

[15] *Ibid.*, p. 269.
[16] Taylor, *op. cit.*, p. 59.

in relation to the child and his studies became a central element in Bobbitt's influential curriculum research and theory a decade or so later. The ramifications of this central production metaphor in educational theory are now widely felt.

Through the first quarter of the 20th century, Bobbitt continued to take the lead in reforming the administration of public schools along the lines of scientific management advocated by Taylor. One such recommendation, for example, took the Harriman railroad system as the model of efficiency. Bobbitt pointed out how that massive enterprise had been divided into 30 autonomous divisions, each with its own specialized staff, resulting in a high rate of efficiency. Extrapolating from this and other examples, Bobbitt went on to comment on the functions of specialized supervisors in schools in determining "proper methods" and "the determination of more or less definite qualifications for the various aspects of the teaching personality." [17] The supervisor of instruction occupied that middle-management function roughly comparable to the foreman in industry.

Increasingly, however, Bobbitt was moving from the mere translation of general principles of scientific management to the management of schools into the domain of curriculum theory. As a kind of quality control, Bobbitt advocated that "definite qualitative and quantitative standards be determined for the product." [18] In the railroad industry, he pointed out, each rail "must be thirty feet in length, and weigh eighty pounds to the yard. It must be seven and three-eighths inches in height, with a head two and one-sixty-fourth of an inch in thickness and five inches deep, and a base five inches wide." [19]

Based on studies by Courtis and others and using standard scores, Bobbitt concluded that:

> The third-grade teacher should bring her pupils up to an average of 26 correct [arithmetic] combinations per minute. The fourth-grade teacher has the task, during the year that the same pupils are under her care, of increasing their addition speed from an average of 26 combinations per minute to an average of 34 combinations per minute. If she does

---

[17] Franklin Bobbitt. "Some General Principles of Management Applied to the Problems of City-School Systems." *Twelfth Yearbook of the National Society for the Study of Education*, Part I. Chicago: University of Chicago Press, 1913. p. 62.

[18] *Ibid.*, p. 11.

[19] *Ibid.*

not bring them up to the standard 34, she has failed to perform her duty in proportion to the deficit; and there is no responsibility upon her for carrying them beyond the standard 34.[20]

Two years later, Bobbitt was to apply principles of cost accounting in business organizations to school subjects. This brought the heart of the school curriculum, the subjects, into the orbit of bureaucratic efficiency. Bobbitt continued to be impressed by standardization in relation to efficiency in railroad administration. He pointed out, for example, that railroad companies know that "locomotive repair-cost should average about six cents per mile-run" and that "lubricating oils should cost about eighteen cents per hundred miles for passenger locomotives, and about twenty-five cents for freight locomotives."[21] Using cost per 1,000 student-hours as his basic unit, Bobbitt was able to report, in terms comparable to those of industry, that the cost of instruction in mathematics in his sample of 25 high schools ranged from $30 to $169 and that Latin instruction was, on the average, 20 percent more expensive than mathematics instruction. The implications of such an accounting procedure were developed later by Bobbitt, his colleagues, and his present-day intellectual heirs.

## Standardization and the Worker

The great bane of bureaucracy is uncertainty. The inevitable course of the bureaucratization of the curriculum, therefore, was in the direction of predictability. As in industry, this was accomplished mainly through the standardization of activity or work units and of the products themselves. In the curriculum field, vague conceptions of the purposes of schooling became intolerable, and "particularization" of educational objectives became a byword. "An age of science is demanding exactness and particularity," announced Bobbitt in the first modern book on curriculum.[22] The curriculum became something progressively to be discovered through the scientific analysis of the activities of mankind. Just as scientific management became associated with virtue, so the incipient field of curriculum looked to scientific curriculum making

[20] *Ibid.*, pp. 21-22.

[21] J. F. Bobbitt. "High-School Costs." *The School Review* 23 (8): 505; October 1915.

[22] Franklin Bobbitt. *The Curriculum.* Boston: Houghton Mifflin Company, 1918. p. 41.

as the source of answers to the great value questions that govern the purposes of education.

The process had a commonsensical appeal. "The curriculum-discoverer will first be an analyst of human nature and human affairs." [23] He would go out into the world of affairs and discover the particular "abilities, attitudes, habits, appreciations, and forms of knowledge" that human beings need. These would become the objectives of the curriculum. When these multitudinous needs are not filled by "undirected experiences," then "directed experiences" would be provided through the curriculum. Bobbitt set forth the basic principle: *"The curriculum of the directed training is to be discovered in the shortcomings of individuals after they have had all that can be given by undirected training."* [24] The curriculum was the mechanism for remedying the haphazard effects of ordinary living, for achieving the standard product which undirected socialization achieved so imperfectly.

One major concomitant of such a conception of the curriculum was the broadening of its scope into the boundless domain of human activity. Instead of being merely the repository of man's intellectual inheritance, the curriculum now embraced the gamut of human experience, "the total range of habits, skills, abilities, forms of thought, valuations, ambitions, etc., that its members need for the effective performance of their vocational labors; likewise, the total range needed for their civic activities; their health activities; their recreational activities; their language; their parental, religious, and general social activities." [25] The standard product would be designed and particularized in every detail.

A lonely voice of opposition to the "blight of standardization" was that of the president emeritus of Harvard University and the chief architect of the Committee of Ten report, Charles W. Eliot. Eliot, then 89 years old, pointed out that while standardization of the worker's movements in industry may have resulted in increased productivity, "the inevitable result was the destruction of the interest of the workman in his work." Standardization, he argued, was also having the same effect in education. What is more, it was antithetical to the true process of education as he saw it. "The true educational goal," he said, "is the utmost development of the individual's capacity or power, not in childhood and adolescence alone,

---

[23] *Ibid.*, p. 43.
[24] *Ibid.*, p. 45. (Original italics.)
[25] *Ibid.*, p. 43.

but all through life. Fixed standards in labor, in study, in modes of family life, are downright enemies of progress for the body, mind, and soul of man." [26] Clearly, the temper of the time would not support such an anachronistic conception of education.

## Standardization and Product Diversification

Apart from its implications for the individual as producer, the production metaphor in curriculum theory carries with it important implications for the individual as product. By the 1920's, a massive effort was under way to reform the curriculum through product standardization and predetermination. As usual, Bobbitt set the tone:

> In the world of economic production, a major secret of success is predetermination. The management predetermines with great exactness the nature of the products to be turned out, and in relation to the other factors, the quality of the output. They standardize and thus predetermine the processes to be employed, the quantity and quality of raw material to be used for each type and unit of product, the character and amount of labor to be employed, and the character of the conditions under which the work should be done. . . . The business world is institutionalizing foresight and developing an appropriate and effective technique.
>
> There is a growing realization within the educational profession that we must particularize the objectives of education. We, too, must institutionalize foresight, and, so far as conditions of our work will permit, develop a technique of predetermination of the particularized results to be obtained.[27]

The technique that Bobbitt referred to, the analysis of man's activities into particular and specialized units of behavior, came to be known as activity analysis.

By the 1920's, Bobbitt had been joined in his campaign to reform the curriculum along the lines of the bureaucratic model by such extraordinarily influential education leaders as W. W. Charters and David Snedden. In the main, the reform in the 1920's took the form of using activity analysis to strip away the nonfunctional, the "dead wood" in the curriculum. Increasingly, this was being done with reference to particular groups in the school. "The curriculum situation has become acute," Charters declared in 1921.

[26] Letter to *The New York Times* 72 (23,946): 12; August 17, 1923. © 1923 by The New York Times Company. Reprinted by permission.

[27] Franklin Bobbitt. "The Objectives of Secondary Education." *The School Review* 28 (10): 738; December 1920.

"The masses who send their children to school are growing restive under what they consider to be the useless material taught in the grades." [28]

Besides his concern for the masses, Charters went on to show how a curriculum could be developed for another identifiable group, women. He developed a curriculum particularly for women as part of the famous study he conducted for Stephens College of Columbia, Missouri. Charters' task was to develop a program which would provide "specific training for the specific job of being a woman." [29] What constitutes being a woman, of course, was determined through activity analysis. Women all over the country were asked to write a complete statement of what they did for a week, and 95,000 replies were received. The replies were then analyzed into about 7,300 categories such as food, clothing, and health. Using these activities as his base, Charters developed the curriculum for Stephens College.

Just as Taylor found it necessary to identify discrete units of work, so were the educational leaders of the period embarking on the task of identifying the units of all human activity as the first step in curriculum planning. As Charters expressed it, the job is one of "finding out what people have to do and showing them how to do it." [30] The possibilities were limitless. Once women were identified and trained to be women, so could almost any other identifiable group in our society be trained for its role. To be sure, all persons would be trained to perform some activities in common, such as some of those involved in maintaining physical efficiency, but their differentiated roles in society could be programmed as well. As in current proposals, such programs could be advertised under the slogans of curriculum flexibility and individualized instruction.

Paradoxically, the effort to diversify the product along the lines of probable destination called for an even greater effort to standardize the units of work than before. Product diversification was not to be accomplished by diversifying work and creating variety in school activity, but by arranging the standard units of work into the most efficient arrangement for manufacturing the particular products. The man who took the lead in this aspect of the social efficiency movement was David Snedden. In 1921, Snedden had written

[28] W. W. Charters. "The Reorganization of Women's Education." *Educational Review* 62 (3): 224; October 1921.

[29] W. W. Charters. "Curriculum for Women." *University of Illinois Bulletin* 23 (27): 327; March 8, 1926.

[30] *Ibid.*, p. 328.

that, "By 1925, it can confidently be hoped, the minds which direct education will have detached from the entanglements of our contemporary situation a thousand definite educational objectives, the realization of which will have demonstrable worth to our society." [31] Snedden devoted the next few years to the realization of that prediction, and also differentiating the curriculum so that the right objectives were applied to the right "case groups."

Case groups were defined as "any considerable group of persons who in large degree resemble each other in the common possession of qualities significant to their school education." [32] Objectives, therefore, would not be applied indiscriminately, but only with reference to the raw material. This was a particular problem, according to Snedden, in the junior high school where "differences of abilities, of extra-school conditions, and of prospects will acutely manifest themselves, forcing us to differentiate curricula in more ways, probably, than as yet suspected." [33] Such a division of the school population into appropriate case groups, in Snedden's mind at least, required sustained attention to the standardization and atomizing of the curriculum. His smallest curriculum unit, the "peth," is probably best illustrated by a single spelling word.[34]

Peths, however, had to be assembled in relation to "strands," classifications of "adult life performance practices" such as "health conservation through habitual safeguarding practices" for which Snedden estimated 50 to 100 peths, and "moral (including fellowship) behaviors" for which the same number was estimated. The vocational participations strand, however, necessitated differentiated numbers of peths, a streetcar motorman requiring only 10 to 20 while a farmer or a homemaker would call for 200 to 500 peths. A "lotment," in turn, was "the amount of work that can be accomplished, or ground covered, by learners of modal characteristics (as related to the activity considered) in 60 clock hours." [35] Thus, as in Taylorism, standards of efficiency were set for individual units

[31] David Snedden. *Sociological Determination of Objectives in Education.* Philadelphia: J. B. Lippincott Company, 1921. p. 79.

[32] David Snedden. " 'Case Group' Methods of Determining Flexibility of General Curricula in High Schools." *School & Society* 17 (429): 290; March 17, 1923.

[33] David Snedden. "Junior High School Offerings." *School & Society* 20 (520): 740; December 13, 1924.

[34] David Snedden. "Planning Curriculum Research, I." *School & Society* 22 (557): 259-65; August 29, 1925.

[35] Snedden, "Junior High School Offerings," *op. cit.*, p. 741.

of work in line with idealized performance levels. Actually, much of Snedden's work parallels the work of one of Taylor's major disciples, Frank Gilbreth, who identified 18 units of motion which he called "therbligs," thereby immortalizing his name in reverse.[36]

Yet the quaint obscurity of the educational terminology of the period tends to mask the underlying serious implications of the bureaucratic model applied to curriculum theory. The schoolchild became something to be molded and manipulated on his way to filling his predetermined social role. Guidance departments probed his inner resources in order to determine which of his potentialities were worth mining. Usually, these policies were followed in the name of bringing the outmoded academic curriculum into line with the new high school population, now dominated by the great unwashed. The curriculum was simply being made more democratic; but as Ellul has pointed out, the individual potentialities that were identified tended to coincide, as if by magic, with the needs of modern industrial society.[37] As the raw material was processed through the curriculum on its way to its ultimate state, simple efficiency dictated a differentiated curriculum in order to achieve the diversification of human labor that a modern industrial society demanded.

Snedden's ideal curriculum of minute standardized work units organized into the most efficient combinations for distinctive case groups was, of course, never achieved. The influence of such a conception of the curriculum was, nevertheless, widely felt. As early as 1923-24, when George S. Counts was conducting his classic study of the high school curriculum, the multiplication of different types of curricula designed for different population groups within the schools was evident. Of the 15 city school systems studied, only two, Detroit and Kansas City, used a system of constants and electives in their high school programs rather than a series of labeled curricula. Los Angeles, where Bobbitt's influence was undoubtedly strong in this period, maintained 18 different curricula in its high schools. Newton, Massachusetts, for example, listed the following 15 differentiated curricula:[38] Classical, Scientific, General, Business, Stenographic, Clerical, Household Arts, Agriculture, Printing, Elec-

[36] Gilbreth's other brush with immortality was Clifton Webb's portrayal of him as the super-efficient father in the film, "Cheaper by the Dozen."

[37] Jacques Ellul. *The Technological Society*. New York: Vintage Books, 1964. pp. 358-63.

[38] George S. Counts. *The Senior High School Curriculum*. Chicago: University of Chicago Press, 1926. pp. 12-14.

tricity, Machine Work, Cabinet and Pattern-Making, Drafting, Automobile, and Carpentry. The principle of predetermination was in this way applied to differentiated vocational roles in addition to one's role as a citizen, parent, church member, and so on.

In the 1923-24 school year, also, the Lynds found in Middletown a "manifest concern . . . to dictate the social attitudes of its young citizens." [39] This was in part reflected in a host of required courses in civic training designed to support "community solidarity against sundry divisive tendencies." [40] The inculcation of appropriate civic attitudes was second only in emphasis to vocational preparation. Upon entering high school, the Middletown student chose among 12 courses of study, 8 of which were distinctly vocational. Education in Middletown was clearly becoming specific preparation for certain community-sanctioned adult roles.

By the mid to late 1920's signs began to appear of a decline in efficiency as the predominant educational ideal and social control as a major function of the schools. Bobbitt's contribution to the influential Twenty-Sixth Yearbook of the National Society for the Study of Education represents a curious denial of some of the basic curriculum tenets he had proposed in his most popular book, published only two years before. In *How To Make a Curriculum,* Bobbitt set forth as one of his major premises that, "Education is primarily for adult life, not for child life. Its fundamental responsibility is to prepare for the fifty years of adulthood, not for the twenty years of childhood and youth." [41] It was on this fundamental assumption that Bobbitt based his case for the analysis of adult activities as the source of curriculum objectives. The efficient performance of adult activities of all kinds was the ideal toward which the whole curriculum was directed. In 1926, however, Bobbitt was to declare:

> Education is not primarily to prepare for life at some future time. Quite the reverse; it proposes to hold high the current living, making it intense, abundant, fruitful, and fitting it firmly in the grooves of habit. . . . In a very true sense, life cannot be "prepared for." It can only be lived.[42]

[39] Robert S. Lynd and Helen Merrell Lynd. *Middletown.* New York: Harcourt, Brace & Company, Inc., 1929. p. 197.

[40] *Ibid.,* p. 196.

[41] Franklin Bobbitt. *How To Make A Curriculum.* Boston: Houghton Mifflin Company, 1924. p. 8.

[42] Franklin Bobbitt. "The Orientation of the Curriculum-Maker." *The Foundations of Curriculum-Making.* Twenty-Sixth Yearbook of the National Society for the Study of Education, Part II. Bloomington, Illinois: Public School Publishing Company, 1926. p. 43.

Such a declaration can only mean a rejection of the production model of curriculum theory, since it denies such central concepts as predetermination and predictability. When, in 1934, Bobbitt was asked to prepare a statement summarizing his curriculum theory, his rejection of his former work was clearly evident and nearly complete.[43] In the 1930's, the ideal of social efficiency in education and the production metaphor as the basis for curriculum theory were obviously in a period of decline, a decline which, however, proved to be only temporary.

## The Contemporary Revival

Just as the first great drive toward standardization, predetermination, and fragmentation in the school curriculum came about in the aftermath of the first industrial revolution, so the renewal of those curriculum tendencies has come about in the aftermath of the second one—what is sometimes called the electronic or technological revolution. To be sure, some differences are evident. In the first place, the theory of behaviorism has been raised to the status of canon law in the social sciences, and so we are admonished to state the design specifications which set forth how a student will turn out in terms of observable behaviors. Second, the 1920s' doctrine of social efficiency has been overlaid with a thin veneer of academic respectability, and so the modern design specifications tend to call for a student to identify certain points on a map or to reel off the valences of a set of chemical elements instead of emphasizing practical, nonacademic activities.

Given these qualifications, Snedden's bureaucratic ideal of a thousand educational objectives to be used as a blueprint for shaping the educational product is now closer to realization than ever before. Teachers may now order from a catalog 96 objectives in language arts 7-9 for $3.00 or 158 objectives in social science (geography) K-9 for $4.00, or 25 objectives in English literature 10-12 for $3.00.[44] Snedden would have considered these a bargain at twice the price. These new objectives, furthermore, are evidently being formulated with such precision and wisdom that one major proponent of the new bureaucracy was led to observe of the period preceding the

---

[43] Franklin Bobbitt. "A Summary Theory of the Curriculum." *Society for Curriculum Study News Bulletin* 5 (1): 2-4; January 12, 1934.

[44] Instructional Objectives Exchange, W. James Popham, Director, Center for the Study of Evaluation, University of California, Los Angeles.

present millennium: "American educators have generally engaged in the same level of discourse regarding the specification of educational goals that one might derive from the grunts of a Neanderthal."[45] "One can only sympathize," he reflected, "with the thousands of learners who had to obtain an education from an instructional system built on a muddle-minded conception of educational goals."[46]

One can avoid muddle-mindedness, apparently, by overcoming a preoccupation with means or process in favor of a focus on outcomes.[47] Current curriculum practice seems to take the form of drawing up endless lists of minute design specifications in behavioral terms and then finding the right "media mix" by which the product can be most efficiently manufactured. "Judgments about the success of an instructional procedure," we are told, "are made exclusively on the basis of results, that is, the changes in learner behavior which emerge as a consequence of instruction. Only if the hoped-for changes in learner behavior have been attained is the instructional process considered successful."[48] The efficient achievement of the end product becomes the criterion by which the means are selected.

Such a sharp dichotomy between ends and means is precisely what resulted from the introduction of the assembly line in the first industrial revolution. Work became important only insofar as it was instrumental in achieving the desired product. The success of the assembly line depends on the fact that it reduces the process of production to units so simple that the predicted outcome is assured. The worker's movements are made so elementary and routine that the product inevitably emerges independent of the will or conscious desire of the worker. John McDermott has observed about the assembly line effect: ". . . since each operation uses only a small fraction of a worker's skill, there is a very great likelihood that the operation will be performed in a minimally acceptable way. Alternately, if each operation taxed the worker's skill there would be frequent errors in the operation, frequent disturbance in work flow, and a thoroughly unpredictable quality to the end product."[49] To

---

[45] W. James Popham. "Objectives and Instruction." American Educational Research Association Monograph on Curriculum Evaluation. Chicago: Rand McNally & Company, 1969. pp. 32-33.

[46] *Ibid.*

[47] W. James Popham. "Focus on Outcomes: A Guiding Theme for ES '70 Schools." *Phi Delta Kappan* 51 (4): 208-10; December 1969.

[48] *Ibid.*, p. 208.

[49] John McDermott. "Technology: The Opiate of the Intellectuals." *New York Review of Books* 13 (2): 34; July 31, 1969.

ensure predictability and efficiency in education, the techniques of industry are introduced with the same effect. Work loses any organic relationship with the end product.

Take, for example, the much publicized program, Individually Prescribed Instruction. Teachers prepare prescriptions—directions for what the child must accomplish. The child, after receiving his prescription, places a recorded disk on some playback equipment, and a disembodied voice asks, "Hello, how are you today?" (Pause for response.) "Today we are going to learn the sounds of the letters. Do you have a pencil?" The child responds and then is directed in the performance of certain tasks. If the child is able to perform these tasks with 85 percent accuracy, he is rewarded with a new prescription. If he fails, he is given remedial training until he meets the performance standard.[50] His progress is carefully plotted by a computer as he passes through the standard work units. Individuality, here, refers to the speed by which one makes his way through the standard work units. Of course, just as corporate management can make the tedium of the assembly line tolerable by scheduling a scientifically determined number of coffee breaks, so can the modern technologist make school work bearable by building into his system an appropriate schedule of other activities. But this would go about as far to create delight in intellectual activity as coffee breaks have in restoring the dignity of work.

In education, as in industry, the standardization of the product also means the standardization of work. Educational activity which may have an organic wholeness and vital meaning takes on significance only in terms of its contribution to the efficient production of the finished product. As in industry, the price of worship at the altar of efficiency is the alienation of the worker from his work—where the continuity and wholeness of the enterprise are destroyed for those who engage in it. Here, then, is one great threat that the production metaphor governing modern curriculum theory poses for American education.

The bureaucratic model, along with its behavioristic and technological refinements, threatens to destroy, in the name of efficiency, the satisfaction that one may find in intellectual activity. The sense of delight in intellectual activity is replaced by a sense of urgency. The thrill of the hunt is converted into an efficient kill. The wonder of the journey is superseded by the relentless pursuit of the

[50] "Individually Prescribed Instruction." *Education U.S.A.* Special Report. Washington, D.C.: National School Public Relations Association, 1968. p. 4.

destination. And to condition the victim to enjoy being conditioned is certainly less humane than open coercion or bribery.

The tragic paradox of the production metaphor applied to curriculum is that the dehumanization of education, the alienation of means from ends, the stifling of intellectual curiosity carry with them very few compensations. In the corporate structure, the worker who has become a cog in a vast bureaucracy is at least rewarded with an improved financial status and opportunity for leisure. The megamachine in ancient Egypt, where the autonomy of human beings was sacrificed in the great cause of the building of the pyramids, at least produced some measure of increased agricultural production and flood control.[51] What comparable benefits accrue from a corresponding regimentation in education? The particularization of the *educational* product, it turns out, is tantamount to its trivialization. A case in point is what happens to history as it is particularized in the highly regarded and liberally financed ES '70s project. One of the more than 50 pilot schools lists among its educational products the following typical examples in the form of items on a computer-printed Individual Student Progress Report (formerly known as a report card):

Given a list which includes Sibley, Colonel Snelling, Father Galtier, J. J. Hill, Ramsey, Fur Traders, missionaries, soldiers, and settlers of Minnesota and several true statements about their contributions, the student is able to match the listed people with the proper true statements.

Given several statements describing early and present day lumbering in Minnesota, the student is able to identify lumbering in Minnesota by writing E -early lumbering-, P -present day lumbering-, or B -both- in front of the applicable statements.

Educational products manufactured at such a level of particularity, even if multiplied a millionfold, could only be trivial. History (assuming that history is the discipline represented by these performance outcomes) simply is not the accurate recitation of bits and pieces of information. Nor is any discipline a specific finite assemblage of facts and skills. So to define it *is* to trivialize it.

This is not to say that instructional objectives, in and of themselves, are useless. They can add a dimension to educational activity; but they have no meaning outside the context of the means toward their achievement. There are, certainly, a variety of ways to consider

[51] Lewis Mumford. *The Myth of the Machine*. London: Secker & Warburg, 1967. p. 12.

the complex interrelationships between means and ends.[52] But the creation of a sharp dichotomy between means and ends or the consideration of means only in the context of efficiency is, pedagogically speaking, a travesty. From an educational point of view, behavior, in and of itself, is of little significance. It is, on the other hand, critically important to know how one comes to behave as he does; whether, for example, a given act derives from mere conditioning or from rational decision-making processes.

Modern curriculum theory, currently being influenced by systems analysis, tends to regard the child simply as input inserted into one end of a great machine from which he eventually emerges at the other end as output replete with all the behaviors, the "competencies," and the skills for which he has been programmed. Even when the output is differentiated, such a mechanistic conception of education contributes only to man's regimentation and dehumanization, rather than to his autonomy.

The mechanistic conception of man, the technology-systems analysis approach to human affairs, the production metaphor for curriculum design all share a common perspective. They represent a deterministic outlook on human behavior. The behavior of human beings is controlled in an effort to make people do the particular things that someone wants them to do. This may take the form of getting people to vote every election day, to buy the latest miracle detergent, or to recite on cue the valences of 30 out of 35 chemical elements. As Von Bertalanffy put it, "Stimulus-response, input-output, producer-consumer are all the same concepts, only expressed in different terms. . . . people are manipulated as they deserve, that is, as overgrown Skinner rats." [53]

[52] See, for example: D. S. Shwayder. *The Stratification of Behavior.* New York: Humanities Press, 1965. pp. 144-64.

[53] Ludwig Von Bertalanffy. *Robots, Men, and Minds: Psychology in the Modern World.* New York: George Braziller, Inc., 1967. p. 12. Reprinted with the permission of the publisher. Copyright © 1967 by Ludwig Von Bertalanffy.

# Part Two

## The Elements of the System

SEVERAL areas of the educational system are reviewed by the writers of this section. These dimensions include the roles which are filled in the system of education by teachers and administrators. Also treated are some of the problems associated with the training of these professional persons at universities and in the bureaucracy of the school.

Larry Cuban speaks a teacher's language when he portrays the crucial problems related to the time and work demands made on teachers. He describes the hierarchical patterning of authority which encourages a dependency relationship in schooling, and he conveys vividly the manner and means by which teachers are inducted into the system.

Speaking to the problem of teacher education, Martin Haberman engages in a series of debunkings regarding the preparation of teachers. Recruitment, selection, program development, the nature of faculty members, and the evaluation of schools of today—all come under sharp attack from Haberman's acid wit. The organizational structure of teacher education is translated in a series of "Haberman's Laws" which delineate some of the areas of concern: change and conflict, preparation for teaching, who should be responsible for organizational change, the press of organizational life, the nature of student involvement, and the nature of evaluation schemes. He offers several ways in which important changes in teacher education could come about.

Supervisory and coordinating roles are, according to Marilyn Gittell, the point at which strong power is exercised within the system of education. Gittell holds that the centralization and bureaucratization of schools have proceeded, along with the controlling and bureaucratization in other urban institutions, under the guise of increased professionalization.

Reviewing the nature of relationships within the schools' bureaucracy, Gittell argues that school boards retain only a very limited control over the actual operation of the schools. Further, the carrying out of policy is indeed, in many cases, the making of policy. Within the administrative hierarchy of urban districts, the central headquarters staff maintains enormous decision-making power in the critical areas of budget, curriculum, and staff promotion.

Gittell further analyzes the move for decentralization, the broader distinction of power, community control, and social change. She feels that the establishment of a new balance of local community participation and the ability of the professional staff to evaluate its new roles may well determine the future of urban schools.

The role of the principal as an educational leader in the maelstrom of bureaucratic procedures is the focus of Harvey Goldman's paper. Goldman points out that the principal is often the person caught in the middle. Strong teacher unions and associations are causing severe stresses for the traditional role of the principal as institutional leader. Courts of law, student power, and civil rights issues bear heavily on the new role which principals must evolve.

Interpreting the program to the community, explaining community concerns to teachers and other administrators, the mediation of conflict at the local level, and the facilitation of the local concerns are what Goldman feels will be the tasks of tomorrow's principal. Goldman prepares a revised program of preparation which will be of help to those interested in the education of principals.

Counseling and guidance and its development in and around the structure of schooling is the focus of John W. M. Rothney's work. As a person who has a long and distinguished history in the field, he is especially able to delineate the major factors which have caused the counseling movement to take its present direction.

Pointing out the vocational impetus in the earlier thrusts of counselors, Rothney develops the theme of current trends toward elementary and post-high school counseling, even though some of these practices are for a "relatively unproven service." The pressure of numbers has dictated many of the practices in counseling with the result that "the lame, the halt, the blind, the disadvantaged, the maladjusted, the failures" receive most of the attention.

Rothney's most pungent comments are directed to the effectiveness of counseling, the direction of the field toward personal-social counseling, the infiltration of the field by pseudo-psychologists and would-be psychiatrists. Most disturbing is Rothney's analysis of the use of counselors, through allotment of money and power, to implement congressional and federal policy for particular groups of students.

Rothney's final comments are reserved for the literature of the field, for the programs of preparation, and for the characteristics of those who enter counseling and guidance. He is especially harsh with the jargon of new counseling procedures. One can only feel that the field of schooling—with all its attendant divisions—would be far better off if such cogent, clear, and honest criticisms were part of the literature.

The chapter by Ann D. Clark delineates a case study of one field of schooling—that of special education. As a field of study and practice it offers rather unusual opportunities to examine, in microcosm, what has happened to the whole of the structure of schooling. Clark presents a clear and timely case study of a field which has drifted into bureaucratic subdivisions and has enormous difficulties in directing attention to the problems of children rather than to the self-serving nature of the divisions. Cutting across these divisions within the field one finds the classification of children, the supportive testing movement, and the steadily increasing bureaucratization over the years as almost inevitable concomitants of the developing field of practice.

In this historical and analytical chapter, Clark documents the crucial importance of the legal structure in recognizing, sanctioning, and legitimating the concept of *particular* disabilities, as well as the growth of bureaucracies about these types of disabilities. Critical note is taken of the testing movement as the vehicle by which children are tracked into preestablished groups. Incredible results follow: tests discriminate some groups; these groups are classified and placed in special categories—all in the name of "objective" measures. As an example, one finds that approximately 9 percent of school children in California are black while over 25 percent of the enrollment in classes for the educable mentally retarded are black! Her excellent summary of the factors which have led to the development of this system will help any educator to explore more critically his own field of practice.

Ernest Becker reviews the leftist, the liberal, and the rightist conceptions of the modern university, with negative and positive features of each viewpoint considered in a historical context. Becker believes that the vision of a scientific society, born out of the French Revolution, is the continuing task of today's university. This scientific society would not only organize knowledge as its contribution to human society, but afford its insights to legislatures, political leaders, and judicial offices.

With this as a background, Becker documents the sad demise of the ideal and of the university itself. He offers both theoretical and practical ways out of the dilemma, making *reform*, not revolution, the center of his program. His compelling suggestions deserve careful thought.

Wilmer S. Cody develops the case of accountability for schooling. His points are in the forefront of current thought and opinion, and he states the case rather well for the development of behavioral objectives and objective measurement of results based on those objectives. The Planning, Programming, Budgeting System (PPBS) is reviewed in his chapter, as are aspects of the recently suggested education voucher system (which he criticizes) and the performance contract (which he does not). His chapter is directed to both teachers and administrators.—V. F. H.

# 5

# *The Administrator Looks at His Practice*

### Wilmer S. Cody

THE organization and consequent administration of public schools in America contains a "structural flaw." This flaw must be eliminated if schools are to be more responsive to their own internal weaknesses and to their failure with a large number of individual students. The flaw emerges as an apparent dilemma. On the one hand, we see the professional teacher's need for freedom and autonomy to be successful with his students; on the other hand, we see the constraints placed upon the teacher by the bureaucracy. These constraints exist to assure his clients (mainly his students and their parents) that he will be successful in the sense of accomplishing what they expect him to accomplish. We also see an increase in collective bargaining that, in part, is a move by teachers to maintain some rights and prerogatives, and correspondingly an increase in demands by the public that schools be more responsive to student needs and interests and be more "successful," particularly with low-income whites and blacks. Such factors are putting the kinds of pressures on the bureaucracy of public schools that, as they are presently organized and operate, will surely lead to a "hardening" of the system, tighter controls, and more resistance to both teacher needs and client needs. This hardly makes for progress.

## The Trouble with School Bureaucracies

Traditionally, public schools have been organized like large manufacturing plants with bureaucratic structures to ensure that the employees are properly supported and controlled so that the objectives of the organization can be met.

The techniques of control have been similar; supervision of employees is used in education as well as in industry and has some merit in both. It does seem especially appropriate to spend a few minutes advising and checking on an employee performing a particular kind of activity that will be repeated many times. A teacher, however, seldom repeats the same activity more than a few times. Teaching activities change from year to year as well as from student to student. Supervision of teachers has considerable value, particularly in spotting problems and assisting teachers who are having difficulty. However, in my opinion, the use of supervision of teachers as a method of making educators more responsive and accountable will never be a major influence in our schools. Because goals and activities need to change so rapidly, the cost of providing supervision for all teachers is simply prohibitive.

The close and frequent supervision that would be required would, itself, be dysfunctional. Numerous research investigations have shown that the performance of any employee, whether teacher or assembly line worker, is depressed by close supervision.[1] Except when an employee is having serious problems, it seems that, to be effective, supervision must be used sparingly. The nature of teaching is simply too complex for infrequent supervision to be of any substantial influence.

Impersonal process mechanisms are also used to control the behavior of employees. Manufacturing companies, in extreme cases, have used assembly lines and specifically prescribed procedures. Schools use textbooks, teaching guides, lesson plans, and more recently "teacher-proof" packages of instructional materials. Doing one's job satisfactorily is a matter of following the rather specific procedures that have been "adopted" by the school system.

Rewards are issued by the administration in the form of praise, attention, and promotion for those teachers who process their students through basal texts. It becomes important that all the students finish the book so they will be ready for next year's teacher and next year's basal text.

There are obvious values in using such process mechanisms to control the work of school teachers. The formal adoption of a new set of curriculum materials accompanied by a program to train teachers in how to use them can be an effective way to bring about rapid innovations in the schools. Modern math and "new" science

---

[1] Alvin W. Gouldner. *Patterns of Industrial Bureaucracy*. Glencoe, Illinois: The Free Press, 1954.

textbook adoptions are good examples of changing the objectives of a curriculum rather rapidly so that students are learning different kinds of things. A wide range of educational innovations is now available in the form of packages that, when successfully implemented, represent improvement over the traditional "packages" of a graded textbook.

Such process mechanisms, however effective they may be for assembly lines, are inadequate for a teacher who must, to be successful, accommodate the various educational needs of many students. Although some teacher-proof packages have built-in features to respond to individual differences, none has been developed to encompass the full range of teacher and student behaviors that must precede learning. More significantly, numerous research projects conclude that the most important ingredient in effective learning by students is in the personal relationship established between the teacher and student.[2] A student works harder and learns more when he believes that his teacher cares about him. No publishing company has yet been able to package "caring." Furthermore, studies have indicated that an overemphasis on packages can lead to depersonalization in the classroom.[3] The package becomes more important to the teacher than is the child.

A third way schools have been organized to hold teachers and administrators accountable is by a system of bureaucratic rules, mostly in the form of school board and administrative policies. In many school systems, extensive and detailed rules exist that, for example, prescribe what the teacher will teach, when he may and may not leave his classroom, and how many staff meetings he must attend; this is a method of circumscribing the work effort of the staff members. Teachers and administrators are doing their jobs satisfactorily when they follow the board and administration policies of the school system.

As with the other control mechanisms, rules have considerable value. They provide guidelines to the individual as to what his job is and, in general, what is expected of him. The absence of some guides can, according to some studies, lead to "role ambiguity" and consequent ineffectiveness on the part of the staff member.[4] Rules can also be valuable in clarifying the relationship between two or

---

[2] James G. Anderson. *Bureaucracy in Education*. Baltimore, Maryland: The Johns Hopkins Press, 1968. p. 156.

[3] *Ibid.*, p. 12.

[4] *Ibid.*, pp. 127-35.

more individuals who must work together. Many educational goals are reached by students in a hierarchical progression. The instructional approach used by the first-year French teacher is very important to the teacher of second-year French. In addition, bureaucratic rules can specify privileges and prerogatives of each staff member, thereby protecting the autonomy, freedom, and flexibility needed by teachers to work effectively with their students.

In spite of these and numerous other benefits, bureaucratic rules also have disadvantages, especially when applied to school systems and other organizations staffed by professionals. The rules of the school can become more important than what the students learn.[5] Extensive rules permit staff members to function in a school without personal involvement and thereby serve as a stimulus to apathy. Rules simply cannot prescribe the deep commitment usually associated with a successful teacher.

Overemphasis on rules also can lead to impersonalization in much the same way as an overemphasis on textbooks. When the impersonal enforcement of extensive rules becomes the major focus of the administrator-teacher relationship, this same pattern is carried over to the relationship between teachers and pupils. Focus is on the impersonal treatment of pupils in relation to rules rather than the formation of personal concern and a feeling of "caring."

To review, supervision, process mechanisms, and bureaucratic rules are valuable and, to some extent, necessary ways of ensuring that school organizations and their staff members are accountable to their clients. None of them, however, is sufficient, and each is accompanied by constraints on the teacher that prevent him from doing an effective job. Existing bureaucratic systems, borrowed from the fields of industrial and business management, are in conflict with the procedural autonomy and flexibility the highly trained professional teacher must have to meet the varied needs of the students with whom he works.

## Other Options

Much has been said about the profession's "policing" itself. Performance would be judged by colleagues. Prior mastery of certain skills would be required before the profession would admit a new member. A code of professional ethics would protect the client

[5] Robert K. Merton. "Bureaucratic Structure and Personality." *Social Forces*, May 1940, pp. 560-68.

from incompetence and malfeasance. The staff member who violates the code would be sanctioned by his colleagues.[6]

This kind of accountability system currently exists, to some extent, in universities and in hospitals. However, it can hardly be considered to be working satisfactorily. While the rewards and sanctions in the academic profession have led to major contributions through research and other creative efforts, the system has hardly held the members of the profession accountable for their effectiveness as teachers of young men and women. The profession offers few incentives for being a good college teacher and no penalties for being a poor one.

The recent flurry of effort on the part of universities and their teachers to improve instruction is more a consequence of college students' (clients') protesting about poor teaching than a consequence of the organized professions' holding their members accountable for their teaching effectiveness.

In the medical profession, doctors, of course, are occasionally sanctioned for malpractice. Usually, however, this occurs only after a patient, or a surviving member of his family, files a complaint or a suit in court. In medicine (and in law as well) the clients hold the professional accountable for the results of his effort simply by exercising the option of firing one and hiring another who may be more successful.

One proposal to increase accountability that has received considerable publicity has been the "voucher" plan in which the government would provide students with vouchers that could be used by students to pay the tuition at either public or private schools. The resulting competition would presumably result in improved quality of schooling. The plan is also favored by persons who contend that schools should foster a pluralistic society rather than "standardization of its products."[7] Advocates of state aid for parochial schools and proponents of a "black separatism" view the voucher plan with some favor.

While this proposal may have some merits, there are a few serious built-in problems that would have to be resolved before it is tried. Presumably, the "free enterprise" system in which schools

---

[6] Peter M. Blau and Richard W. Scott. *Formal Organization.* San Francisco, California: Chandler Publishing Company, 1962. pp. 60-63.

[7] Charles Benson. *The Economics of Education.* Boston: Houghton Mifflin Company, 1961. pp. 328-31. Also see: Edward J. Fox and William B. Levenson. "In Defense of the 'Harmful Monopoly.'" *Phi Delta Kappan* 51 (3): 131-34; November 1969.

would compete in the market place would lead to a better product. One look, however, at other markets would indicate that quality is not the only basis for "comparison shopping" in America. Infecting American education with a Madison Avenue advertising campaign will not likely be beneficial to either teacher autonomy or student needs.

As a more serious problem, the voucher plan would very likely develop into a system that contradicts the basic belief in equality of educational opportunity or in equality of results. Students would quickly become separated according to how much each could supplement the state allotment for his education. Students from poor families would select a school where the only cost is the state voucher. Parents who could afford to add a few hundred dollars a year to the state voucher would select a "better" private school. Wealthy parents would continue to send their children to the "best." The results would be that poor children would all attend the more poorly financed schools and the wealthier children would attend the better financed schools. This, of course, would not be too different from the way public education is currently supported. The change to a voucher plan would hardly result in progress.

## Professional Autonomy Through Accountability for Results

In summary, the attempts of the bureaucratic system to achieve accountability from teachers result in constraints on the teacher; self-control by the profession does not seem likely to produce accountability, nor does a voucher plan. The question is how to organize and administer toward such an end in a way that satisfies the teacher's need for freedom and the public's demand for accountability.

This dilemma will be resolved as an administrative system of tools and procedures is developed that will permit accountability to be expressed in terms of the *results* of the school's and the individual teacher's efforts. Bureaucratic control mechanisms will be reduced if and when the system is able to measure results in terms of the needs of its clients and in terms of the effect of schooling. Perhaps we should view the matter as a negotiated agreement between the teachers and the public in which the public says: "You give me evidence of how effective you are with my child. On this information, I will decide whether to continue your services. In exchange, use whatever means you think is best to teach my child. You're demanding freedom. I'm demanding results!"

The reality of such a public demand is present throughout the United States. In hundreds of instances general dissatisfaction with schools and the consequent demand to show results have been at the heart of bond issue and tax increase failure. The dissatisfaction with the results of schooling is further expressed by the numerous calls for "community control" of schools.

The pitfalls of developing systems for professional accountability for results of schooling are numerous. Most of the existing tests of student achievement measure the level of a student's educational development but do not provide an assessment of student learning that has resulted from schooling. The difficulty of distinguishing the effects of schooling from the broader effects of experience outside as well as inside school is a real one and has led some educators to shy away from assessment proposals.[8]

If the learning to be measured is not carefully selected to be consistent with the objectives of schooling, a distortion of the teacher effort could easily result. Research by Blau in a state employment agency revealed that the quantity of interviews conducted by employees was one of the performance measures used by the agency to evaluate employees. This resulted in employees' spending more time conducting interviews than in finding jobs for their clients.[9] Argyris found that a quota system could lead employees to select the easier tasks.[10] Such findings only point out, however, the importance of carefully selecting the bases for evaluation, not that performance criteria should be avoided.

Competition between teachers could easily develop to the point of being dysfunctional. Blau found that this occurred in the state employment agency to the degree that productivity was hampered.[11] This problem could be one of the more serious ones since cooperation among staff members is one of the major trends in education, for example, in team teaching and staff differentiation. In many elementary schools, the development of reading skills may be the joint responsibility of the student's "regular" teacher, a special reading

[8] Herbert C. Rudman. "National Educational Assessment." *Educational Administration Quarterly* 3 (2): 115-29; Spring 1967.

[9] Peter Blau. *The Dynamics of Bureaucracy.* Chicago: University of Chicago Press, 1955. pp. 33-48.

[10] Anderson, *op. cit.*

[11] Blau, *op. cit.*, pp. 33-48.

teacher, and a volunteer tutor. Who, then, is to be held accountable? It would seem reasonable that, when the development of certain educational objectives is the responsibility of a team, then the team effort be assessed.

The ambiguity of some objectives of schooling and the present lack of assessment procedures could easily lead to a distortion of the school's efforts. Assessment procedures in the form of tests are already well developed for many of the cognitive goals of schools such as reading and mathematical skills, but procedures for assessing the learning of music appreciation and citizenship are not so advanced. A distortion in the teacher's or the school's effort could easily occur with an overemphasis on those goals that can be measured to the detriment of those that, at present, cannot. Before any system of teacher or student accountability is implemented, it should be comprehensive enough to cover the wide range of goals.

## Some Promising Signs

In spite of the obvious difficulties in assessing the effects of schooling, there are a number of developments within and outside education that give some support to the emergence of new accountability systems that would be a more viable substitute to bureaucratic controls.

The improvements in the measurement of academic achievement have been extensive during the past 15 years.[12] One of the important improvements in standardized tests in recent years has been the trend to include critical reasoning as well as recall of facts and concepts.[13] More benefits will come as assessment methods are developed to measure the learning of complex behaviors such as scientific investigation.

The intensive efforts being made to develop behavioral objectives will also, in my opinion, benefit the emergence of systems to assess the effects of schooling. One of the current difficulties in trying to measure the results of schooling is that many of the goals of schools are stated in broad, vague terms. Such statements have seldom been analyzed to even superficially describe the wide range of educational goals, including complex behaviors and values as

[12] Harold F. Bligh. "Trends in the Measurement of Educational Achievement." *Review of Educational Research.* "Educational and Psychological Testing." 35: 34-52; February 1965.

[13] Rudman, *op. cit.*, p. 119.

well as knowledge and skills, which must be developed if the tools and procedures to assess the results of schooling are also to be developed.

Inverting the evaluation process may prove to be one of the most useful components of a new accountability system. Faithful to the concept of bureaucratic management, schools now typically evaluate performance and effectiveness from the top down. The superintendent evaluates principals, principals evaluate teachers who, in turn, assess the learning of students. A new accountability system would, as proposed, focus on results, that is, on knowing what and how much a student has learned. We also need to know why a student learns, or at least the teacher needs to know why, so he can improve his effectiveness. Currently, the school system provides a supervisor who observes what the teacher does, then makes an analysis that relates to how the student views the teacher. Student perception of the classroom teacher would seem to provide very useful data in determining *how* a teacher is succeeding or failing. The teacher may be better off by simply asking the students rather than by inviting in an observer. Likewise, the principal could learn a lot about his effectiveness by asking his teachers, and the superintendent by asking his staff.

Although such an assessment procedure is not uncommon in education, it has not received widespread use because school systems are organized like manufacturing plants, with student learning viewed as a product. Students, however, are clients as well as "raw material." Teachers are professionals who need technical assistance and not simply management and control. Assessment, in the form of analyzing strengths and weaknesses of personnel, should be a two-way street.

Another development that is prominent in federal government organizations but is just now being tried in several school systems is the planning and budgeting procedure called PPBS (Planning, Programming, Budgeting System).[14] This budget planning and review system organizes the budget around educational objectives rather than the traditional functions and stresses program evaluation on a cost-effectiveness basis. Ultimately the system, if successful, will develop to a point where not only the effectiveness of a program (or personnel) can be assessed, but the benefits can be compared to costs. Every year, school boards must decide where to invest tax

---

[14] Harry J. Hartley. "PPBS and Cost Effectiveness Analysis." *Educational Administration Quarterly* 5 (1): 65-80; Winter 1969.

funds for the greatest student learning. We really do not know whether higher salaries, or smaller classes, or special teachers, or more materials would be the best investment in a particular system. Thus, the annual decision process is primarily a political one, with various interest groups, including teachers, administrators, or segments of the public, vying for prominence with their proposals.

PPBS has a long way to go in adding some rationality to this annual hassle, but at least this process is on the right track and provides a sound structure to an eventual accountability system based on results. While objective ways of measuring the outcomes of schooling are needed, the emergence of such methods will result from "political" influence as well as rational persuasion.

One potentially powerful influence that appears just over the horizon is the move to base some educational financing, particularly federal and foundation grants, on performance contracts. Leon Lessinger, an Associate Commissioner in the U.S. Office of Education, has made a strong appeal for making federal grants on the basis of performance contracts.[15]

Another potential influence toward accountability for results and professional autonomy are the contract negotiations that occur annually between school boards and teacher organizations. The typical contract contains agreements by both sides that each will fulfill certain commitments. To my knowledge, there has been no contract with a union or professional association that provides any assurance that student learning will take place. The contracts are, of course, labor contracts outside of education and usually establish performance criteria which can be used as the basis for assessing an employee.

Teacher organizations should and, in fact, must negotiate with boards to protect the freedom and autonomy that teachers need to be effective. School boards, however, will not and should not agree to extensive teacher autonomy until the teacher can provide some way to assess results.

If such negotiations seem implausible, note should be taken of the entry of private firms into the teaching field. Such firms are not selling equipment or materials; they are selling a total service and are guaranteeing results as part of a contract. In the fall of 1969, the Texarkana, Arkansas, School Board signed a contract with

---

[15] Leon M. Lessinger and Dwight H. Allen. "Performance Proposals for Educational Funding: A New Approach to Federal Resource Allocation." *Phi Delta Kappan* 51 (3): 136-37; November 1969.

Dorsett Educational Systems which guaranteed to raise the reading and mathematics achievement level of a certain group of students in one year within 80 hours of instruction for $80. For each student who reached this goal in less than 80 hours, the company was paid a higher bonus rate. If more than 80 hours was required, the payment rate was reduced.[16] This project may or may not succeed, but already other private firms are offering to teach boys and girls and be paid on the basis of *results*. Such a movement may convince public school educators that they must pay much closer attention to the results of their efforts.

In summary, the "structural flaw" in public education can be eliminated. The current accountability function of the school system bureaucracy places dysfunctional constraints on the teacher and does not even perform the accountability function very well. If teachers, administrators, and other staff members could be held accountable for the results of their efforts, then the bureaucratic constraints could be lessened to the extent that the professional educator would have the freedom and autonomy he needs to perform his job effectively.

Accomplishing such a change in public education will not be easy. The objectives of schooling need better articulation and specificity. Existing assessment tools and procedures are far from being adequate to such a task. Educational bureaucracies must be reexamined and given a changed role. Hopefully, they will devote less time to management and controls and more time to a service function, that of assisting teachers in improving the learning of boys and girls. That is what schools are supposed to make possible. To get closer to this purpose, I believe, extensive changes in public education will be needed.

[16] *Phi Delta Kappan* 51 (3): 135; November 1969.

# 6

# *Educating the Teachers: Changing Problems*

## Martin Haberman

WHAT is "It" that mass-produces large numbers of a product for which it takes no responsibility; is an establishment without an identifiable organization; is impervious to change but has no power structure; is completely decentralized but offers nationally uniform processes and content; is vitally important to the social welfare but removed from social control; is influenced by advances in knowledge of human behavior but cannot be evaluated in terms of what it actually does for people; and is controlled by state law on the basis of criteria which are irrelevant to its practice? Although the institution of marriage and other systems satisfy these conditions, the discussion which follows deals with *teacher education*.

Simplistic analyses have homogenized the ideas of layman and expert into a popular litany of what is wrong with teacher education. A brief consideration of these misconceptions is helpful for dispelling such non-problems and for pointing out the conditions and processes we use to defend ourselves against having to deal with real problems.

### Problems in Present Problem Statements

No facet of teacher education is spared the attacks of "common sense." Statements of obvious truth frequently advocate solutions and leave to others the definition of the problems they solve. Consider some of the more popular truisms regarding the components of teacher education programs.

## Recruitment

- *"We need more successful black male teachers who can serve as models for ghetto children."*

This non-problem neglects the fact that, by definition, teachers cannot serve as success models in American society. Able blacks can do more for society and themselves by functioning as bankers, businessmen, government officials, physicians, and military leaders than by teaching third grade in Peoria—even though such service is desirable.

Are we willing to fault corporate executives who neglect "their own people" and American society by not teaching hillbillies of WASP background? At present, our societal need for more minority group members in positions of power and status trumps the needs of any single profession. What is needed to recruit promising blacks into teaching, therefore, is simply monumental insensitivity. Creative educators can conceive of ways to involve people in the role of success models without recruiting them as career teachers.

## Selection

- *"We need to attract more able people into teaching."*

This non-problem ignores the facts. Although the number of students in teacher education programs is increasing, 30 percent of those who are graduated and certified never begin actual teaching and an additional 60 percent quit in less than five years, most of these in the first year.[1] With the exception of highly specialized areas, public schools can meet all their personnel needs by increasing the retention rate only one percent.[2] These data can be used to support the contention that teacher education is actually a process of helping people learn that teaching is not for them rather than of how to teach. The "problem" is to identify and retain available talent rather than to seek new populations. One helpful process would be to screen out the ineffective, experienced teachers who drive out promising beginners in much the same way they turn off pupils.

---

[1] *School Board Notes* 15 (8): 27; May 1969. Published by State Federation of District Boards of Education of New Jersey. (This citation refers to a national, not a state, statistic.)

[2] Edward Zabrowski, Judith R. Zinter, and Tetsuo Okada. *Student-Teacher Population Growth Model.* Document Number OE-10055. Washington, D.C.: U.S. Department of Health, Education, and Welfare, Office of Education, 1968. pp. 35, 36, 47.

No selection criteria used thus far have been reliable predictors of future success. The most widely used criteria are usually irrelevancies, such as grades, citizenship, and chest X-rays, which offer no theoretical justification for correlation with future performance. Self-selection on the basis of firsthand knowledge of the role to be filled is the most effective procedure for identifying the initially motivated and the potentially successful. A relevant selection process would be one year's work in some real school-neighborhood job. Neither college nor public school organization is capable of facilitating such selection.

## Program

• "*Teachers should: know more subject matter; go through sensitivity training;*[3] *learn verbal and nonverbal teaching strategies; diagnose, prescribe, and evaluate learning; consume and conduct research; learn to work in teams; create, select, and evaluate media and materials; teach aides, students, and interns; function as change agents.*"

These popular panaceas burlesque the overabundance of needs attributed to teachers. There has, to my knowledge, never been a study of a supposed lack among teachers which did not substantiate the contention that teachers were weak in the particular information, skill, or perceptions prized by the investigator. Yet, teacher educators inevitably specialize in something they perceive teachers lack; we assume, with little or no evidence, that more of our particular "X" will lead to improved instruction.

Advocates of additions to programs are more persuasive than those seeking deletions and, in this regard, programs of teacher education are not unlike those of public schools. Yet the most critical element in program development is also the most neglected—the establishment of priorities regarding what teachers should be taught to do.

## Faculty

• "*We need more clinical professors and field-oriented people as teacher educators.*"

This truism neglects the fact that the operating organizational

[3] In one of the more prestigious urban-intern programs, "insensitives" are sought for ghetto schools on the ingenious criterion that more of these types survive.

norms, in the colleges and universities which control programs, reward faculty for other things than field work. Getting involved with schools and teacher problems actually interferes with writing proposals for grants, mimeographing manifestos with activist students, and doing the flashy but hollow kinds of things for which education professors receive merit and promotion. Yet there is an even more important reason that the improvement of faculty cannot be conceived as a simplistic need for more clinical types. Because the role of teacher educator is tainted by irrelevance, pomposity, and lack of self-understanding, the experienced clinical teacher forfeits his influence to the practicing classroom teacher immediately upon his assumption of the role of teacher educator.

Recent trends in the administration of schools of education support the classroom teacher's perceptions of teacher education. For example, increasing numbers of beginning faculty (new doctorates) with no teaching experience; emphasis on special programs for public relations value with little attention to fundamental revisions of the regular programs; over-concern with problems of organizational life within the university which neglect the basic relationships between professionals in teacher education and in the classroom.

Dubbing a classroom teacher "clinical professor," however, not only puts him with undesirables, it removes him from a powerful in-group. Even the Yale Club is no match for the feelings of identity rampant among classroom teachers. Those who work with pupils have credence; everyone else is suspect. While blatant prejudice is frequently justified, it mitigates the potential usefulness of any teacher education program, given our present system of locating such education in colleges and using faculty (whether professors or clinicians) who do not simultaneously teach youngsters.

## *Evaluation*

• *"Public school instruction should be evaluated in order to determine which teacher education program is doing the best job."*

Follow-up of graduates into their actual teaching is a threat to both the competence of the faculty and to college control of approved programs. Advocating this kind of evaluation (accountability), however, sounds noble and is safe since public school organization precludes teacher evaluation and college organization limits the resources which are required.

The cost of "training" a teacher averages less than $1,000 per year.[4] As low as this investment is in comparison to other professional preparation, it is substantially higher than the amount expended for liberal arts students—the usual group college administrators use as a comparison. As long as future teachers are organized into groups that take classes, rather than into teams that work in schools, the money and resources for follow-up will remain nil.

Professional educators justify this institutional irresponsibility for graduates by pointing out that schools stink (although they use more scholarly jargon) and that good teacher education programs cannot be evaluated because their graduates have been dropped into sewers ("nonconducive instructional environments"). Similarly, educational researchers are reluctant even to try field studies in schools because reality does not match the rules of research design. Our behavior as teacher educators says something like this: "We have prepared our graduates for the best of all nonexistent worlds. Now shape up, world! If you don't provide a suitable environment for our graduates to be successful in, we can't be held responsible. Your problems resist our solutions, muck up our practices, and contaminate our research."

What other institution but a school of education could prepare 90 percent of its graduates for quitting or failure and still continue to expand in size and influence?

## The Real Problem of Educating Teachers

Which organizations and social systems should be changed to improve the education of teachers? Until we delimit some parameters, trying to "improve" organizational impact on teacher education is like attempting a trip around the world in 80 days. The press of each cultural situation could have an educative effect if examined in depth; in a brief tour, the result is more likely to be cultural shock than understanding. And if we have not agreed to the purpose of the journey, the search for environmental impact is pointless. For those whose purpose is "just going," the environment of the airplane itself may exert the most powerful situational impact.

At present, multiple sets of purposes are advanced for teacher education which are not connected with functions for implementing them. Purposes do not readily translate into what people do, unless stated initially in behavioral terms. The conceptual model, there-

[4] At a large state institution where I served as Director of Teacher Education Programs, the figure was under $500 per student for an entire two-year program.

fore, is an undifferentiated set of vague, do-good kinds of social service objectives which still identify the organizational structure that supports or inhibits the education of teachers.

Current literature on the effects of organization on people and products is still largely influenced by industrial and business models and by the knowledge (and lack of it) in sociopsychological explanations of human behavior. Even good summaries of what is known about organizational impact are singularly innocent with regard to the multiplicity and interrelationships among organizations and their subsystems.[5] They deal with one environment, one set of purposes, or one group, one at a time, as if a university—or even a shoe factory—were like a submarine with watertight compartments rather than like the institutional carnival in which we all participate daily. The world seems too complex for social scientists unable to whistle and shower simultaneously.

Teacher education is an interlocking, uncoordinated set of social systems. Governmental agencies, both state and national, universities, public schools, neighborhood organizations, social agencies, private foundations, industry, and other social professions each represents a complex of interdependent organizational systems which impinge upon teacher education programs. Tracing power lines in this maze is not unlike trying to untangle a large ball of rubber bands. In one sense, the social system of the university is the locus of "ideal" teacher education, and the public school is where "real" teacher education occurs. ("Ideal" means desirable but impractical; "real" means actual but self-administered by those who survive.) Conceptually, the analysis of teacher education can proceed with either the university or the public school as the center of the universe, but it is important to be clear about the terms of reference.

The preceding citation that 90 percent of teacher education graduates quit or fail in less than five years does not, by itself, support the contention that programs controlled by colleges have failed the profession.[6] It seems to me that teaching children and youth

[5] Richard C. Lonsdale. "Maintaining the Organization in Dynamic Equilibrium." In: *Behavioral Science and Educational Administration*. Sixty-Third Yearbook of the National Society for the Study of Education, Part II. Chicago: University of Chicago Press, 1964. Chapter 7.

[6] Actually, this statistic is probably an *under*estimate. My own approximations, as well as those of Robert A. Poppendieck, Specialist in Teacher Education, U.S. Office of Education, based on averaging data from a variety of sources, lead me to believe that about four-fifths of the certified graduates never begin teaching, or leave the profession in less than one year.

demands the full measure of one's physical, emotional, and intellectual capacities and can only be done for a few years before deteriorating in quality. On what basis dare we assume that the ability to teach—to offer any creative effort under pressure—will improve with age when all the evidence indicates that the contrary expectation is more likely?[7] I look forward to the day when we consciously plan for teaching careers of two to five years. The burden of proof will be on those exceptions who wish to continue, to demonstrate that they still retain their vitality, enthusiasm, and strength. Teachers should be recertified. We should approach the assumption of their competence as if they were airline pilots rather than priests. On this assumption of temporary competence, university programs can continue to prepare people for short periods but in more deliberate ways.

Knowing what the problems *are not* and appreciating the complexity of the organizational maze which affects teacher education represent merely a beginning. What principles of organizational life influence teacher education most? What are the connections between these principles and some real problems of teacher education?

## Haberman's Laws: Connections Between Organizational Life and Teacher Education

LAW I. *The further one is from a conflict situation, the more certain one is about its solution.*

Other people's problems are not only simpler but more amenable to dispassionate analysis. Teacher educators and their students (the practitioners) do not readily communicate because their participation in conflicting groups and in different work situations leads them to disparate perceptions of teaching problems and how to solve them. The professor can carefully define and propose alternative solutions for the classroom teacher, who can in turn work similar wonders on how to solve the problems of the school of education. Neither of them, however, places much credence in the other's advice since it rarely works in practice. How could it? Ignorance of another's reality is the surest path to becoming an expert.

Without a faculty directly engaged in instruction of youth,

---

[7] Jack Botwinick. *Cognitive Processes in Maturity and Old Age.* New York: Springer Publishing Company, 1967.

there is little likelihood that the intellectual-psychological-status gap between teacher educators and practitioners can be bridged. Professors, even clinical types, should be moved out of controlling, dominant roles into new roles as on-call, resource consultants whose use (and disuse) is decided by teachers and other school personnel.

LAW II. *Reducing conflict prevents change.*

The natural process by which an organization survives is to seek equilibrium to temper sharp attacks and to counterbalance shifts in its operation. But conflict, within and between organizations, is also a natural condition; and it is contention, not cooperation, which leads to important change.

Compromise is an organized effort to take the edge off differences in order to proceed as usual, while continued contention with a polarization of interests is the process which leads to a clear victory (or defeat) for some group. It is not possible for organizations to respond to both of these natural drives. To the extent that cooperation dominates, differences will be resolved (underplayed) and the organization will reestablish its old balance. When differences lead to clear-cut triumphs for some contending force, however, the organization is jarred into seeking a new kind of equilibrium. Most of us have been conditioned to value cooperation, not conflict; in this sense most of us are predisposed to resist important organizational change.

Successful organizations absorb their threatening competitors, water down their differences, and make minimal adjustments. Hotels merge with motels, motion picture companies merge with television stations, and department stores hire competing fashion designers. The result of such cooperation is that present systems survive by replacing extreme demands for change with changes small enough to be equalized.

Teacher educators, who realize they cannot really change the public schools which offer clinical experience to future teachers, frequently advocate laboratory schools. Public school people, who realize they cannot really change schools of education, seek to control their own teacher education programs. In other instances, public schools and colleges cooperate by watering down their legitimate complaints against each other. The result is that both systems are maintained rather than jarred into a search for new equilibrium—professors protect their irrelevant expertise and school people guard their irrelevant curricula.

Genuine competition among colleges, public schools, neighborhood groups, teachers unions, professional associations, college student groups, and others would result in significant changes in the ways teacher education is organized. Presently, colleges subvert such drives by a bear-hug type of cooperation which inevitably results in their retaining the unique right to offer state-approved programs of teacher certification; these other groups remain junior partners. Imagine the scope of change which might occur if any of these other groups were to compete long enough to win similar authority!

The usual funding practice is to give money to the very institutions and people to be changed. The willingness of these organizations to do themselves in is understandably low. Tinkering rather than overhaul has become the order of the day. Public schools receive tens of millions to innovate (Title III of the Elementary and Secondary Education Act), and they engage in the revolutionary behavior of buying library books. Colleges receive millions to revolutionize teacher education (National Defense Education Act) but restrict their vision to summer institutes.

Hoping for organizations to radically change themselves is a victory of expectation over experience. Competition, in the tradition of economic liberalism, is a more effective process of change. It may be that those who influence and manage the sources of educational funds are making a conscious effort to prevent significant change. How else can all this support for only existing organizational structures to change themselves be explained?

LAW III. *As content ideas become scarce, organizational tinkering increases.*

In teacher education this dynamic is curricular rigor mortis. We simply do not know enough instructional behaviors for overcoming pupils' obstacles to learning. When teachers ask for specific behavioral advice most professors dodge by asking for more information about the pupils or by advocating irrelevancies. The cumulative process of more and more instructional problems for which professors have fewer and fewer answers leads to an unfortunate defensiveness. Professorial defensiveness is manifested in our proliferation of academic hoops which, taken together, become programs but which, taken apart, do not include ideas which can be used in practice.

Most change agents in teacher education demonstrate they do not know the difference between piddling with the way teacher education is organized and making significant changes in what teachers are able to do as a result of completing a program. Infinitely more time and effort are devoted to altering faculty staffing patterns, financial allocations, credits and hours, time schedules, sequence of activities, material resources, and the certification requirements based on these modifications, than on making important changes in potential teacher behavior.

Even when we do get involved in changing content, we often create a new orthodoxy without relevance to practice. Although teachers express pleasure with their new workshops in Black History, Learning To State Behavioral Objectives, and Sensitivity Training, they do not see how these contents are useful solutions to their day-to-day instructional problems. Simply stated, teachers who know more blacks and their contributions to American Society, who can specify objectives in behavioral terms, and who "have been sensitized up" continue to feel helpless about the same old problems; that is, discipline, achievement, and motivation. Unless we consciously strive for more new content usable by classroom teachers, we will continue to drift with the organizational pressure for more artificial requirements.

LAW IV. *Individuals strive to do (and not do) what they feel like doing and attribute organizational value to their behavior afterward.*

Problems, like facts, never speak for themselves. The easiest and most common ways in which we seek to enhance ourselves are first, to recast organizational purposes in terms of our personal contributions and second, to redefine organizational problems as obstacles to our functioning.

In teacher education, the faculty's perception of "what teachers need to know" is so blatantly "what I like to teach" that it has a childlike, humorous quality: "more learning theory," says the educational psychologist; "more how-to-do-it," says the methods teacher; "more understanding of the social forces," says the educational sociologist; "clearer objectives," says the researcher. This is no different from the delusions of professors of arts and science; however, professional educators must derive, test, and revise their knowledge on the crucible of professional use.

In the larger sense, this law contends that the function of organizational change is not possible—unless performed by individuals with no vested stake in the performance of particular functions within the organization. In teacher education the message is clear—professors not only do not deal themselves out but overgeneralize and defend their specializations as the most vital requirement of professional practice.

LAW V. *The opportunity to self-actualize (that is, "to do one's thing") increases as the number of people performing in similar roles decreases.*

Many devotees of the assumption that human needs arrange themselves in a neat hierarchy also believe that the highest form of human motivation "refers to man's desire for self-fulfillment, namely, to the tendency for him to become actualized in what he is potentially. This tendency may be phrased as the desire to become more and more what one is, to become everything that one is capable of becoming." [8] Abraham Maslow, the high priest of this cult, has speculated that as few as one percent of the population will ever achieve this level of self-actualization in their needs satisfaction.[9]

Actually looking at man's behavior leads to a more credible assumption that human motivations are simultaneous and complex rather than structured into a sequence of prerequisites. Man's search for connectedness, power, and love is an interrelated search—and operates even when he is hungry.

"To do one's thing" or "whatever turns you on" is currently the common cry of many groups fighting the established systems of government, business, the military, colleges, and schools. Those who think they agree with and understand these mottoes interpret them as the basic right of the individual to be himself—even in rebelling against restrictive moral systems.

Organizational functioning, by definition, is a form of group life in which the individual neglects or transforms his personal whims in order to maintain membership in a group that is significant to him, that is, a group he uses as a reference to define and evaluate himself as a person. For me, the Hawthorne Effect is not the simplistic notion that people who know they are in an experiment will work harder, but that people who give up their identity to the point of valuing their participation in a work group become controlled by the norms of that group. Attempts to motivate or demoralize them as individuals are filtered through the group's value structure.[10] Even morale is commonly viewed as:

[8] Abraham H. Maslow. *Motivation and Personality.* New York: Harper & Brothers, 1954. pp. 91-92.

[9] Cited in: Richard C. Lonsdale, *op. cit.*, p. 157.

[10] F. J. Roethlisberger and William J. Dickson. *Management and the Worker.* Cambridge, Massachusetts: Harvard University Press, 1938.

... a combination of (a) perceived productivity or progress toward the achievement of the tasks of the organization, and (b) perceived satisfaction of individual needs through the interaction of the participant in his role within the work group and the total organization.[11]

There is no new knowledge to be derived from casting the issue of organizational life as the individual versus the system; but much can be learned from developing new ways in which individuals can realize themselves through their required participation in groups.

As individuals move to higher status, more powerful occupational levels, their peer groups shrink and become dispersed geographically. Professional isolation is an occupational affliction more common among corporate presidents than production workers. The freedom of the boss to "do his thing," therefore, is derived from both his status (that is, no one who values continued participation in the system tells the emperor that he is naked) and the fact that his idiosyncratic behavior does not shake up any co-workers since he has no genuine peers. In operation, it is the flexibility of *groups* of subordinates that makes the chief's *individuality* possible. Maslow may be right when he says only one percent ever fully realize their potential. The reason, however, is organizational (too few presidents) and not personal.

Occasionally, an individual in a staff or consultant role enjoys the same freedom as the chief. In most systems it has become fashionable to tolerate and publicize a few divergent characters in much the same way as "the white Jew" or "the house nigger"—to prove the organization's basic democracy and humanness. Yet people who really do what they feel like doing are organization's most dangerous natural enemies. The simple fact is that psychiatrists who advocate that each man live out his feelings and values are simpleminded about the societal need for organized social systems and man's basic need to participate in them even at his personal expense.

The implications of this dynamic for education professors who believe they should prepare teachers to face themselves, or to be truly creative in public school settings, are obvious. But at the same time we teacher educators denigrate public schools that cannot absorb all our creative graduates, we punish colleagues who dare to rock the university organization which is significant to us. Creative people are driven out of schools and colleges not because the people in these systems are evil and stupid but because we are organized.

[11] Richard C. Lonsdale, *op. cit.*, p. 165.

The very process of joint activity requires some repression of one's divergence, pizazz, distinctiveness.

LAW VI. *Those most prone to disrupt an organization are least able to administer it.*

Student activism has resulted in take-overs of some teacher education programs. In truth, abdication of responsibility by professional educators, not student power, has often forced student take-overs since education students tend to be like other nonmilitant, vocationally oriented types.[12] Shifts from faculty to student domination will be even more common in the future.

While there is little to defend in most present programs, there is even less in completely controlled student efforts. One program, which I observed at close range for one year, began by asking 60 juniors in two liberal arts colleges what they would like to learn. Complete student control in this case became the freedom to not think, to not experience, and to not participate.

The very process of winning control destroys the value of student control. "Doing one's thing" is antithetic to any organization—even if that organization is now controlled by "the good guys." (See Law V.) It is the nature of the organizational process and not the particular people in the power structure which mitigates the opportunity for individualism.

When grades, course requirements (even student teaching), compulsory attendance, and examinations are done away with, the focus is still on organizational change which may or may not affect content. (See Law III.) Other fundamental errors in running out and sticking the students with the program are: (a) to confuse general-liberal education with professional education which includes the mastery of techniques, and (b) to expect middle-class late adolescents to know what they need to learn *prior* to any experiences in communities and neighborhoods, in schools, or in various professional roles.

Complete student control of teacher education programs is a naïve process if it derives from the dissatisfactions of college youth, most of whom are even more ignorant than education professors regarding the problems of education in an urban society. Substituting youthful passions for faculty's pet ideas is merely the creation of new kinds of irrelevancies. Genuine relevance in teacher educa-

[12] Jonathan R. Warren. "Student Perceptions of College Subcultures." *American Educational Research Journal* 5 (2): 213-32; March 1968. Washington, D.C.: American Educational Research Association.

tion should mean the development of competencies in field situations. The objective of equalizing educational opportunity in an urban society is a more valid reason for conducting a program of teacher education than the need to pander to college youth in the throes of biochemical change.

I recognize the risk that I will be misread by some as one opposed to student involvement. Quite the contrary. I am dedicated to student involvement—even control, provided the students respond to their experiences gained in the organizations of the public school and community, and are not merely overreacting to the organization of the university. At a White House conference in 1962 President Kennedy indicated a similar distinction between the need for passion and know-how:

> The fact of the matter is that most, or at least many of the problems we now face are technical and administrative problems. They are very sophisticated judgments which do not lend themselves to the great sort of passionate movements which have moved the country so often in the past. Now they deal with questions which are beyond the comprehension of most men and most government administrators, over which experts differ.

LAW VII. *Accountability is always the first criterion for evaluating other people's programs.*

The organizational implication of this law for teacher education is clearest when we say things like: "Our graduates go all over the country." Or, "The evaluation techniques for connecting what a teacher does in practice with what happened to him as an undergraduate are not developed." Or, "The organizational press of the public schools is so deleterious that it is impossible to assess the potential of beginning teachers who are simply trying to survive." Regardless of the reasons, valid and invalid, colleges and schools of education do not take responsibility for the professional practice of their graduates.

Actually, there are two other reasons why teacher education is organized against accountability: college administrators do not value teacher education, and it takes financial resources to follow graduates into practice. Higher education is organized to sell courses, not to sustain losses for improving public education. Individual graduates who are willing to continue to pay for credits and degrees will be "followed up"—but even here, there is no institutional accountability for their professional practice.

Tax-supported state universities are particularly culpable for their lack of responsible action. I recall conducting a meeting of deans who represented the various colleges of a large, well-endowed state university. We served as the policy-making body of the university regarding all teacher education programs. Prior to one meeting, I informed the council of a telephone call from the office of the state commissioner reporting that 12,000 elementary school teachers were needed immediately. The council discussed this item for less than three minutes and then passed a unanimous motion that the university, in keeping with its traditions, would continue to offer only programs of secondary education. These administrators would not have had the luxury of sitting on their "traditions" if there had been any process whatever for holding them publicly accountable for the expenditure of public funds in disregard of the general welfare.

Social activists may be sufficiently aware to picket a community action project, but few have enough organizational savvy to trace any community problems back to schools of education. If they did, more deans would be held hostage. As long as we in teacher education can snuggle in among the complex systems operating in large universities and as long as social militants remain unsophisticated about organizations, our programs will remain insulated from public pressure and held unaccountable.

Law VIII. *As scientific study of organizations increases, correct predictions of organizational change decrease.*

Post hoc analyses are the essence of the work proffered by social scientists concerned with organizations. They are not unlike Casey Stengel who, having completed a lengthy and exhaustive analysis of why the New York Yankees had lost the preceding day's game, turned his expertise to predicting the next game and stated: "The team that gets the most runs will win." Experts are people who can create complex but arbitrary definitions of capricious constructs which inevitably explain past events. Concepts of leadership, administrative style, organizational press are clever, but soon take on a life of their own. If life does not fit the constructs, then life, not the neat way of explaining it, is rejected.

In teacher education, analyses of past programs are more typical than efforts to learn enough to state that *if* students experience "X" activities *then* they will be likely to have "Y" behaviors, perceptions, knowledge. Such effort is rare because it demands hard thinking and because it is more vulnerable to methodological criticism. Businessmen, accountable for future payoff (See Law VII), have a better record than educators in assessing the values of social science analyses of organizations.

The foregoing connections between organizational truisms and problems of teacher education do not describe the nature of the *changes* in problems of preparing teachers. Our tacit assumption is that more change has occurred in conceptual schemes for analyzing teacher education than in the problems themselves. Any one way of seeing, however, is also a way of not seeing. Whoever reveals the problems also reveals his ignorance of the limitless range in ways of knowing.

Given *my* insights and blinders, therefore, it seems to me that the present state of the changing problems of teacher education indicates some patterns that are worth sharing. These trends are related to the laws discussed above.

*What Organizational Changes Would Affect Teacher Education in Peripheral Ways?*

1. Grants to colleges and universities (Laws I, II, III, IV, V, VI, VII, VIII)

2. Grants to public schools (Laws II, III, IV, V, VI, VIII)

3. Recruitment of new populations—Peace Corps returnees, returning war veterans, VISTA Volunteers, and others (Laws I, V, VI, VII)

4. Packaged materials and media developed by private industry (Laws VII, VIII)

5. Utilizing a new breed of teacher educator as directors of teacher education programs (Laws I, IV, V, VI)

6. The intern approach (Laws III, V, VI)

7. Clinical professors (Laws IV, V)

8. "Crash," "experimental," and "demonstration" programs in urban areas (Laws I, II)

9. More black faculty (Laws II, IV, V)

10. Changing public school organization (Laws I, II, VI, VII)

11. Initiating new organizational forms for educating teachers, such as centers or regional laboratories (Laws I, II, III, VII, VIII).

## What Organizational Changes Would Affect Teacher Education in Important Ways?

1. Permit state departments of education to allow institutions other than colleges and universities to offer approved programs for teachers and other personnel.

2. Put a five-year time limit on all teacher education programs; require colleges (and other agencies) to submit new proposals for state approval at least this often.

3. Do away with the issuance of "teaching" licenses and substitute new role definitions, for example, specialist in materials and planning, community resource coordinator, skills tutor, action researcher, media consultant, and instructional value-clarifier.

4. Prepare future personnel in cross-role teams of people performing actual functions.

5. Replace the "right" of graduates to take a position, as individuals, in any system they choose, with the "obligation" to work for a given period in the schools where they were prepared, with the very team members they worked with.

6. Use observation of teachers and other professionals in the school system to credit practitioners with equivalency certificates—in lieu of course work.

7. Put a five-year termination on teaching licenses. Require continuous reevaluation on the basis of observed competencies.

8. Evaluate and certify teacher educators on the basis of behavioral competencies and on the basis of evaluation submitted by teachers and others who have studied with them.

9. Assess the content of teacher education programs in terms of its applications to field situations.

10. Promote competition among teacher education programs offered by teachers unions, community groups, college students, professors, professional associations, government agencies, religious groups, and industry.

The likelihood is that processes of tinkering will continue to be more common than those which might lead to fundamental changes. This assumption leads me to question why I am hopeful. I suppose my faith in the future derives from the belief that chance, which may be the most powerful change agent of all, will not prove as fruitless as tradition.

# 7

# Educating the Administrators

## Harvey Goldman

THIS paper will consider the preparatory programs for educational leaders, as exemplified in the principalship. It is necessary, therefore, to define certain terms prior to dealing with them at length.

The term "leadership," when referred to in this paper, is defined as:

... the initiation of a new structure or procedure for accomplishing an organization's goals and objectives or for changing an organization's goals and objectives.... the leader is concerned with initiating changes in established structures, procedures, or goals; he is disruptive of the existing state of affairs.[1]

To ensure clarity of terminology, "administration" is defined here as:

... the utilization of existing structures or procedures to achieve an organizational goal or objective.... the administrator is concerned primarily with maintaining, rather than changing, established structures, procedures, or goals. Thus, the administrator may be viewed as a stabilizing force.[2]

For the purpose of this paper the principalship will be conceived of as a leadership position. That it also involves administration is recognized, as is the fact that principals have not always manifested leadership behaviors.

[1] James M. Lipham. "Leadership and Administration." In: *Behavioral Science and Educational Administration.* Sixty-Third Yearbook of the National Society for the Study of Education, Part II. Chicago: University of Chicago Press, 1964. p. 122.

[2] *Ibid.*

The remainder of this paper will focus on the emergent role of the principal, the factors affecting that role, and the necessary adaptations that will have to take place in training programs for such personnel if building-level administrators are to play a leadership role in the educational arena. The decision to emphasize this one role was based on the following criteria: (a) it is the administrative/leadership role with the largest number of position incumbents; (b) it is the administrative/leadership role that is closest to the classroom instruction; (c) the impact which teacher militancy and the negotiations process have had upon the teacher-principal relationship is similar to, albeit somewhat more intensive than, that which has been felt by other line-staff personnel at various levels of the formal organization; (d) the principalship is often viewed as the most desirable entry level administrative/leadership position and, as a result, includes among its ranks a significant number of persons with little or no prior administrative/leadership experience.

The available evidence indicates that the principalship is in a transitional period, one filled with conflict and uncertainty. Elementary and secondary school principals are well aware of the fact that traditional responses are often inappropriate when dealing with contemporary problems.[3]

The emergence of powerful and militant teachers organizations has proven especially threatening to principals. To a considerable extent, principals' anxiety over this development is due to the fact that they, alone among the administrative hierarchy of the schools, spend the greater portion of their working day in close proximity to teachers and are most affected by the vicissitudes and demands of their staffs. Most students of the principalship seem to agree that the existence of strong teachers unions and the resultant negotiation process portend major changes in the principals' roles and in their relationships with teachers, even though there is considerable disagreement over the form these changes will take.

Redfern sees the principal of the future playing an active coordination role for teachers committees within schools.[4] Apparently, whatever influence is to be possessed by principals in this setting would be a direct result of the degree to which their expertise

---

[3] The fact that both the April and May 1968 issues of *The National Elementary Principal* were devoted to the theme "The Changing World of the Principal" is indicative of the soul-searching that is being carried on regarding this transitional state.

[4] George B. Redfern. "Negotiation Changes Principal-Teacher Relationships." *The National Elementary Principal* 47: 20-25; April 1968.

was of value to teachers as they functioned within their classrooms and committees. Another view of the effects of negotiations is set forth by Taffel [5] when he points out the impact of that process as it serves to restrict the latitude which principals traditionally have possessed with regard to such areas as assignment of teachers, program development, transfer of teachers, and handling of grievances.

The courts, too, have rendered decisions which have numerous implications for principals as well as administrators at other levels. That recent court decisions have had the effect of severely delimiting the perceived alternatives available to principals who must cope with students on a day-to-day basis is eminently clear; that such decisions have at the same time provided students with a legal basis for attacking the existing school structure is also obvious. The challenge of curbing inappropriate student behavior without encroaching on students' constitutional rights is potentially a problem that could drive principals to distraction.[6]

Students, as we all are well aware, are increasingly discontent with the manner in which the schools relate to them and to the society as a whole. That the student rebellion to which we have become so accustomed on college campuses will also infect secondary schools seems a certainty. Some of the reasons for this change in the nature of the secondary school student body are briefly and insightfully treated by Glatthorn.[7] Principals will find it necessary to initiate new structures and processes for incorporating students into the policy-making aspects of the schools and for providing them with an effective means of voicing their concerns without having to resort to the methods which serve to intensify rather than reduce existing levels of conflict.

Clute [8] points out that recognition of the existence of students' rights also implies that principals have a direct responsibility to effect those curricular and organizational changes that must ensue

---

[5] Alexander Taffel. "The Principal and Teacher-School Board Negotiations." *The Bulletin of the National Association of Secondary School Principals* 52: 71-83; September 1968.

[6] William E. Griffiths. "Student Constitutional Rights: The Role of the Principal." *The Bulletin of the National Association of Secondary School Principals* 52: 30-37; September 1968.

[7] Allan A. Glatthorn. *The Principal and the Student Council.* Washington, D.C.: National Association of Secondary School Principals, 1968. pp. 1-9.

[8] Morrel J. Clute. "Rights and Responsibilities of Students." *Educational Leadership* 26 (3): 240-42; December 1968.

to comply with recent court decisions. Most of the changes must be directed toward rearrangement of organizational structures and instructional programs in a manner consonant with the ideals which the schools profess to value—that is, due process, responsibility, allegiance to the Constitution, participatory democracy, freedom of speech, and the right to personal privacy.

The cause of students' rights is also being championed by the American Civil Liberties Union, as evidenced by its recent publication entitled *Academic Freedom in the Secondary Schools*.[9] This pamphlet attempts to delineate the parameters within which teachers *and students* should be free to act.

Pressures are exerted upon school administrators at all levels to include within the school curricula information regarding topics that a great many principals would prefer to ignore. Among them are demands upon the schools to provide students with information about sex and its role in our society,[10] about conscientious objection to war and military service,[11] and about the nature and use of drugs.[12] Principals often do not feel such topics should be included within the curricula of the public schools; others are opposed to the dissemination of such information by any public agency. Simultaneously, principals are asked to cope with concerns such as militant parents, extremist groups, community involvement, and decentralization.[13]

Particularly in urban areas, desegregation and decentralization pose an enormous threat to school building administrators. Even though everyone agrees that New York City is atypical, the conflict which has surrounded that city's attempts to desegregate and decentralize has only served to intensify already existent fears that

---

[9] The American Civil Liberties Union. *Academic Freedom in the Secondary Schools.* New York: The American Civil Liberties Union, 1968. 20+ pp.

[10] David I. Bednarek. "Right Wingers Fight Sex Education." *The Milwaukee Journal,* "Accent on the News" Section, May 15, 1969. pp. 1-2. The article provides a brief description of the various forces most intimately involved with this issue and the bases on which these forces are justifying their positions.

[11] Dean A. Allen. "Responsibilities of the High School for Providing Information on Conscientious Objection to War." *Phi Delta Kappan* 50: 145-47; November 1968.

[12] George D. Demos. "Drug Abuse and the New Generation." *Phi Delta Kappan* 50: 214-17; December 1968.

[13] David Lewin. "The Changing Role of the Urban Principal." *The Elementary School Journal* 68: 329-33; April 1968.

the principal's autonomy will be further circumscribed.[14] Certainly, the increasing demand of urban minorities for the ever-larger "piece of the action" with respect to those agencies which affect (and to some degree control) their destinies also serves as a threat to the principal's autonomy. Indeed, if community control is to be defined as it was in an issue of *Foresight*,[15] then it will clearly result in a complete restructuring of most larger school systems and in a new set of roles for parents, students, and teachers.

## The Principal's Role

Although it is possible that the worst fears of some students of the principalship will come true, there is also a distinct possibility that the role, rather than being diminished, will instead be enhanced and redefined to encompass areas of responsibility not presently within its domain.[16] The accomplishment of this redefinition would be a rather delicate undertaking and would necessitate considerable thought and effort on the part of those principals desirous of maintaining leadership positions within the schools. Any such redefinition will have to account for the fact that the roles of teachers, parents, and students will also be undergoing modification concurrently. The direction that these changes might take can be hypothesized after an examination of existing trends.

Teachers are, hopefully, finally accepting responsibility for defining their own role and for ensuring that they have a more prominent and influential part in the conduct of the schools. As teachers continue to redefine the parameters of their own role, they will undoubtedly exclude principals from some task areas for which the principals have previously assumed responsibility. This will be particularly true with respect to such responsibilities as assignment of teachers to teaching stations and supervision of instruction. Thus,

---

[14] Arthur E. Salz. "Local Control vs. Professionalism." *Phi Delta Kappan* 50: 332-34; February 1969. Also see: David Rogers. *110 Livingston Street: Politics and Bureaucracy in the New York City Schools.* New York: Random House, Inc., 1968. 584 pp.

[15] Preston Wilcox. "The Meaning of Community Control." *Foresight* 1: 9-14; February 1969. Detroit: The Black Teachers Workshop. In essence, the view is set forth that ghetto schools should be controlled and operated for blacks by blacks and not be subject to review by any other agency.

[16] Harvey Goldman. "Principals for Community Schools." *The Community School and Its Administration.* Flint, Michigan: The Flint Board of Education and the Mott Foundation, Volume 7, Number 1, September 1968.

any definition of the emerging principalship will have to take into consideration the current trend in which teachers are "staking out" and defining those areas of the instructional program for which they, *and they alone,* shall be responsible.

As society continues the already apparent trend toward measuring the worth of people in terms of the number of certificates, diplomas, and degrees possessed, the importance of the schools to society will increase markedly. Although this trend is not necessarily desirable, all indications point to its continuance. Therefore, parents in both our urban and suburban areas are more likely to vocalize their demands of the school. As a result, and in what they will view as a way of protecting their children, parents will seek means by which they can play a more influential role with respect to the determination of policy and evaluation procedures for the public schools. Any redefinition of the principalship must provide for the maintenance of adequate relations with parents while ensuring the opportunity for the preservation of institutional integrity. Admittedly, this will be a rather difficult task—one which approximates walking a tightrope that is unattached at both ends.

The role toward which the principalship will evolve will very likely consist of the following:

1. *Interpreting the educational program to the community.* This will involve the identification of those formal and informal groupings within the school district which are concerned with the educational processes and assisting them to develop an understanding of the organization. As a part of this task, principals will find it necessary to determine majority and minority groups within their districts, and to reach both with equal effectiveness.

2. *Explaining community concerns and problems to teachers and other administrators.* This task area will, of necessity, require that the principal accept responsibility for the organization and conduct of research studies on a continuous basis within his school district, and for the development of processes by which teachers and central office administrators can be continually informed of the results of these studies. A major aspect of this role will be to help teachers incorporate the data gleaned from the research into the school curricula to ensure continued relevancy on the part of the school.

3. *Mediation of conflict at the local level.* Both the incidence and intensity of conflict affecting the schools will increase in the years ahead. This occurrence will result in a situation whereby

principals will be required to solve most or all of this conflict at the building level to avoid the inundation of central office personnel with such matters. Principals will have to be granted the authority to make such determinations.

4. *Facilitation of extra-local concerns.* Some concerns of teachers or community representatives will clearly be of such a nature that solutions cannot be sought at the building level. In such cases the principal will be responsible for bringing together the persons who can make authoritative decisions relative to such matters and for all necessary follow-up activities to ensure that all concerned are apprised of the final decisions as well as factors which prompted their determination.

If principals are to successfully carry out the role described here, those aspiring to the position will require extensive training in the social sciences in addition to that portion of their preparatory programs which is oriented toward an understanding of schools. Although a number of principals have acquired such skills in the course of their professional activities, the matter can no longer be left to chance.

Specialized training in such areas as communications analysis, the nature and psychology of poverty and affluence, group dynamics, the evaluation of behavior, community development, and conflict mediation will be a distinct asset for future principals.

To cope effectively with the four task areas listed previously, principals will need to perceive and develop more adequate means of making the bureaucratic structures that characterize most school systems more responsive to building-level needs.

Principals do not seem to understand that many of the urgent reforms of public education mean changing the bureaucratic structure to allow it to respond to societal pressures which it is currently unable or unwilling to meet. . . . It is difficult for principals to realize that it is their position which holds the old autocratic organization together and thus provides it stability. . . . By denying the necessity for changing themselves, they preserve the rigor mortis of the educational bureaucracy.[17]

Anderson, speaking of the manner in which principals relate to their staff members, suggests that they are fearful of the risks involved in assigning authority and autonomy to teachers and also

[17] Fenwick English. "The Ailing Principalship." *Phi Delta Kappan* 50: 159; November 1968.

of being held responsible for the evaluation of staff performance.[18] As a result, they rely on the centralization of authority and on the establishment of rules which serve to control, rather than liberate, teachers. "Thus, the administrator can measure teacher compliance with those norms rather than teacher effectiveness since, unfortunately, for many administrators the two are synonymous."[19]

A clearly stated indictment of the extent to which bureaucratic procedures dominate the orientation of schools is set forth by Rhea:

> It is possible to substitute planning and control for professional competence and autonomy, it is cheaper, and that is what we have done.... and the price of bureaucratization has been a virtual redefinition of the term *education* itself. We may still talk of student-centered education and of the need to maximize human growth, but what we actually do and what we actually accomplish are not at all what Rousseau or Dewey or their followers had in mind. The actual student-teacher relationships found in most schools, the interpersonal methods which they employ, are largely bureaucratic in nature, and the bureaucratic methods are very far from ideal educational ones.... in virtually every important respect the behaviors and attitudes appropriate for bureaucracies are quite the opposite of those appropriate for education.[20]

In essence, there are two points of view from which all bureaucratic structures can be considered.[21] The first is to view bureaucracy as a tool or mechanism designed to facilitate the accomplishment of institutional goals. The second is to view bureaucracy as a means of exercising power and control over persons. From the first point of view, bureaucracy can be seen as a rather flexible entity, subject to modification as either conditions or goals change. When examined from the second point of view, bureaucracy is a rather rigid structure which rebuffs attempts to influence its nature. To the extent that principals encourage the development of bureaucracies as control institutions, they diminish the probability that instructional personnel will be creative, independent persons who foster creativity and independence on the part of students.

[18] James G. Anderson. "The Authority Structure of the School: System of Social Exchange." *Educational Administration Quarterly* 3: 130-48; Spring 1967.

[19] *Ibid.*, p. 136.

[20] Buford Rhea. "The Large High School in Its Social Context." *The Bulletin of the National Association of Secondary School Principals* 52 (331): 35-45; November 1968.

[21] N. Eisenstadt. "Bureaucracy, Bureaucratization, and Debureaucratization." *Administrative Science Quarterly* 4: 302-20; December 1959.

It seems certain that if principals are to promote the development of bureaucratic organizations which facilitate goal attainment, they will have to devote a significant portion of their time to determining and refining primary and secondary institutional goals.[22] Without any doubt, the ability to determine and refine goals is one measure of leadership capacity. It is interesting to note the results of a recent central office reorganization in the Milwaukee, Wisconsin, Public Schools. In effect, responsibility for the day-to-day operations of the school was assigned to a deputy superintendent, but the superintendent retained primary responsibility for three divisions not engaged in the daily operations of the schools.[23] One of those is the Division of Long-Range Planning, the agency responsible for determining what the schools ought to be doing and where they ought to be going as well as what changes in goals (or emphases) are necessary. The superintendent was very probably well aware of the fact that participation in the purpose-defining role constitutes a major aspect of any leadership role and enables a person to have a significant impact on the total pattern of organizational behavior.

## The Preparation Program

In an article commenting on administrator preparation programs, Cunningham and Nystrand point out that professors have been slow in modifying existing programs which have emerged in recent years.[24] As stated, "Perhaps a major reason that our training programs lack sufficient relevance to the behaviors required of administrators in the field is that the interest and involvement of professors in problems associated with the field have declined."[25] Although the authors point out that administrator preparation programs and internships should be the result of joint university/public school planning, they indicate that little of this has taken place and that

[22] James G. Harlow. "Purpose-Defining: The Central Function of the School Administrator." In: Jack A. Culbertson and Stephen P. Hencley, editors. *Preparing Administrators: New Perspectives.* Columbus, Ohio: The University Council for Educational Administration, 1962. pp. 61-71.

[23] The Milwaukee Public Schools. *'69 Facts ... Figures: Superintendent's Annual Report, 1968.* Milwaukee, Wisconsin: Milwaukee Public Schools, Division of Relationships, 1969. pp. 16-17.

[24] Luvern L. Cunningham and Raphael O. Nystrand. "Toward Greater Relevance in Preparation Programs for Urban Administrators." *Educational Administration Quarterly* 5: 6-23; Winter 1969.

[25] *Ibid.*, p. 11.

efforts to define the purpose and nature of such internship programs have not thus far proven especially productive.

If programmatic relevance is to be sought, it is evident that public school systems and universities will have to develop continuing cooperative relationships that are based on mutual trust in one another, and this may prove to be extremely difficult. There is little doubt that schools and universities can jointly plan and administer programs; there is considerable doubt regarding whether or not they do have mutual trust in one another. Fortunately or unfortunately, depending on one's point of view, the state of mutual trust referred to here implies a minimal loss of autonomy for both agencies; each will find it necessary to modify its demands and to curtail its insatiable appetite for increased influence and empire-building in order to accept the "give" as well as the "take" of such a relationship.

The cooperative enterprise also implies an organizational willingness to invest the time and energies of personnel as well as some monetary resources to ensure the necessary coordination of efforts. Logically, the cost of such services should be shared by the participating institutions. This investment of resources should be directed toward a structural addition to both administrative hierarchies, one which acts as a bridge between the university and the school system and which is staffed with members of both.

It is also apparent that interorganizational cooperation of the type suggested here requires that both agencies reconcile their differences with respect to organizational purposes. Few would question the fact that the fundamental reasons for the existence of universities in our society differ from those which underlie the existence and maintenance of public school systems. However, if the two groups are to work together with some degree of harmony, both will have to accept the fact that the two organizations ought to complement, rather than contradict, each other and that both have much to gain from, as well as to give to, a state of interdependency.

As noted previously, our society places a great deal of emphasis on the formal credentials possessed by individuals. Within our public schools the master's degree is considered a virtual necessity for those who hope to advance themselves financially or in terms of position. Both salary schedules and certification beyond that of classroom teacher commonly depend upon advanced academic preparation as represented by additional degrees or certificates. In fact, the relative importance of the educational hierarchy in our society is largely based on its power to confer or withhold those formal credentials which facilitate the attainment of employment and permit access to additional education. In this manner the public schools and colleges unintentionally (or perhaps intentionally) act as screening agencies which reduce the number of persons available for particular positions and, thus, simplify the personnel selection and promotion processes of the nation's employers.

Simultaneously, a curious phenomenon occurs: the prestige value of a particular degree or certificate diminishes in direct relation to the number of persons holding that degree or certificate. Hence, administrators from the principalship to the superintendency are increasingly required to possess either the Educational Specialist Certificate or the doctorate. This trend will continue and we can anticipate that those desirous of securing certification for the principalship in the future will be required to possess, at a minimum, the Educational Specialist Certificate (usually granted upon successful completion of one full year of advanced study beyond the master's degree).[26]

Requirement of two years of graduate academic training in administration will serve a number of purposes, one of which is to enable prospective candidates to attain a solid foundation in one or more of the social sciences. Schools of education around the country will increasingly seek candidates for their Educational Specialist Certificate programs who have received their master's degrees in fields other than education entirely (for example, sociology, psychology, economics, anthropology, political science, urban development, linguistics, communications, and social welfare). A second requirement will be that the year of study leading to the Educational Specialist Certificate be a full-time endeavor and that it include a carefully planned, supervised, and evaluated internship.

The preparation program itself will involve the following elements:

1. Formal classwork
2. Interdisciplinary seminars
3. Internship
4. Independent study and research.

[26] Glaydon D. Robbins. *Preparation of Elementary School Principals.* Washington, D.C.: Department of Elementary School Principals, 1967. 9 pp. In this pamphlet the author summarized some recommendations of the Department pertinent to administrator preparation programs. One recommendation is that the Educational Specialist Certificate should be the minimum academic level required for principals.

The formal coursework should focus on the technical aspects of educational matters with which principals ought to be concerned. Introductory courses in school law, plant, finance, curriculum, statistics, supervision, and personnel would fall into this area. In this manner future principals can be exposed to the technical areas in which they will later be expected to exhibit competence. Hopefully, these courses would exemplify the best teaching currently being carried on in our universities.

The interdisciplinary seminars should focus on the application of concepts and facts acquired in the formal coursework to actual and simulated educational problems facing principals in the schools. Such seminars would focus on the analysis of complex problems related to effecting change within bureaucratic structures. Instructional inputs from teams of social scientists representing the various disciplines would be continuous in these seminars and would enable prospective principals to examine the complex nature of most educational problems. This would provide them with problem-solving and strategy-building techniques which would enable them to cope with such problems once in administrative assignments. At least one of these ongoing seminars should be restricted to consideration of the internship and the relating of theory to practice as represented by the problems faced daily. Large segments of these seminars would be devoted to the determination of long-range institutional goals and appropriate strategies for accomplishing them.

A major contributor to the ineffectiveness of contemporary principals is their inability to conceive of and implement long-range goals which would give direction to their role behaviors. Instead, all too commonly we find principals reacting to changing times and conditions rather than initiating action which would influence the nature of future conditions. Thus, the professional behaviors of most principals tend to be random and reactionary rather than purposive. The acquisition of skills which would facilitate the establishment of long-range goals and their refinement over a period of time would constitute a major contribution toward the improvement of professional competence on the part of principals.[27] An interdisciplinary approach [28] would also enhance the ability of principals to serve a

---

[27] Harlow, *op. cit.*

[28] Norman J. Boyan. "Common and Specialized Learnings for Administrators and Supervisors: Some Problems and Issues." In: Donald J. Leu and Herbert C. Rudman, editors. *Preparation Programs for School Administrators.* East Lansing, Michigan: Office of Research and Publications, College of Education, Michigan State University, 1963. pp. 1-23.

mediating function between the organization and the community, a function that will be of increasing importance as the incidence of school-community conflict continues to escalate.

Administrative personnel from the public schools should be assigned instructional responsibilities within the university program if relevance is to be assured and if the academic classroom is to maintain a continuous link with the realities of day-to-day school operation.[29] Simultaneously, university staff members should be assigned to positions in the public schools and given long-range administrative responsibilities within the school system.[30] Assuming that only a small portion of university staff members were given such assignments, they would be in a unique position to assist in the in-service education of their colleagues.

An internship should be *required* for certification for the principalship.[31] This should represent the equivalent of a half-time assignment spread over the year of advanced study and funded by the school district *in return for services rendered.* The experiences suggested for inclusion in the internship might involve work in such areas as instruction, personnel, finance and business, plant, community relations, auxiliary services, and social issues.[32] Another listing includes research and evaluation.[33] Both lists break each of the areas into its component elements to provide a comprehensive set of experiences for the interns.

The internship should include two types of experiences for the interns. The first type is referred to by Cunningham and Nystrand [34] as targeted field experiences "which provide students with brief, but intense, exposure to important realities of administrative life." In

[29] Cunningham and Nystrand, *op. cit.*, pp. 18-19.

[30] The Detroit, Michigan, Public Schools have maintained such a relationship in which a Professor of Educational Psychology also serves as Assistant Superintendent for the Division of Child Accounting and Adjustment.

[31] Conrad Briner. "The Role of Internships in the Total Preparation Program for Educational Administration: A Frontier Perspective." In: Stephen P. Hencley, editor. *The Internship in Administrative Preparation.* Columbus, Ohio: University Council for Educational Administration, 1963. pp. 16-18.

[32] Cooperative Program in Educational Administration. *Selected Activities of Interns in Educational Administration* (CPEA-MAR). New York: Bureau of Publications, Teachers College, Columbia University, 1953. 9 pp.

[33] Clarence A. Newell. "Leadership Training Program." Washington, D.C.: American Association of School Administrators, December 1965. 11 pp. (Mimeographed.)

[34] Cunningham and Nystrand, *op. cit.*, pp. 19-20.

such situations an intern might spend one-, two-, or three-week periods with a superintendent, a teachers organization, a principal, an urban renewal agency, a juvenile police department, a mayor's office, or any one of the broad range of available observation posts that could serve as valuable experiences for an intern. A second type of internship which ought to be included is the long-range administrative assignment to a particular school, with accompanying authority to act in that role.[35]

Both types of internship should be evaluated jointly by a member of the university Department of Educational Administration, a representative of the social science area in which the student claims some degree of expertise, and the school system. This will ensure that interns make every effort to apply the concepts presented in their academic training to the solution of daily in-school problems. It is also important for the internship to include extensive opportunities for contact with the many and varied facets of the community. Since involvement with the community will constitute a major aspect of his professional role, the prospective principal should be exposed to the groups which comprise a community and become aware of the influence that community members will have on the schools as well as the impact of the schools on the community.

During the course of this academic training, every intern should select for independent study a problem of interest to him and related to, or directly concerning, administration.[36] This study should be reported in written form by the intern and examined at some point by the same persons responsible for evaluating his internship experiences. Preferably, this problem would be closely associated with his continuing internship assignment and would, therefore, provide another opportunity for the blending of theory and practice.

Responsibility for the evaluation of the total preparation program should be a joint activity of the schools and the university, and should include three components: (a) ongoing evaluation of the program in operation to determine immediate modifications; (b) evaluation of the program in retrospect upon completion of each class of interns; and (c) long-term follow-up studies with a view toward refinement of the intern selection process and determination

---

[35] Both types of internship referred to here are utilized by the Mott Inter-University Clinical Preparation Program for Educational Leadership, Flint, Michigan, as one aspect of the program in which the participants are involved.

[36] Studies of this nature are in some cases an integral part of the Educational Specialist Certificate program.

of the conditions which best foster success on the part of interns after completion of the program.

One evaluation conducted solely by university staff members dealt with the following areas: the effect of internship on the interns; the effect of the internship on the field agency and its personnel; the effect of the internship on the university; and the administrative practices of field agencies relative to internships.[37] Other areas of concern should include a study of the effectiveness of interns while in internship and an extension of that research to determine whether the degree of effectiveness while in internship is predictive of the quality of administrative behavior manifested at various points in a principal's career. The development and refinement of processes and instruments through which the quality of administrative behavior can be measured should also be a primary goal of the evaluation process.

Existing procedures for certifying administrative personnel should, in the future, undergo considerable modification. At present, the entry level administrative certificate is usually issued by a state department of public instruction upon the recommendation of a university after the applicant has completed a specific number of academic credits and two or three years of teaching. Hopefully, this process will soon be discarded. Entry into the principalship should be dependent upon the successful completion of a full-time, graduate academic program which includes an internship of the type described earlier. Certificates should not be issued until an individual has successfully completed two years of administrative service on what might appropriately be called an interim permit.

The two years of administrative duty would be undertaken after completion of the previously mentioned graduate preparation program. These two years of service should be evaluated by a representative from the university, another from the social science area in which the intern possesses special training, and a third from the school system. There is available at least one framework which would enable these persons to evaluate effectively such a two-year "residency" while taking into account the individual nature of the assigned tasks.[38] This two-year interim period would be somewhat analogous to the residency requirement that exists for doctors of

---

[37] Clifford P. Hooker, editor. *An Appraisal of the Internship in Educational Administration.* New York: Bureau of Publications, Teachers College, Columbia University, 1958. 58 pp.

[38] Arch Patton. "How To Appraise Executive Performance." *Harvard Business Review* 38: 63-70; January/February 1960.

medicine, but would be served at full salary. Thus, the residency becomes an extension of the training program.

Another major change should also be effected in the certification process. When the team which evaluates the residency of a given intern completes its investigation, its recommendation, accompanied by supporting data, should then be forwarded to the appropriate committee of the National Association of Elementary School Principals (NAESP) or the National Association of Secondary School Principals (NASSP) for evaluation and, quite possibly, for an interview. Common sense would dictate that this task be undertaken at the state level by committees responsible to the national agencies. After extensive examination of a person's credentials by this committee, a recommendation would then be forwarded to the appropriate office of the state department of public instruction which would issue the certificate.

As is obvious, this recommended procedure is somewhat similar to those utilized by the legal and medical professions. It would place the major responsibility for certification in the hands of the profession *where it belongs*. This procedure would effectively put an end to the wholesale certification of unqualified persons upon recommendation by school districts, and would also ensure that the bases on which certification is issued would be more rational, defensible, and consistently applied.

The same two organizations referred to in the preceding paragraph (NAESP and NASSP) should also organize committees at the state or regional level which would be assigned the responsibility for evaluating existing university programs for preparing administrators and for approving or disapproving of them. Although these committees would most likely lack the power to control the nature and quality of university programs directly, this authority would exist indirectly since members of those organizations working in the schools could refuse to accept administrative interns from disapproved graduate programs.

Causes for disapproval could include such items as unqualified instructional staff, inadequate facilities, the continuation of preparation programs for part-time students, inadequate internship opportunities, and unethical practices. In addition, the increasingly influential role which these two organizations would play in the certification process would enable them to refuse certification of those individuals not graduating from approved preparation programs. This, in effect, would bring about a situation in which qualified prospective administrative candidates would not apply for admission to disapproved programs and the universities involved would then find it necessary to "shape up."

The implications of a preparation program of this nature for the universities involved fall into two general categories. The first category includes all elements relative to the fact that a significantly larger investment of resources, both monetary and human, would have to be made for each intern enrolled. Ratios of staff to students would be diminished greatly and, in fact, would no longer serve as an effective measure of the utilization of professional talent. Increased concern with internship, program development, and evaluation of administrative behavior would all necessitate a greater investment of instructional resources, an investment that would be justified on the basis of effectiveness rather than efficiency. A second category relates to the fact that fewer students would be admitted to preparation programs for the principalship. At the present time any student who qualifies academically can enter and complete such a program and, thereby, receive an administrative certificate—and most do exactly that.

As a result there is a large number of certificated potential administrators "on the loose" who will in all probability never receive an administrative position. In effect, such persons represent a waste of university resources since they may never utilize their training.

In the future, there are three factors which should contribute to a reduction in the number of persons prepared for the principalship. One is the increased educational training that will be required; the second would be the requirement that the additional academic training be undertaken on a full-time basis; the third relates to the fact that as universities and school systems jointly select prospective administrators for such preparation programs they would choose only enough persons to fill anticipated administrative vacancies. Given the nature of the proposed internship and residency requirements, and their intimate relationship to the certification process, it would be necessary for the schools and the universities to participate jointly in the selection of prospective administrators for preparation programs.[39] Certainly, the public schools cannot be expected to accept interns about whom they express reservations and, similarly, universities should not find it necessary to consider applicants who are not intellectually able. Therefore, it can be anticipated that the requirements for admission to administrator preparation

[39] Cunningham and Nystrand, *op. cit.*, pp. 14-15.

programs will increase in number and sophistication, and the admissions process will become more complex.

A great many in-service preparation programs for principals should be carried out through an Academy for Educational Development which would be organized and maintained by one or more of the major educational organizations equipped to mount such a program. Albright has proposed the creation of an Administrative Staff College for Education and suggested that the University Council for Educational Administration accept responsibility for its maintenance.[40] He has also gone into considerable detail in developing the framework for the nature and role of such an entity. In many ways the College would play a role analogous to that of the military staff development colleges and those that currently exist throughout the world in the areas of hospital administration, business administration, and public administration. Since the writing of Albright's article, a National Academy for School Executives has been established by the American Association of School Administrators, one which will fill a similar function for top-level central office administrators.[41]

What is proposed here is that the National Association of Elementary School Principals and the National Association of Secondary School Principals jointly sponsor a similar organization to provide advanced training of a relevant nature to building principals. Depending on the nature of the problems to be dealt with, these in-service programs could be held at the national, state, or local levels. Whenever necessary or desirable, selected universities and public school personnel could also be involved. Specialized and sharply focused in-service programs, varying in length from one week to one academic year, could be presented as part of the total in-service program. The program would have a small permanent administrative staff and should engage instructional staff members as needed from the public schools and universities who possess specific skills and/or knowledge that would be of use to building principals.

Participation in such "clinics" over a period of time should be *required* for maintenance of administrative certification. Possibly,

[40] A. D. Albright. "An Administrative Staff College for Education." In: Jack A. Culbertson and Stephen P. Hencley, editors. *Preparing Administrators: New Perspectives.* Columbus, Ohio: The University Council for Educational Administration, 1962. pp. 133-50.

[41] Stephen J. Knezevich and Michael J. Murphy. "The Emerging AASA National Academy." *Phi Delta Kappan* 50: 224-27; December 1968.

certificates attesting to attendance or levels of achievement attained could be presented to successful participants.[42] Certificates of achievement would indicate that given individuals had realized increased levels of professionalization and skill development as a result of their involvement in the in-service preparation programs. At least one state medical association now requires the participation of medical doctors in in-service training programs, with failure to comply resulting in the revocation of the license to practice.

At this point it is again imperative to examine the future role of the principal in terms of the type of training required for success with a specified set of responsibilities. We might at this point ask the question that has been both asked and answered so many times before: Should the principal be a "perceptive generalist" or a "specialist"? The answer must be *both!* If the principal of the future is truly to act in the capacity of an educational leader—one who initiates constructive and orderly change and who ensures that the institution has adequate direction—then the ability to perceive the relationships between the various segments of society and integrate them into a meaningful whole will constitute a necessary skill. Certainly, this integrative skill represents the *sine qua non* of the "perceptive generalist"! However, his role as a social scientist who acts to ensure that the organization is in balance with the society in which it is situated will also require a measure of specialization.

Training programs for principals must reflect the nature of the tasks for which they are increasingly being asked to assume administrative and leadership responsibility. As our society continues the trend toward inter-institutional dependency and concomitant complexity, we can anticipate that the schools will also be in the midst of the maelstrom and that they will continue to become more, rather than less, bureaucratic. As stated by Walton, ". . . if we are to enjoy the advantages of a highly organized society, we must be prepared to deal with the undesirable concomitant effects."[43] Despite the tendency toward further bureaucratization, the challenge will be to ensure that the schools provide students with the

---

[42] Certificates of attendance will be earned by participants at the AASA National Academy. See: *Ibid.*, pp. 226-27.

[43] John Walton. "The Education of Educational Administrators." In: Jack A. Culbertson and Stephen P. Hencley, editors. *Preparing Administrators: New Perspectives.* Columbus, Ohio: The University Council for Educational Administration, 1962. p. 100.

personal freedoms to which they are legally and morally entitled.

If we are sincere when we state that it is both desirable and necessary for public school principals to play a leadership role in order to ensure both the effectiveness and efficiency of the institution, then the preparatory programs for such personnel must also respond to the challenge. As we are well aware, leadership behaviors are not today characteristic of most principals, and it is highly unfair to expect from them leadership behaviors for which they are not personally equipped or professionally prepared.

The programmatic and institutional changes suggested here are not radical in nature; some have been proposed previously and others which have not appear feasible. There is little doubt, however, that the successful accomplishment of these programs would require a sustained effort on the part of concerned persons if they are to be generalized to the majority of existent programs within the coming decade. Directors of programs designed to prepare administrators for other levels of the educational spectrum might also find that some of the suggestions discussed in this paper could quite appropriately be incorporated into those sequences after some modification to account for the differential nature of the positions and related task areas.

# 8

# *Teaching the Children: Does the System Help or Hinder?*

## LARRY CUBAN

THE "system" provides a little help, much hindrance, and a great deal of hounding. Before pursuing this further, I must set two matters straight. First, I cannot out-write Bel Kaufman so I dare not recreate an Admiral Ass to make my point; nor can I out-analyze Edgar Friedenberg in isolating those elements of the school system that cripple both students and teachers; nor can I, finally, reproduce visually Frederick Wiseman's "High School" which captures the way the system steamrollers students blandly yet viciously. Given these major shortcomings, the best I can dredge up is a series of impressions drawn from the past 13 years, primarily as a teacher but also as an administrator.

Second, some definitions are in order. When I refer to "system," I mean two distinct but interrelated systems. First, there are the connecting parts of the public school apparatus such as teachers, administrators, supervisors, and school board members that interact upon one another. Often criticized as lethargic, incapable of reform because of a mandarin style and Byzantine ways, this is the Operating System that, according to critics, destroys children.

Every member of the organization is concerned with keeping his superior happy, and he develops . . . an elaborate con game. Nobody is interested in real problems of the "outside" world. Rather, students are interested in figuring out what the teachers want and trying to give it to them, the teachers do the same with the principals, principals with the superintendents, and the superintendents with the school boards. . . .[1]

---

[1] Harvey Pressman. "New Schools for the Poor." Washington, D.C.: Citizens Crusade Against Poverty, January 1966. p. 15. (Mimeographed.)

Second, there is the apparatus of 18 years of school running from kindergarten through graduate school which, for lack of a clever phrase, I call the Training System. From this system, students absorb certain ideas, feelings, and practices which subsequently bubble to the surface and are incorporated into the Operating System. The linkage between these two systems is complex. One reinforces the other, and the worst in both is perpetuated. The cliché about teaching as one was taught perhaps best captures the connection between the systems.

Both systems are hierarchical and concentrate heavily upon obedience to authority and dependency. This fact suggests that Jerry Farber's likening students to slaves in his celebrated essay, "The Student as Nigger," may well apply to teachers as possible niggers in the Operating System. Farber saw clearly the intersection of the two systems when he described his teaching at a West Coast university:

As hard as I may try to turn students on to poetry, I know that the desks, the tests, the IBM cards, their own attitudes, and my own residue of UCLA methods are turning them off. . . . Students don't get emancipated when they graduate. As a matter of fact, we don't let them graduate until they have demonstrated their willingness—over 18 years—to remain slaves. And for important jobs like teaching, we make them go through more years, just to make sure. What I'm getting at is that we're all more or less niggers and slaves, teachers and students alike. . . .[2]

Suggesting this metaphor and drawing a rough distinction between Operating and Training Systems may or may not be useful in understanding how deeply the complex act of teaching is shaped by these two systems. Postpone, if you can, judgment on the validity of the two systems and the consequences of their interaction.

Perhaps a few specifics at this point are necessary to flesh out these abstractions. Let us turn to a teacher I know. This description of him and one day at his school is not a straw man to be pulled apart. If he is typical of any group, it is that group that tries to do a good job in the classroom yet does not fully understand how these two systems shape much of what they do.

## Consider David Brown

Consider David Brown (not his real name), a seven-year veteran teacher in a Midwestern inner city school. A graduate of the

[2] Jerry Farber. "The Student as Nigger." Washington, D.C.: Students for a Democratic Society. No date, no page number.

city's teacher education institution, Brown worked his way through college and he is proud of it. On a recent questionnaire, he replied that he enjoyed teaching and although he was uneasy about the low caliber of new students, he was satisfied with the working conditions and liked the children in the school.

Arriving at 8:30, he signed the time sheet, picked up the keys to his homeroom and the notices in his mailbox. In his room (this year, Brown has it the whole day; last year he shared it with one other teacher, and the year before, he "floated" from room to room to teach his five classes), he began reading the daily bulletin.

### BULLETIN No. 27
October 13, 1969

**Thought for the Day:**
Difficulties strengthen the mind as labor does the body. (Seneca)

*(Whoever Seneca was, Brown thought, he knew about this school.)*

1. Do not admit to class without a note from Mrs. Jones:
Raymond Miller 417
Forest Pettigrew 203
Timothy Calloway 409

*(Pettigrew is in my 4th period class. I wonder what trouble he's in now. His whole family is bad news.)*

2. Time Correction: Senior Class will have rehearsal for the Convocation today at the 2nd period.

*(Well, there goes that class. And I stayed up late last night clipping those pictures for the lesson.)*

3. Candy Sale: Please turn in all your candy money NOW.

4. Varsity football at home. Students with tickets will be excused the 7th period.

*(I figured they'd do that; I didn't prepare for that class anyway.)*

**TEACHERS**

1. All male teachers are expected on duty at football game today. Mr. Smith will be around with the sign-up sheet.

2. Beginning TODAY daily absence sheets will be placed in each teacher's box and may be picked up at any time after 11:10. Students will make **no** deliveries.

*(I guess the kids found another way of cutting class.)*

3. NO teacher is to send a student on an errand outside the school **without express permission** from the office.

4. Faculty meeting next Wednesday. Be prompt. Attendance will be taken.

*(Oh, hell, another afternoon shot. If he reads to us like he did last meeting, I'll walk out. Aw, no I won't; I always say that but never get off my duff.)*

5. Some homeroom teachers have failed to complete the attendance cards, Request for Information Sheets, and triplicate program cards for each student. Students are ABSOLUTELY not to fill out these cards. Do not use ball-point pens to complete forms.

*(That's me, I'll have to take those damn things home this weekend to finish them.)*

6. The following schedule for the submission of records and reports for upcoming report card grades is listed for the information of all teachers:

   Grading period closed on November 9, Thursday.
   Thursday, November 9—All attendance cards are due in Room 109 at 9:45 a.m.
   Monday, November 13—All Form 40's are due in the Business Office at 8:45 a.m.
   Thursday, November 16—Report cards will be distributed to pupils at 2:50 p.m.
   Friday, November 17—Form 39's and Form 40's are due in the office at 9:00 a.m.

*(Oh, God!)*

Brown finished the bulletin as his homeroom began to fill up with youngsters. His 37 youngsters are with him about 20 minutes and then they move into their first-period class. He is supposed to provide guidance for members of the homeroom, but rarely does he have time to lift his head from the records he must complete for the office. While he takes roll (since it is Friday, over eight students are absent), the tardy bell rings. Two latecomers appear. To one who has been chronically late, he assigns an after-school detention. He does not like the idea of a detention hall, but Brown fears that the others in the homeroom might come late if he does not assign detentions.

He calls the homeroom to order, reads the announcements, and asks for comments or questions. Since there are none except for the stout girl in the last row who wants to go to the bathroom (permission granted), Brown asks all students to take out their books and study or do homework until the bell rings. Some do that. Others put their heads down and go to sleep. A few copy homework from one another. And the rest ignore what Brown has said and begin talking until sharp glances and mumblings from Brown end the conversations. Brown runs a tight classroom and is proud of it.

In the remaining minutes of the homeroom period, he writes assignments for his five classes on the blackboard. He has three 11th- and two 12th-grade English classes. Though it seems to the layman that he would only have two different preparations—one for the 11th and the other for the 12th—for the 25 classes he teaches a week, he really has more. Or at least he did at one time. Two of his five classes are college preparatory, two are general academic, and one is in a business curriculum. When he first began teaching, he spent an enormous amount of time preparing detailed lesson plans, reading background materials, and the like. But the caliber of students changed and academic standards seemed to fall and he got married and, well, he does not have five preparations now; he has two. He still feels uneasy about all 11th graders reading *The Scarlet Letter* and all 12th graders analyzing 18th century poetry, but he has learned to live with it.

The first three periods of the day go well enough for a Friday. Two P.A. announcements ("Will June Taylor of homeroom 201 please report to the office immediately," and "There is a blue Mustang blocking the principal's car in the parking lot. Unless it is moved, it will be towed away.") interrupt his first-period class, but this isn't more than a nuisance since the class is answering questions on the character of Hester Prynne. Brown has lifted the questions from an English literature workbook.

He does get irritated, however, in his third-period class of Business English when four students leave for the nurse's office in the middle of a discussion on symbolism in Alexander Pope's poetry. It isn't exactly a discussion, since only five of the thirty students present are answering the questions that Brown has assigned; the others have not done their homework. What irritates Brown is that, of the five who left, three have been active in the discussion. Now he is left with a small three-way conversation in a class of thirty. Again, it seems to Brown that the quality of youngsters in the school is deteriorating.

At lunchtime (the teachers union has secured 40 minutes of uninterrupted time), Brown joins the "gripe" table. Four to six veteran faculty members often spend the period complaining about the latest stupidity of the administration, or about an encounter with a troublesome youth. Consensus is invariably reached that if parents were more interested in their children, then the teacher's job would be much easier. But Brown always feels uneasy when the griping turns to uninterested parents because he has met so few parents (only twelve of the parents of his 150 students had visited him at the last PTA meeting) and because he remembers how difficult it was for his folks to attend school functions. Anyway it is different for these parents because many are on welfare. His parents, while poor, never took handouts.

The next class is a disaster. The homework he assigned two days ago is still undone by a majority of the class. He gives them a sermon about responsibility, the importance of education for "you people," why laziness leads to dropping out, etc., etc., and orders the whole class to open their textbooks and begin doing the homework. Most students comply, including the ones who have already done the assignment, but within 10 minutes a few students have their heads down on desks ("resting my eyes," one student tells Brown) and clusters of buzzing kids materialize. Brown rises from his desk and walks back and forth in front of the class for the remaining 25 minutes, glaring at individuals when they begin talking.

Finally the bell rings and Brown goes to the faculty lounge. It is his planning period and he usually grades papers or catches up on homeroom records, but today he does not feel like it. He needs a smoke. In the men's lounge (the school was built over 50 years ago and the lounges are still segregated) a few of the men teachers are playing bridge, one is snoring on the divan, and a small group is gossiping about the school. He joins the last group. He stays for two periods since his last class is excused early. In the middle of the last period of the day, a P.A. announcement calls him to the principal's office, generating some humorous remarks among the loungers.

Brown knows the call has to do with his application to a federally-sponsored summer institute for teachers of the disadvantaged operated by a local university. The principal shows him the strong recommendation he has written to the director of the institute. The principal has singled out Brown as a stalwart of his staff, responsible in fulfilling professional obligations (he turns in most of his reports on time), high moral character, effective teacher, etc., etc. Even though the principal has seen Brown teach twice in seven years and was in his classes for no more than 20 minutes altogether, the principal knows that Brown controls his classes and rarely sends youngsters to him for disciplinary measures. The principal gives Brown a copy of the recommendation and wishes him luck. Just then the final bell rings and Brown returns to his room to clear his desk. At 3:30 David Brown turns in his candy money and signs out.[3]

David Brown is a nice guy. His principal rates him superior. His colleagues respect him, but his students yawn. And the sad truth is that, as nice as Brown may be, he is ineffective. He does not stimulate interest, involvement, and expression in what is being taught or learned (the two are not the same); he sees control of a class only as a nasty task to perform; he does not listen well or modify methods or materials; he does not communicate.

Does ineffectiveness stem from Brown's genes? (Nowadays we ask this question.) Probably not. My guess is, and it is only a guess, that whatever drabness Brown possesses has developed out of the interaction between the two systems mentioned earlier. An examination of the administrative structure and the incentive system, with their supporting rules and regulations, reveals the effects of the Operating System on the teacher.

In many schools (including Brown's), the principal and his assistants call the shots, from arranging the teaching schedules to setting the agenda for the faculty meeting to disbursing funds from the school kitty. Of course, the more enlightened administrators consult, seek advice, and weigh the pros and cons—they smooth out the rough edges of authoritarian decision making. But when you get right down to it, the principal decides.

## The Silent Language

Now, this observation of authoritarian leadership—rough-edged or gilded—is not new nor meant critically; it is an observation made by many persons who are more eloquent and caustic than I am. With the principal having responsibility for the school, authority is placed in his hands. Fine. Yet authority is double-edged; it cuts both ways. In many Operating Systems, buttressed by rules and

[3] Larry Cuban. *To Make a Difference*. New York: The Free Press, 1970. pp. 25-31.

administrative measures, authority slips into authoritarianism, thereby strangling initiative, and thus dull conformity is the only means by which the teacher can survive. I can only state that the Operating System with its apparatus of do's and don't's oppresses teachers such as David Brown not loudly, beating them over the head with a sledgehammer, but like the drip-drop of a leaky faucet, slowly and silently and relentlessly numbing brains and paralyzing independence.

Consider what excessive bulletins, bell schedules, and regulations communicate to teachers like David Brown. First, they tell him that, at best, he is a technician, a mechanic, one who cannot be trusted with too much responsibility. This silent language of the school quickly and effectively eliminates all that garbage from university courses on professionalism given to prospective teachers. After all, how many professionals do you know who would tolerate the language of David Brown's bulletin—written in the second person, imperative? Bells at odd minutes may suggest factory efficiency, but at the cost of telling teachers with every gong, clang, and buzz that they are incapable of deciding when to begin or end the class.

Second, the silent language of bells, rules, and bulletins communicates clearly and loudly that teachers are dumb children. Teachers cannot read bulletins carefully; that is why there is a public address system to repeat what was written in the bulletin. Teachers cannot follow directions, which is why faculty meetings are held to impress upon them the importance of certain tasks. Teachers are not permitted to collect or spend money without the permission of the principal. Childlike dependency results from excessive strictures and demands.

The bells, bulletins, and administrative rules that David Brown and others are required to follow (many schools still require teachers to sign in or punch in on a time clock) are but the tip of the iceberg that extends deep throughout the school system and freezes teaching behavior.

Consider how the teaching load and daily schedule—both important organizational supports of the Operating System—isolate teachers from one another and curb intellectual growth, keeping teachers docile and childlike. The Operating System conspires against the formation of an intellectual community by teachers. At the elementary level—even with all the talk about team teaching, nongradedness, and individualizing instruction—most teachers still have self-contained classrooms. This means that for about five hours a day the teacher is responsible for at least seven different preparations, over one thousand interactions with 30 kids, and the complex but necessary business of getting materials and children ready for learning. At the secondary level, teachers have, for the most part, five classes with about 150 to 175 students, two to three preparations, an additional assignment, and clerical trivia.

## If the Brain Shrinks

Such teacher loads and scheduling, aside from sapping all vitality, conspire to separate teachers from one another, locking them into their rooms (or lounges, out of desperation) and preventing any meaningful cooperation or exchange from taking place. The low level of intellectual give and take, the simple conceptual framework that teachers use to explain what goes on in class and school (see Philip Jackson's *Life in Classrooms*[4] on this point), stem not from any inherent incapacity to deal with issues but from fatigue and lack of opportunity to play the game of intellect. It is quite easy to come to school at 8:15 and leave at 3:30 five days a week and not have one chance to discuss meaningfully and undefensively an instructional or curricular or student problem. Seldom are there opportunities for teachers to grapple with the tangled issues of identity, child or adolescent development, and behavior as affected and shaped by the school program.

In short, many promising teachers enter the profession and starve to death intellectually. It is as if the brain shrinks to the size of a pea while the rest of the body continues operating as usual. The fact is, as teachers know so well, that they have no time to read, write, or think about theory or techniques. The cliché about the 20-year veteran teaching the same thing 20 times catches the intellectual sterility of the teacher. The onerous teaching load confronting teachers is just another structural support of the Operating System that keeps teachers docile. If this is the case, one can ask legitimately and angrily: how can teachers who are restrained from growing mentally be charged with the responsibility of stretching youngsters' minds? It is rhetorical and loaded yet a valid question; few ask it and fewer still answer.

Let me briefly consider the anxieties and ethical dilemmas that the other half of the System—the Training System—presents the teacher with. The stated objective of marks, of course, is to assign students grades that represent their performance. As many critics

[4] Philip W. Jackson. *Life in Classrooms*. New York: Holt, Rinehart & Winston, Inc., 1968.

have pointed out, however, the real function of grading in the public school is to sort out those students who accept the unstated values of the school, that is, conformity, docility, attentiveness, and scholarliness, from those who reject those values. Thus, behavior, academic performance, and relative progress get hopelessly tangled up and each teacher has to wrestle with himself over each student's marks, knowing that the grades he "gives" are the coinage of success in and out of the school.

A teacher, from the first day of school, is forced to judge children on performance and citizenship with very little data that are reliable or valid, such as homework, test scores, attendance, daily behavior in class, or number of times recited in class. Teachers construct elaborate point systems; complicated scoring systems with varying weights are assigned to diverse activities that students are compelled to perform. Yet all of these designs only end up justifying conclusions that the teacher has already arrived at impressionistically.

Of course, some teachers relish such a responsibility since grading is an important tool for maintaining authority; other teachers rationalize marks on the ground that the "real" world sorts out individuals, therefore the school had better start doing it. Whatever the justification, grades destroy the spirit of inquiry and learning. Marks rather than learning often become the goal of schooling.

Rhetoric about the noble aims of the school aside, kids know what the score is: it's not what you have learned; it's what is on the report card. And the kids' perceptions prepare them for further dependency.

Grades and an exhausting teaching regimen represent only a few of the Training System's organizational devices that help shape teacher and student behavior into dependency, docility, and ineffectiveness. There are, obviously, many teachers who try to escape the crippling effects of the two Systems by leaving the classroom. Those who do come to realize, however, that the same pressures constraining them as teachers operate similarly for nonteaching personnel.

Administrators, supervisors, and curriculum workers soon discover that they are caught on the fishhook of the Operating System. Their roles, like that of the teacher, are so circumscribed that their maneuverability and independence are limited.

While principals appear to have a great deal of autonomy, they are transfixed by a peculiar double vision: one eye focuses upon pleasing supervisors, for advancement in the system goes to those who "play ball with the team" (schools, like prisons, as some have observed, pay off for good behavior); the other eye focuses upon running a tight ship with a minimum of boat rocking from students and teachers since waves cause trouble.

## To Effect Changes

Subject supervisors are also trapped by the Operating System's endemic distrust and regulations. They are powerless to effect changes and therefore are irrelevant to those they are pledged to help. Teachers need fewer students a day and more contact with those they have, fewer classes to teach, no clerical duties, and more time for planning. Supervisors are incapable of resolving these basic problems. Charged with responsibility, yet empty of authority, supervisors can only advise, cajole, and supplicate. Confronted by powerlessness, supervisors turn inward. They conduct workshops, collect information, visit classes, and prepare sample lesson plans. Like loyal house slaves, to continue with the metaphor, administrators, supervisors, and the like are devoted, dependable, and nice to have around. They give class to the operation but they are expendable.

That all personnel are stuck in the organizational flypaper of the Operating System suggests only one dimension of the system's influence upon what happens in the classroom. Consider at another dimension beyond organizational policies the negative incentive apparatus that drives teachers from the classroom.

Every institution, including the schools, has a motivational structure to spur professional improvement and performance. This is not so in the Operating System, or at least the incentive system is not structurally compatible with improving what happens in the classroom. Currently, dollars and status are in the principal's office, in the counselor's cubicle, or in central administration—any place but in the classroom. Teachers who haven't seen one another for a while commonly ask: "Are you *still* teaching?" The fact is you make more money the further you are from the kids. The incentive structure is clear: get the hell out of the classroom. Such negative motivation degrades the act of teaching and signals loudly to all who care to listen that the classroom is the final resting place for the unambitious, the dependent, and the untalented. Dedication, idealism, and contact with youngsters remain prime incentives for new teachers but within a few years wear thin. Security through tenure is attractive, at least it was for the generation that experienced the Depression, but even now this does not mean very much to a highly educated, mobile generation of college graduates.

In short, one does not make a career of classroom teaching in the public schools. Yearly, classrooms are decimated by promotions as ambitious teachers opt for nonteaching, higher salaried positions. Money, of course, is not the only magnet pulling teachers, especially men, out of the classroom; the factory-like environment, the anti-intellectual climate, and the impossible work load push people out. The promise of higher salary measured against the daily grind accounts in part for the high annual turnover of experienced and effective classroom teachers. Such an annual rape of the system's best people may augur well for administration but plays havoc with kids.

With the increasing militancy of teachers unions and associations, one can argue that low salaries, intolerable working conditions, and the like will disappear. I think that this is accurate. But I also think that unions have already discovered that, even with higher salaries (although they are still insufficient), erosion of experienced teaching talent continues. Militancy and élan are not yet a substitute for the incentives (illusory as they may be) that drive effective teachers from the classroom.

## Staff Development

There is, finally, one other element of the Operating System that I will mention, aside from the lack of a positive incentive structure and the existence of counterproductive organization policies and procedures. The Operating System is incapable of training and retraining its professionals.

I mean staff development. While virtually every school system in the country has the facade of an in-service program, the fact remains that most Operating Systems do not yet train adequately those who enter the classroom for the first time deficient in survival skills and functional knowledge. In addition, the Operating System does not invest in retraining existing staff to cope with changes. Without mechanisms for continuing and sustained renewal of professionals, the Operating System, like water in a stopped-up sink, can only stagnate. Most staff development operations are minimally funded and are usually at the top of the superintendent's list in rhetoric and at the bottom in funding priority.

Moreover, in-service training is usually located in the Division of Personnel, safely locked away from ever having intimate contact with operating heads of departments. In-service courses are generally taught by tired supervisors and administrators after school, or are hack courses taught at the local college; seldom does staff development provide the cutting edge of people-change in a school system. Like the carefully circumscribed roles of administrators and teachers, the efforts of staff developers are constrained by policies designed to minimize impact.

Few systems build in released time for professionals to be trained during the work day; few systems attempt coordinated efforts across the board to provide services to teachers on-site. I could go on and on. The point is that a potential lever for shoving the system off dead center is often seen as a window dressing, a frilly program that lends pizazz to public relations handouts, but little more.

Yet this is almost to be expected, given the extraordinary confidence and faith that the public schools have in the training programs of universities. The public schools are one of the handful of institutions that contract out the training of their professionals to other agencies (who kindly give "field experiences"—called student teaching—to those preparing to be professionals in those very institutions). It is extraordinary, since the record of universities in training teachers for the schools is not one to admire. This is the major part of the intersection between the Training System and the Operating System, which reinforce each other shamefully.

If the Operating System encourages dependency, docility, and distrust, universities do not help matters much. Consider how so many preservice college programs inhibit imagination and flexibility when professors, removed from the classroom for some years and lacking recent clinical experience, force-feed potential teachers with "truths" about children, learning, and teaching. In case the force-feeding does not go down smoothly, grades lubricate the journey.

Distrust becomes evident when students hear about the critical importance of students' discovering concepts for themselves— through lectures. Distrust emerges when they hear about how important it is to know your students well so that wise instructional decisions can be made. When they go around to discuss this with the professor, his office hours are between 2:00 and 3:00 on Fridays. These inconsistencies are forms of nonverbal communication and, as in any classroom, tell undergraduates much more about the integrity of the professor and the particular program than pieties or advanced degrees.

Conditioned by the Training System to accept the primary authority of knowledge, the privileges of rank (that is, being The Teacher), and the truth of grades, teachers fit well into the Operating System. The cycle is complete.

The analogy between slaves and teachers was a metaphorical attempt to capture the essence of being a teacher in most public school systems. Like most metaphors, there is slippage around the edges and the fit between the two is clumsy. Yet there is something to it. Anyone who has spent time in large urban schools can see its validity in teachers kowtowing to principals, in the plodding dependency of too many teachers, in the unmanly tone of so many schools, in the rumblings of resistance followed by runaways (called teacher attrition), or by petty obstructionism pursued by angered teachers. I do not want to push the metaphor too far but I feel it has a flash of truth to it that burns itself into the imagination and makes it difficult to push out of one's mind.

I did not want to turn this chapter into a finger-shaking prophecy of doom for public education. Yet the next decade does not seem to promise a way out of the bind that the Operating and Training Systems have gotten all of us into. As long as nothing is done to alter sharply the traditional teaching load of public school teachers to, say, half of what it is now—no amount of rhetoric and gush will convert teachers into decision makers or agents of change. *This* is the reality that must be dealt with if the teacher is ever to crack the constraint of the two systems, for dependency is, in the deepest sense, the chain that binds teachers to the system.

# 9

# *Supervisors and Coordinators: Power in the System*

## Marilyn Gittell

ANALYSTS of city power structures are generally agreed that bureaucratic specialization and professionalization characterize modern urban institutions. Power has shifted from the political parties to bureaucratic elites who control a major share of the decision making in their area of specialization. Professionalism has been reinforced by civil service requirements and procedures producing what is best described as an internalization of the political process.

Insulation of the professional bureaucrat originally was conceived as a defense against the inequity of the patronage system and continues to be defended as essential to independent and objective action without political interference. As a result of these trends toward internalization of politics, however, decision making has become more professionally contained, minimizing public input. The large urban school systems in America reflect these general institutional trends.

### Status of the Professional in Urban School Systems

Throughout the nation, school people are emphatic about the need to assure professional controls. Public officials are excluded from direct involvement with public education issues by charges of political interference. In addition, parents and other community interest groups have been sidelined in educational policy making by constant reminders from professionals of their lack of expertise.

The insulation of public education institutions stems from

bureaucratic centralization which, although in large part a product of size, is reinforced by an ideological rationale of professionalism. The administrative structure of urban school systems has increased in complexity over the years. In all cities the size of the administrative staff or educational bureaucracy has greatly increased. The student population, however, has not expanded in proportion to the significant increase in specialized personnel.

The establishment of a rather strict merit and seniority system has considerably restricted discretion and flexibility in all aspects of school policy making. Personnel recruitment is circumscribed and the constraints are significant. In urban school districts the administrative hierarchy comes from the teaching ranks. Principals and assistant principals are promoted by examination and are required to have teaching experience. Oral and/or written competitive examinations of some form are generally required to satisfy civil service regulations. Movement from school teaching or administration to headquarters staff, normally considered a promotion, is achieved by examination, personal contact and favor, or based on experience and performance.

This procedure generally closes off the system to out-of-city residents and non-education professionals. Even in the more specialized areas, such as budgeting, public relations, and personnel, staff members are selected from the teaching and school administrative ranks. Such procedures result in a system of administrative inbreeding.

The larger the school system, generally, the more complex the headquarters structure. As a rule one will find certain key divisions in the organization of the central staff. Secondary and elementary school administration are usually structured separately. Special curriculum, budgeting, and planning subdivisions are common. Audio and visual aids and school guidance programs are found as separate agencies in almost every headquarters operation. More recently, federal aid project directors and staffs have been established centrally.

Organization charts for most city school systems indicate anywhere from 3 to 60 assistant superintendents in charge of the major divisions, which vary according to the size of the city and the extent of bureaucratic development.

Size, however, may not be the sole determinant of the extent of bureaucratization. In a comparative study of six urban school systems, this author found that several larger cities had not increased their central staffs as much as those with comparatively smaller school populations.[1] Also, systems with constant or declining school populations tended to increase their staffs. This may have something to do with the relative ability of professional groups to promote their own development in different cities, but may also reflect the willingness of city political leadership to support additional educational costs.

Most urban school systems have become highly professionally oriented; the extent of specialization is reflected in the multitude of special divisions in headquarters staff. These specialists are responsible for policy for the system as a whole. Such policy is implemented through headquarters directives to school principals and regional staff. As is true of all highly bureaucratic structures, formal standards and guidelines in written form provide the primary basis of communication between central and field staff. Periodic conferences and meetings allow for additional although limited contact.

In some of the larger cities, regional districts have been created to administratively decentralize the system. The number of districts may range from 3 (Baltimore) to 31 (New York City). District or field superintendents are appointed to supervise regions; the extent of delegation of power to district or regional administrators varies in different cities. In some cities, field administrators operate from headquarters; in others, local field offices and staffs have been established. Mounting concern in recent years with the inability of headquarters staff to respond to local needs has resulted in the delegation of somewhat increased discretion in decision making to field administrators. Generally, however, headquarters personnel retain strong controls over city-wide education policy and there is limited power delegated to field administrators.

## School Board-Supervisory Staff Relationship

A board of education is the chief policy-making body for all urban school districts. The method of selecting the school board influences to some degree its status and power. Almost all fiscally independent districts elect school board members, generally in off-year, nonpartisan elections. They are most often elected at large rather than by wards. A number of fiscally dependent school districts, particularly in the larger cities, have appointed school boards. In the latter cases, the mayor appoints members of the board for a

---

[1] Marilyn Gittell and T. Edward Hollander. *Six Urban School Districts: A Comparative Study of Institutional Response*. New York: Frederick A. Praeger, Inc., 1968.

term overlapping his own. In recent years, the appointment procedure in three large cities (New York City, Chicago, and Philadelphia) has been modified by the provision for a selection panel which recommends to the mayor possible candidates for appointments to the school board. This procedure was intended to reduce political influence in such appointments. (Under the 1970 School Decentralization Legislation the procedure was changed in New York City.)

The maintenance of a board of education, independent of the city government in American cities, is in keeping with the strong tradition of separating the education function from all other city functions, in order to assure its apolitical status. Periodically, recommendations emerge, particularly from academic sources, to abolish the boards and establish education as a division or department of city government under the mayor.[2] These suggestions are short-lived and face strong opposition from several quarters, particularly from the professionals in the system.

The size of the boards of education in American cities may range from 6 to 15 members. For the most part, the members of the board of education are recruited from the middle and upper classes and are recognized community leaders who have established some prior role in educational circles. According to a U.S. Office of Education study, the members of boards of education include largely professionals (doctors and lawyers) and business-management types.[3] Seldom are board members blue-collar workers, teachers, small businessmen, or lower management people. Most boards include some minority group representation. The average age level of members is generally over 50.

Board of education members are unsalaried and assume their positions as a civic responsibility. However, in some instances board membership can be a stepping-stone to higher political offices and will therefore attract more political types. As the chief policy-making organ of the school system, the school board meets regularly

[2] Thomas H. Eliot. "Toward an Understanding of Public School Politics." *American Political Science Review* 52: 1032-51; December 1959; Nelson B. Henry and Jerome G. Kerwin. *School and City Government.* Chicago: University of Chicago Press, 1938; Mayor's Advisory Panel on Decentralization of the New York City Schools. *Reconnection for Learning: A Community School System for New York City.* New York: Frederick A. Praeger, Inc., 1969.

[3] Alpheus L. White. *Local School Boards: Organization and Practices.* Washington, D.C.: Office of Education, U.S. Department of Health, Education, and Welfare, 1962.

to determine guidelines for the administrative staff. The board, which seldom has many staff members directly and wholly responsible to itself, must rely on the superintendent and other school professionals for most of its information and recommendations. Weakness or ineffectuality of the boards of education in American cities is often attributed to this lack of staff and to the limited time available to board members as part-time unsalaried officials.

The relative strength of school boards varies somewhat from city to city and may be related directly to the character of leadership on the board itself. A member of the Chicago School Board has written of the frustrations of school board members in the face of overwhelming problems and the lack of time and resources.[4] Often the school board will be caught up in day-to-day administrative problems and eschew long range policy issues. The great dependence of boards of education on the superintendent of schools makes his appointment one of their key functions. The other areas of major concern are budgetary and financial policies, especially in the fiscally independent districts. Personnel matters are yet another segment of school decision making on which boards must focus considerable attention.

The potential for conflict between the superintendent and top supervisory personnel and the board of education is ever present. The professionals are naturally jealous of their expertise and resent interference by a lay board in areas they perceive as technical. However, these areas may include most aspects of school policy making. The board, on the other hand, can hardly compete with the accumulated knowledge and advantage of the full-time role of the professional staff. Therefore, the usual distinction between policy and implementation is virtually impossible to achieve in practice. Generally the staff can, with its highly effective resources, direct and influence policy more successfully than the school board. The staff's major power appears to be manifest in veto action, preventing decisions from being made or, once made, negating them in implementation.

## The Superintendent and His Staff

Increased size and specialization of labor in the large city school systems have steadily complicated the role of the chief school administrative officer, the superintendent of schools. Up to

[4] Joseph Pois. *The School Board Crisis: A Chicago Case Study.* Chicago: Educational Methods, 1964.

the turn of the century the job of the superintendent in many cities was shared by two officials appointed separately by the board of education—a business manager (who usually had the upper hand) and a school administrator. Their tasks were divided accordingly and the distinction in their roles was the source of divided authority and conflict.[5] Administrative reorganization in most cities has revised that structure, establishing a single chief administrator with all staff directly responsible to him.

The superintendent is generally a person with advanced credentials in education and considerable training and experience in school administration. Increasing staff size has resulted in a sizable headquarters staff operating under the superintendent. The superintendent is hired by the board of education under a contract, generally for a four- to six-year period. In most of the larger cities the superintendent is someone who has risen through the ranks of the city school system. Recently there has been some tendency to go outside the local system to fill the office. However, there is strong, internal pressure to appoint a superintendent familiar with the local structure. Some authors have noted the precariousness of the superintendent's job in large cities, suggesting that his length of tenure is diminishing.[6] The sensitive issues which have developed in recent years as a result of the vast changes in city population and the pressing educational needs in urban areas are no small part of the mounting pressure on the superintendent. Educational failures are often placed at his doorstep, and probably this explains the shorter life-span of the office.

Administrative or supervisory staff can be viewed in two general categories: (a) the headquarters staff; and (b) operational field staff (comprised mainly of school principals and their various assistants). Generally a small core of the headquarters staff holds the decision-making power rather tightly. These senior staff people are bred in the system and are, therefore, responsive to the internal reward structure; this means they are primarily concerned with the maintenance of the system. Few headquarters supervisors in any of the large city school systems are brought in from outside the system. Some few exceptions can be noted where new superintendents (such as Mark Shedd in Philadelphia in recent years)

[5] Joseph Marr Cronin. "The Board of Education in the Great Cities, 1890-1964." Ph.D. dissertation, Stanford University, 1965.

[6] Allan R. Talbott. "Needed: A New Breed of School Superintendent." *Harper's Magazine* 232: 8 and 87; February 1966.

seek reform through a circulation of key personnel. Whether or not tenure in job and rank is legally granted to supervisory personnel seems not to matter in practice. New York City is the only large city to grant such tenure, yet a survey of the large city school systems would indicate that supervisory personnel have a "common law" tenure once they are promoted into that position. Rarely are headquarters staff demoted or transferred to the field after assignment to the central office.

The range of policy control exercised by school supervisory staff is indeed comprehensive, if not complete. The top supervisory staff members exercise considerable influence and power in budgeting and curriculum matters. They are generally the source of promotion decisions whether or not these are made formally or informally. Requirements for promotion and review give incumbent administrators the key role in the process. In all cities written and oral testing are the criteria for promotion to principal and other supervisory staff positions. Studies of the bureaucratic personality in the school system indicate the scope of the problem in relation to reforming the system. In a recent analysis of school principals in New York City, a major conclusion of the study was that the group was committed to the status quo. As a group they agreed that they were doing all that could be done or all that could be expected of them.

The superintendent of schools in large city school systems is increasingly recognized as an important political leader, whether viewed from his role within the system or in the total context of city politics. Within the system he suffers from the conflict of an expanding executive role with rather limited flexibility and constraints on his powers. Those constraints are largely a product of the formal procedures established in the merit system (for example, the appointment and removal of personnel) and the informal powers which the professional staff has gathered to itself over the years. Union contracts and comprehensive regulations further limit his ability to act as the chief education officer. Without the full support of his board and some key city officials, even an imaginative superintendent's task is necessarily reduced to day-to-day administrative procedures.

In several cities (for example, Detroit, Pittsburgh, and Philadelphia) superintendents have been the source of reform because they have been able to develop political support. In each case, however, the superintendents have faced considerable opposition from their professional staffs.

## Centralization of Urban School Systems and the Protection of the Status Quo

Within any school system, the potential participants in the policy-making process are essentially the same. Legal power is usually divided between a board of education and the superintendent. The bureaucracy breaks down into the central administrative bureaucracy, field administrators, top supervisory staff, and middle management. Organizations representing each of these groups are common in the larger school districts, and the activities of each can be significant. Teachers and teacher organizations, parents and parents' organizations are also potential participants. Specialized education interest groups (*ad hoc* and permanent) have been active in many communities, and their role can be vital. In the general community, there are other potential participants—local, state, and federal officials, civic groups, the press, business organizations, and individual entrepreneurs seeking the rewards of the school system. Interrelationships between these potential participants, the relative power of each, and their role in particular decisions differ with the nature of the issues and the political environment of the school system.

Participation in school policy formulation can take three forms: (a) *closed*—only the professionals in the system participate; (b) *limited*—the board of education and/or the mayor and specialized educational interest groups participate; and (c) *wide*—groups not wholly concerned with school policy participate. Most school systems fall into category (a) or (b) as a result of their highly centralized structure. Efforts at decentralization have been noticeably ineffective.

In the study mentioned earlier in this paper, the author reviewed the efforts for administrative decentralization in these cities. The study concluded the following:

1. The district superintendents, almost without exception, are nearly totally powerless. They have not served as an innovative force in their school systems. Their potential for doing so is very sharply limited because they do not have the power necessary to initiate programs on their own.

2. The district superintendents' chief function seems to be to serve as a liaison between the central administration on the one hand and the schools, parents, and other community groups on the other. They tend to act as a buffer protecting the central staff from parental dissatisfaction.

3. Secure tenure is a relevant factor characteristic of district superintendents. Even in Philadelphia, where there is an annual appointment, they are always reappointed. None of the cities, except Detroit, provides for review of the district superintendents.

4. In nearly all the cities, recommendations have been made to increase the power and responsibility of the district superintendents. The delegation of power at this point, however, might be extremely difficult. James W. Fesler has pointed out that if authority is not delegated soon after the creation of an agency, the agency will not be able to attract good men to its field service. This lack of good men in the field makes later decentralization even more difficult because mediocre men are not likely to be trusted enough to have authority delegated to them.[7]

While there have been efforts to make school systems more responsive to client needs, the growing importance of the professional role appears to counterbalance such action.

Supervisory staffs in several cities are organized into professional associations, often by school level and rank. Their primary interest is to protect the members' status and salaries, but there is growing concern with maintaining the system as it is. In many ways these associations serve as participants in policy making through public statements and direct pressure on the board of education and on city and state officials. The Council of Supervisory Associations in New York City, which represents some 4,000 professionals, has been a major voice of opposition to board policies on school pairing, bussing, dropping the IQ examination, and decentralization plans of every kind. These groups are emerging in other cities in the same type of role.

Teacher organizations and unions have proliferated over the past several years and have emerged as a primary influence in school affairs. Union leaders are important participants in school policy making, and the union contract is one of the more important documents of school policy, particularly in the areas of working conditions, salaries, and fringe benefits. Priorities for the allocation of school funds are greatly influenced by the settlement of wage and salary levels for teachers. In several of the larger cities, unions and other teacher organizations have been directly involved in other related areas of school policy, often with the result that such provisions become an integral part of the contract arrangement. Such matters as team teaching, class size, and compensatory educational programs are becoming issues for negotiation.

[7] Marilyn Gittell and T. Edward Hollander, *op. cit.*, p. 76.

The American Federation of Teachers, in fact, has adopted a national policy favoring the More Effective Schools program (a compensatory education program initiated by the United Federation of Teachers in New York City) and is seeking its adoption in several cities. Teacher organizations and unions have worked with school administrators on problems of recruitment and training as well. In some cities the union has shared directly in the campaign for teacher recruitment. In New York City and Detroit the union has argued strongly against any extensive delegation of powers to local decentralized districts. Although historically the teacher organizations and supervisory staff have been in conflict on many issues, in more recent years one can discern an alignment of the professionals in the system. In some cities, supervisory staff organizations and unions have joined forces in opposition to school reform measures. It is likely that joint action will increase over the next decade.

The constantly expanding role and power of the school professionals in the policy process seriously diminished movements toward increased public roles. Yet the lack of responsiveness of the centralized bureaucratic urban school system is under serious attack.

## Reforming the System

The most significant trend today in urban schools, particularly in the larger cities, is the movement toward greater decentralization and increased community participation. This movement was an outgrowth of the U.S. Supreme Court decisions (*Brown* v. *Topeka*) in 1954, which called for school desegregation. Civil rights groups took up the challenge of integration and exposed the great inequities in city schools, focusing on the lack of adequate programs and facilities in the ghetto communities. The general failure of integration efforts as well as compensatory educational programs indicated the inadequacy of the urban school structure and its insulation from community interests and demands. Without revision of the total school structure, it was thought, little could be accomplished with special programs. Consequently, new reformers and, particularly, ghetto groups in several large cities have been pressing for urban school reorganization. Most of these plans call for an increased role for the local community through the election of local school boards and the delegation of personnel, budget, and curriculum powers to these boards.

These reformers argue that those who have controlled the schools have been unable to produce results. They have failed to educate large numbers of students and have excluded the public from its rightful role in the policy process. A participatory role for the community is not conceived as an abandonment of professionalism, but rather an effort to achieve a proper balance between professionalism and public participation in the policy process. Community control implies a redistribution of power within the educational system. The definition of community includes not only parents of schoolchildren but also other segments of the public which, over the years, have been excluded from a role in public education. It is directed toward fulfilling the demands of a democratic system. In relating to the educational failure of urban school system decentralization, community control is intended to create an environment in which more meaningful educational policies can be developed and a wide variety of alternate solutions and techniques can be experimented with. The argument assumes that a school system devoted to community needs, which serves as an agent of community interests, will provide a more conducive environment in which children can learn.

Properly instituted, community control is an instrument of social change. The redistribution of power is in itself an aspect of that change. If adequate provision is made for the technical resources to carry out this new role, community control has the potential for providing new insights into our concept of professionalism as well as our general theories of educational expertise. If community boards have the resources to engage a variety of professionals and nonprofessionals in the policy process, institutional changes can be anticipated. The business community, university faculty, and research centers may become more actively involved in the schools.

The opposition of the school professionals to the demands for increased community control of the schools has been clear and insistent. Teachers and administrators view the movement as a threat to their status in the system. Their historical emphasis on insulation of the system and reliance on professional decision making is in conflict with these new concepts. Their power and prestige, they apparently believe, would be considerably diminished by this movement. It is understandable that they would therefore struggle to maintain the system which protects all their interests.

The general movement toward decentralization/community control appears to be gathering support even in the face of professional opposition. In some states, legislation has been introduced to encourage city action; in Michigan and New York more specific legislation calling for restructuring of city school systems has been approved. These efforts are likely to be expanded in coming years and the largest city school districts will probably become more decentralized in their structure. The extent of community control granted to neighborhood boards may vary, but certainly they will be given a more direct role in educational policy making.

*Conditions for Community Control*

In recognition of their expertise, school professionals will maintain a strong basis of power in any school structure, but two new conditions are likely to occur in community-controlled school districts. First, there will be, at least initially, less reliance on and trust in the professionals by parents and community leaders and, second, it is likely that the more traditional types of school professionals will not monopolize administrative and classroom jobs. There will be a tendency to choose people from outside the system and of minority ethnic backgrounds as well as to encourage greater acceptance of the role of the paraprofessional.

Local school boards elected by the community will be anxious to use and test their powers. They will expect to be involved in matters traditionally considered a part of the administrator's domain. Particularly in the area of personnel selection, the local board is not likely to want to yield any of its newly acquired prerogatives even to its own administrator. There is no question but that the appointment of principals and teachers is something in which the local boards will want a strong hand. The local administrator (superintendent) will certainly feel the traditional need to choose his own staff members and have them be responsible to him; this would include principals and assistant principals.

Achieving a proper balance of power between the local board and its administrator will be fraught with many of the same problems as have been observed between city-wide boards and their administrators, but there will also be significant differences. Because the power of the local boards will be so newly acquired and untested, there will be a far greater interest in using it. The racial issue will be a primary factor in ghetto areas.

There will be more emphasis upon hiring more congenial and supportive staff members. There will be stronger constraints on the professional, though he may himself be a member of that ethnic or racial group.

The failure of urban school systems throughout the country

and the ineffectiveness of those solutions which have been offered will persuade large segments of the urban community of the need for more fundamental reform of school systems. More and more pressure will be brought to bear on school professionals to reevaluate their role in urban schools. The future of city schools may well rest on the kind of response which is forthcoming.

# 10

# Who Gets Counseled and For What?

### John W. M. Rothney

WHEN many persons look at counseling they get very unfavorable impressions. There will be much in the following pages which suggests that such impressions are fully warranted. Before passing generally unfavorable judgments on counseling, however, one should consider the fact that many school counselors carry loads that would be comparable to that of a teacher who had sixty or more students in each of his classes. If one were to appraise the effectiveness of the teaching of English or any other subject under such circumstances it seems likely that there would also be unfavorable impressions. As he reads this chapter the reader should recognize that, despite the impressions he may get about the general ineffectiveness and uncertainties of the counseling movement, there are many individuals within it who can demonstrate that they contribute a great deal to the accomplishment of the objectives of education.

Counselees often ask counselors to give them answers to questions about the desirability of actions they propose to take. If the counselor is a good one, he will often preface his answer with the statement, "It depends on . . ."; then he names some circumstances which might influence a choice, and offers some possible outcomes for consideration. Similarly, when one tries to answer the questions given in the title of this chapter, the "It depends . . ." response must be utilized.

The "depends" circumstances are many and varied. They encompass, among others, such matters as the personal characteristics of the counselee and the counselor. They include the locale in which the counselor works, the preparation he has had for his profession, and the state of affairs on local, regional, and national scenes. And all of the above can be subdivided in so many ways that the permutations and combinations seem endless. The subdivisions in turn are so complicated by the individual idiosyncracies of counselors and counselees that the complexities become astronomical. In view of such complexity, no general answer to the question of "Who Gets Counseled and For What?" can be given unless one can be satisfied with a statistical tabulation. Some statistics follow which may conceal more than they disclose.

Counselors in secondary schools currently have average loads of 400 or 500 counselees, while the counselor-pupil ratios in elementary schools are approximately one to 700. A quarter of our secondary schools have no counselors, and approximately one-third of our elementary schools employ only one counselor for every 1,000 pupils. Statistics about counselor-student ratios in higher education are so confounded by the employment of many part-time counselors that any figures can be misleading. Yet all the figures, crude as they are, suggest that counseling is not offered to every student, and that some selective factors must operate in the determination of who gets counseled.

## Selection of Counselees: Historical Perspective

Selective factors have operated in the guidance movement from its inception. Frank Parsons,[1] who is generally credited with starting guidance in 1908, was concerned with youths who were about to seek employment, offered nothing for young children, and gave college-going youth only some general exhortation about behavior and good citizenship. All of these, he hoped, would result in the development of a socialist state. Anna Reid and Jesse Davis, who followed Parsons in the early part of the century, were concerned with the guidance of adolescents. Reid wanted to be sure that they secured employment which would enhance the profits of businessmen, and Davis wished to develop in them what he called good moral character.

John M. Brewer, the first man to hold a prestigious position as a professor of guidance at Harvard (and this writer's first instructor in this field), advocated guidance as a means of making education more realistic for adolescents.[2] When the first group to promote guidance was organized in 1913, the members called it the National Vocational Guidance Association and implied by use of that title that counseling would be concerned primarily with persons who

[1] Frank Parsons. *Choosing a Vocation.* Boston: Houghton Mifflin Company, 1909.

[2] J. M. Brewer. *Education as Guidance.* New York: The Macmillan Company, 1932.

needed vocational counseling. In the depression years of the thirties, determined efforts were made to help youths to find the kind of employment for which they seemed best fitted. The aptitude testing movement which began a few years earlier was designed primarily to offer assistance in that endeavor.

The advent of the progressive education movement in the thirties and early forties brought greater concern for the whole person.[3] Concern about early growth and development of individuals resulted in a limited amount of guidance for the preadolescent, although counseling had always been, and still is, primarily for youth. However, the efforts of the Veterans' Administration after World War II provided counseling for young adults, while the development of counseling centers in colleges and universities expanded the age range. Yet the emphasis in guidance changed again when the provisions of the National Defense Education Act, as originally conceived in 1957, were limited to secondary school youth.

Until very recently, then, the persons who got counseled were adolescents and young adults, and they were counseled primarily for vocational choice and placement. One did not get counseled unless one had reached the secondary school or beyond; and even when those stages had been reached, one had to be preparing for or seeking employment, talented (by NDEA prescription), or (because some interest in counseling had developed in mental hygiene clinics and correctional institutions) in serious trouble.

Although there has always been some interest in the counseling of elementary school children, professional personnel did little about it until the current decade. C. G. Wrenn [4] provided a great stimulus to elementary school guidance in 1964 by suggesting that counselors could do on a grand scale what had previously been done by school psychologists, family welfare workers, remedial specialists, curriculum consultants,[5] teacher educators, and good classroom teachers. (The wide acceptance of this suggestion illustrates how guidance

---

[3] L. A. Cremin. "The Progressive Movement in American Education: A Perspective." *Harvard Educational Review* 4: 251-70; 1957.

[4] C. G. Wrenn. *The Counselor in a Changing World.* Washington, D.C.: American Personnel and Guidance Association, 1962.

[5] It is often amusing to note the naïveté of many workers in elementary school counseling. They propose, for example, to add courses and units in occupational information to the curriculum. In doing so they seem to ignore the inability of small children to grasp the complex concepts involved, and fail to realize that good teachers have always done some work in this area at a level that children can understand.

workers are quick to use the filling station approach—if they think that something needs repair, they rush in to repair it whether or not they are qualified or have the equipment to do it.) A recent amendment to NDEA, which permits and supports counseling and guidance in the elementary grades, has stimulated a movement to place counselors in all schools. Although substantial evidence of their accomplishments is lacking, there is considerable current pressure to employ them, and to pay them well for a relatively unproven service. Some of the pressure has been effective and, for the first time in the history of the guidance movement, elementary school children in substantial numbers can be counted among those who get counseled.[6]

It seems clear from the preceding statements that the answer to the question of who gets counseled in educational institutions has changed over the years. The guidance movement has developed from initial concern with job-seeking adolescents to the current concern with elementary school children and young adults in post-high school educational programs. It is often proposed that there should be counseling for all children but, in practice, the problem student steals the show. Regardless of the professed interest of counselors in all students, a student is more likely to get counseling if he is among the lame, the halt, the blind, the disadvantaged, the maladjusted, the failures.[7] One sure way to get the attention of the counselor is to be very unusual in some way. Thus, the counselor tends to become more a salvage and repair man than a worker whose primary concern is for development of all the children.

## What Counselors Do

Despite the faulty mechanism for the selection of prospective counselors, there can be no doubt about the need for adolescents to discuss their career choices when they begin to feel grown up, see the end of formal schooling approach, and seek to become less dependent on their families. Recognition that some one-fifth to one quarter of a person's waking hours are spent in employment, and that a considerable proportion of this time will continue to be so spent even with the anticipated decrease in length of the work week, convinces some counselors that providing assistance in choice of

[6] V. Faust. *History of Elementary School Counseling.* Boston: Houghton Mifflin Company, 1968.

[7] V. F. Calia. "The Culturally Deprived Client: A Reformulation of the Counselor's Role." *Journal of Counseling Psychology* 13: 100-105; 1966.

careers is an important part of their work.[8] It is interesting to note that the new emphasis on the use of the computer in guidance has been directed primarily toward helping students in the processes of career consideration and choice. The ancient process of fitting the square peg to the square hole is now being attempted electronically.[9]

Since there is an ever-increasing tendency to require educational guidance, counselors find that they must be concerned with this function. The process is usually one of considering with a student the choice of electives within the school, or selecting an institution for post-high school training. Since we do not commonly give elementary school children the privilege of selection among school experiences, educational guidance is limited largely to secondary and post-secondary school youth. This does not, however, prevent elementary school counselors from professing that educational guidance is part of their job. When pressed for a definition of educational guidance, they usually describe it as remedial work in subject fields.

Although there is little evidence that either career or educational counseling is effective,[10] there seems to be rather general acceptance of the belief that these tasks are within a school counselor's legitimate domain if he also works cooperatively with parents and school personnel. When, however, he gets into the realm of what is often called personal counseling, the legitimacy of his activities is likely to be seriously questioned. If he claims that he is working in the area of personal-social adjustment, which involves such matters as value, emotional balance, or correction of unacceptable social behavior, his troubles begin. Doubts about his proficiency in working in such areas are often raised and considerable skepticism about his effectiveness is often expressed.[11]

At no time in the history of the guidance movement has the

[8] American Personnel and Guidance Association. "The Counselor: Professional Preparation and Role." *The Personnel and Guidance Journal* 42: 536-41; 1964.

[9] D. V. Tiedemann. *Information Systems for Vocational Decisions.* Project Report No. 12. Cambridge, Massachusetts: Harvard Graduate School of Education, 1965.

[10] See the *Review of Educational Research* reports on Guidance and Counseling which have appeared in 1969, 1966, 1963, and 1960. Good reviews of evaluation of counseling are presented in: L. E. Tyler. *The Work of the Counselor.* New York: Appleton-Century-Crofts, 1969.

[11] G. P. Moore. "A Negative View Toward Therapeutic Counseling in the Public Schools." *Counselor Education and Supervision* 1: 60-68; 1961.

matter of personal development been neglected, but emphasis upon it has increased significantly during the past two decades. Even the pioneers of the guidance movement saw the importance of acceptable personal behavior in their concern over career choices, although they tended to be highly moralistic and judgmental about the behavior of their subjects. They recognized, even more than many current workers, that the areas of careers, education, and personal behavior were so interrelated that work in one of the areas involved concern for the others.

Contrarily, there has been a strong tendency for many current counselors and counselor educators to consider vocational and educational counseling to be too mundane for their attention. Influenced by the pseudopsychologists and would-be psychiatrists who have infiltrated the guidance movement, they tend to seek out for counseling only those students whose behavior is highly unusual or bizarre. Borrowing from clinical psychologists, whose concern was for persons referred for treatment of abnormal behavior, counselors began to use their concepts, their jargon, and their techniques.[12] They tended to overlook the fact that what might have been effective treatment for neurotic little old ladies of another generation might not be suitable in helping young people in the process of coming of age in America.

Although there seems to be fairly general consensus that almost all youths can profit from considering their educational and vocational choices with a counselor, the pressure of numbers often results in the neglect of that activity so that salvage and repair work can be done with the student whose behavior is so unusual that he becomes highly visible in a school situation. The answer, then, to what one gets counseled for, depends too often on the counselor-student ratio. This ratio can be an overriding factor in any counselor's use of his time, but it is not the sole determiner. Some of the other factors are considered below.

## Other Factors Influencing Counselor Behavior

Counselors are not free agents who can decide what they will do regardless of the concerns of those who employ them. As members of a school staff they must serve the community needs (even

---

[12] V. A. Boy and C. J. Pine. *Client-Centered Counseling in the Secondary School.* Boston: Houghton Mifflin Company, 1961.

while trying to change them) as expressed in the objectives of the institution. No counselor is likely to be effective if he is constantly at odds with his contemporaries, colleagues, and co-workers in an educational enterprise designed to meet the needs of society. If he cannot resolve differences with the institution, he should withdraw from his position.

The counselor cannot be expected to be complaisant about conditions which he thinks are unsatisfactory, but he is not likely to be an effective counselor if his aims differ significantly from the aims of the school in which he works. If, for example, the school, in response to community needs, decides that major emphasis will be placed upon the career counseling of the disadvantaged with resultant neglect of the development of the gifted, and the counselor believes that this is an undesirable emphasis, he must express his opinions, work for a change, and, failing to see change, seek another position.

Who gets counseled and for what will depend, then, in part on the goals of the institution of which he is a faculty member. Counselors are not institutions in themselves; they help to meet the goals of the institution.[13]

Bureaucracy can be a nasty term which implies unreasoning behavior on the part of its members. It can also imply a helpful organization of persons united in the service of a worthy cause. Counselors find that both interpretations may influence who gets counseled.

In the forties, the work of the federal government in guidance first became independent of the Vocational Education Division. Federal sources then provided valuable reports of current practices, offered stimulating suggestions, and supported cooperative efforts to enhance counseling in the schools. With the passage of the National Defense Education Act, however, the suggestions became, by allocation of funds, mandates for counselor action.

The counseling aspect of NDEA was definitely a manpower utilization concept (to get more capable students into mathematics,

---

[13] In reporting his long-term follow-up studies of counseled and noncounseled youth, the author has indicated his findings in this manner: "Intensive counseling of youths during their high school years and the close collaboration of counselors with the school staff do assist materially in the accomplishment of some of the objectives of the American secondary school." John W. M. Rothney. *Guidance Practices and Results.* New York: Harper & Brothers, 1958. By reporting in this manner he was emphasizing the helping and cooperative roles and the commonality of ultimate objectives.

science, and the foreign languages); and bureaucratic, arbitrary regulations forced counselors, if their schools were to get funds, to emphasize testing and counseling of the most able.[14] Although large numbers of counselors evaded the situation by claiming that they had to examine all students to find the most able, they were forced into making some superb rationalizations and highly questionable interpretations of the intent of the act. Whether the NDEA had positive or negative consequences (and one does not know, since the planned evaluation was not carried through), it served as a good illustration of how public pressures exerted through a bureaucracy determine who gets counseled and for what.[15]

A further illustration of how public pressures on counselors influence what they do may be seen in the current emphasis on education of the underprivileged. Disturbing evidence of poverty, unemployment, unequal educational opportunities, and differential treatment of members of minority groups became highly visible; and although the source of such difficulties had their major roots in broader economic and social circumstances, much criticism for the shortcomings is aimed at educational institutions. Since counselors were commonly considered to be the persons who help students to make wise educational decisions (including the matter of dropping out of school), the pressure was on counselors to work more with the culturally disadvantaged, underprivileged, and handicapped. Work with the talented, which had received such high priority in the early sixties, has been relegated to a lesser place as distribution of funds and public demands require more attention for the less favored students.[16] The frantic efforts throughout the nation to correct shortcomings in the education of the disadvantaged are reflected in the determination of which students get most coun-

[14] This following statement in Section 101 of the act indicates the purpose of the NDEA: "We must increase our efforts to identify and educate more of the talent of our nation. This requires programs that will give assurance that no student of ability will be denied an opportunity for higher education because of financial need; will correct as rapidly as possible the existing imbalances in our educational program which have led to an insufficient proportion of our population educated in science, mathematics, and modern foreign languages, and trained in technology."

[15] The author was a member of a group brought together to devise procedures for evaluation of the counseling part of NDEA. It was very clear that appraisal should be expressed in terms of numbers of students placed in mathematics, science, and foreign languages.

[16] John W. M. Rothney. "A State-wide Approach to Discovery and Guidance of Superior Students." *School & Society* 89: 271-74; 1961.

selor attention and what these students get counseled about.[17]

National pressures on what counselors do are often supplemented by state regulations. Most states have counselor certification requirements and, although they are not currently as rigid as they were initially, they do influence who will do the counseling in schools. This, in turn, affects the kind of counseling that is done and to whom it is offered. There is an increasing (and this author believes an unfortunate) tendency to certify as counselors persons who have not had teaching experience. This change permits persons to become counselors who have made no serious commitment to education, who do not really know schools, and who are not likely to be accepted by experienced teachers. It encourages the recruitment of persons who want to practice an amateur kind of psychiatry and psychotherapy, but who do not want to undertake the long period of study and internship required to become professionals in those fields. Such persons tend to see counseling as a remedial rather than a developmental process, and they prefer to counsel only those who are troubled. Guidance people, whether or not they are capable of doing so, always seem willing to try to fill up what they think are gaps in the performances of others. Likewise, certain kinds of state regulations can foster or inhibit that process. Current trends suggest that they foster such an approach. If state regulations do not change, it seems likely that a student will get counseling only if something has gone wrong. If he wants to talk with a counselor, he will not get the chance unless he is among the neurotic, the delinquent, or the potential dropouts.

State certification can determine in part the kind of counseling that is done. If there is a requirement that the counselor-in-preparation have some credits in group counseling, it implies that groups of students can be counseled simultaneously;[18] that sensitivity can be developed readily in persons by exposing them briefly to some of the nonsense offered in T-groups; and that confrontation, so frequently avoided in counseling the individual, can bring about quick development of desirable personality characteristics. Many values may accrue from state certification for counselors, including, of course, the exclusion of obviously unfit persons; but the very presence of

---

[17] Current emphasis may be seen in the program of the national convention of the Personnel and Guidance Association for 1969. Nineteen presentations on the culturally disadvantaged, 18 on elementary school guidance, and 3 on the gifted were offered.

[18] J. J. Muro and S. L. Freeman. *Readings in Group Counseling.* Scranton, Pennsylvania: International Textbook Company, 1968.

regulations does influence the choice of who gets counseled. The very fact that there is certification for elementary school counselors suggests that counseling, previously reserved for secondary school youth, will be offered in pre-high school years.

University programs for counselor education are related to state certification since many departments of education work closely with counselor educators in formulating their requirements. It is axiomatic, therefore, that some of the effects described here will be exerted in counselor education. However, the actual program of studies can have influences that go beyond mere course titles. Professors in counselor education departments who have strong beliefs about any or all phases of counselor preparation can, by their research, writing, political manipulation, and arrangement for staff inbreeding, influence graduates of a counselor education program in the selection and nature of their work with counselees.

Thus, one counselor education department may graduate counselors whose chief concern is that all their counselees will be tested and inventoried ad nauseum and ad absurdum, while others send out counselors who are primarily listeners and reflectors and givers of unconditional positive regard to the troubled who seek them out. Still others graduate counselors who are, in the current jargon, behavior counselors, who try to see that all their counselees are "conditioned" as well as any dog, monkey, pigeon, or caged kitten.[19] And some even try to draw from several schools of thought so that their graduates are eclectic in their approach. The result is that the kind of counseling and to whom it is offered vary according to the institution in which the counselor did his graduate study. Such variation may or may not be desirable, but the net effect is that who gets counseled and what he gets counseled for are highly unpredictable [20] in any particular school.

---

[19] G. M. Grossberg. "Behavior Therapy: A Review." *Psychological Bulletin* 62: 73-88; 1964; L. P. Ullman and L. Krasner. *Case Studies in Behavior Modification.* New York: Holt, Rinehart and Winston, Inc., 1965.

[20] A traveler from a foreign but friendly country recently visited many of our colleges and universities. In writing about his impressions he commented specifically on guidance courses. "Guidance," he said, "struck me as a hybrid melange of watered-down child psychology, mental health, tests and measurement, and non-practical clinical psychology. The subject never struck me as having an academic significance and its existence presupposed that the teacher was a fool. The less distinguished the institution the greater was the proliferation of its courses in guidance." Perhaps our critic was too harsh, but we cannot deny that there is much truth in what he said. The implications should be clear to those who would teach guidance.

Counselors are hired, and presumably supervised, by administrators. Their tenure must, in part at least, be determined by the extent to which administrators think that they assist the school to attain its objectives.[21] Their thoughts range from the belief that counselors should do clerical chores, accept disciplinary roles, arrange schedules, and substitute for absent teachers, to the conviction that they should perform as truly professional workers acting as specialists in the areas for which they are prepared. When unsuitable demands are made on them, counselors frequently become submissive, congenial flunkies, and counseling becomes a minor part of their activities. Fewer and fewer students get counseled and, since time is always limited, even the few who are counseled get only cursory attention. Until counselors can define their roles more effectively and provide convincing evidence to administrators about the extent to which they can contribute to the attainment of the school's objectives by doing their real job, it seems likely that the who and what of counseling will continue to be contingent partly on administrative fiat.

The literature of counseling has variously been described as illiterate, repetitive, elaboration of the obvious, confused, and confounding.[22] And the language is said to be a semantic jungle. Yet in-service and preservice counselors are required to study the literature, and it must influence what they do on the job. The availability of books is determined by the extent to which publishers think they will be "commercial." That term is defined as those books which will sell in large numbers. In order to sell quantities of books the authors must not be critical of others' ideas and practices, and they must not move far beyond what is currently popular. Even if a book seems likely to make a contribution to the field, it will not get into print unless a commercial publisher can see the possibility of selling several thousand copies a year. Under these circumstances, counselors are encouraged to study some of the most uninspiring literature of any professional field. If their reading does influence whom they counsel and for what (perhaps a hazardous assumption), commercial textbook publishers exert considerable influence on the work of counselors.

Finally, of course, the characteristics of persons enrolled in

[21] R. L. Wrenn. "Counseling Orientation: Theoretical or Situational." *Journal of Counseling Psychology* 7: 40-45; 1960.

[22] In deference to the proud authors no specific examples will be given here. The reader is invited to read some of the widely-used textbooks or books of readings and decide whether he concurs with such descriptions.

counselor training programs, regardless of how the factors mentioned above will influence their development, must affect the work that is done.[23] It is perhaps symbolic of the state of the guidance field that a profession concerned with choice of careers has found no satisfactory way of selecting candidates for degrees in its own area. Some misguided efforts to select them on the basis of scores on ridiculous interest inventories and so-called personality tests have produced nothing of value. Other attempts to rate applicants on their responses to naïve questions about what they would do if confronted by statements of inadequately described potential counselees have produced only that nothingness which oversimplified procedures can provide. Multiple-guess testing procedures have been inadequate, interviews have shown little predictive efficiency, and grade-point averages, which have been only fairly effective in forecasting course grades, are less than adequate in selecting for training those persons who can work well with people. Where no suitable criteria exist for the selection of persons for training in a profession, a proportion of the graduates will certainly be unfit for the work it demands. Some of their inadequacies will almost certainly be revealed in their selection of counselees and what they do with them.

Space does not permit detailed consideration of the many other factors which may determine who gets counseled and for what. Much could be written about parental pressures, teachers' attitudes, students' concepts of the role of the counselor, the brevity of the school year, and the competition among school personnel for the money available in the school budget. All of these and many other conditions operate in schools so that it is almost impossible to give a general picture of what the offering of a counseling program means and to whom it will be given.

## The Future

Perhaps better answers to the questions contained in the title of this chapter would be possible if counselors stated their objectives in terms that permitted evaluation and did some evaluation in terms of their stated objectives. Professionals who avoid evaluation of their work, as guidance counselors usually do, are likely to be uncertain about their purposes, variable in their activities, and extravagant in their claims of accomplishment.

[23] E. J. Shoben. "The Counselor's Theory as a Personal Trait." *The Personnel and Guidance Journal* 40: 617-21; 1962.

If school counselors would recognize that they are helpers in an educational institution rather than institutions in themselves, would really clarify their roles as specialists in a community of specialists, and would provide some evidence that they can make significant contributions to the attainment of a school's objectives, it seems likely that one could begin to recognize what counselors are trying to do, and with whom. As of now the best answers, or the best guesses, must be prefaced by the statement, "It all depends...."

## References

R. Carle, C. Kehas, and R. Mosher. "Guidance—An Examination." *Harvard Educational Review* 34: 373, 574; 1962.

D. C. Dinkmeyer. *Guidance and Counseling in the Elementary School.* New York: Holt, Rinehart and Winston, Inc., 1968.

C. H. Miller. *Foundations of Guidance.* New York: Harper & Brothers, 1961.

John W. M. Rothney. *Guidance Practices and Results.* New York: Harper & Brothers, 1958.

B. Stefflre. *Theories of Counseling.* New York: McGraw-Hill Book Company, 1965.

D. V. Tiedemann and R. P. O'Hara. *Career Development: Choice and Adjustment.* New York: College Entrance Examination Board, 1963.

L. E. Tyler. *The Work of the Counselor.* New York: Appleton-Century-Crofts, 1969.

W. H. Van Hoose and J. J. Pietrofesa. *Guidance and Counseling in the Twentieth Century.* Boston: Houghton Mifflin Company, 1970.

E. G. Williamson. *Vocational Counseling: Some Historical, Philosophical, and Theoretical Perspectives.* New York: McGraw-Hill Book Company, 1965.

C. G. Wrenn. *The Counselor in a Changing World.* Washington, D.C.: American Personnel and Guidance Association, 1962.

# 11

# Crisis of the Modern University[1]

## Ernest Becker

> ... democracy lives dangerously. For humanity is dangerous, and is not to be controlled by committees of men. But the danger from its freedom—from a program which asks it what it can be rather than tells it what to do—is less than the blind risk that is run when the program is to mislead and miseducate it. ...
>
> Mark Van Doren [2]

NEXT to the death of the planet from atomic war or pollution, the most important problem of our time is the crisis of the university. For it is the nature of the university, and the role it plays in any particular society, which gives that society its quality and its direction. Which is to say that if we are lucky or intelligent enough to save our planet, the major question then becomes: What is to be the character, quality, and direction of human life? The crisis of the university, then, touches directly on the matter of evolution itself.

### Three Views of the University

In matters of such gravity we should not wonder that the present world struggle in and around the university is such a passionate, bitter, diehard, life-and-death matter. It is as if all the factions knew exactly what was at stake, and each was determined to usher in a future which bore its stamp, and its stamp alone; like proud and jealous fathers intent on the continued dominance of their

---

[1] This paper draws on an unpublished essay: "The Tragic Paradox of Albion Small and American Social Science"; and on a paper to appear in the *Festschrift* for Herbert Blumer: "The Social Role of the Man of Knowledge: A Critical and Historical Sketch."

[2] Mark Van Doren. *Liberal Education.* Boston: Beacon Press, 1959.

unmistakable personal traits. "Over our own bodies . . ." shout the leftists; "we will suppress the agitators to a man" hiss the rightists; "we will not hesitate to call upon whatever force is necessary to preserve this institution" say the liberals, matter-of-factly, with no variation in tone.

In this kind of three-way monologue we know we can expect disaster and tragedy, and this is exactly what we are living, and will continue to live, until we can devise and implement a reasonable solution and agreement. The purpose of this essay is to present such a solution, the most reasonable and natural one possible, to my mind. It is the same solution that the founders of modern democracy themselves proposed—as we shall see—which is why I introduce it with confidence and temerity into the present bitter dispute. As it turns out, there is no way out but the best way. Let us begin by reviewing the three main positions or conceptions of the university, involved in the present struggle.

## *The Leftist Conception of the University*

The position is simple and straightforward, as far as I can tell. The university is considered to be the ideal base for revolutionary ferment, for total upheaval, for a brand-new social order. This ferment takes two forms: first, the use of the university as a physical base for agitation, and for militant and disruptive sallies into the larger society: the university as an *active* moral conscience, as the instrument of social justice. And second, the complete internal reform of the university: student control over their own activities; student power in faculty hiring and in curriculum planning; student control over admissions from minority groups; all in all, autonomous departments, run or controlled by students.

This program represents such a brutal break with all habitual student activity of the past, with the halcyon days of fraternal fracases and panty raids, that it shivers the spines not only of alumni, but of most students themselves, whose hearts drop at the thought of such independence and power. Like most programs it has two sides, a positive and a negative one. The positive aspects appeal to many people: the striking courage and largely unexpected idealism discovered in youth so long pampered, in limbo through so many years of elementary and high school. These people are awake, active, struggling for self-determination, fighting against the massive alienation to which their society has condemned them. And it is not a selfish struggle either; in its second aspect it is a struggle which puts forth many of the basic tenets of democracy itself: self-determination, local decision making, anti-paternalism, anti-racism, and anti-exploitation by the large minorities in our society. Its basic credo is Jeffersonian: that the society should renew itself *for* the youth, for youth's unknown energies, for the new solutions that a new epoch and a new generation will need to devise; society, if it is to survive and grow creatively, must not warm its youth over for its own stale designs, its already failing adaptations, its old and ebbing energies.

So much for the positive side. Before pausing on the negative one, I think it is important to do something to the program that the students themselves seem to have failed to do: I mean, to separate the first part of it—the social agitation—from the second part, the growth of student power in the university. It is the second part that is attractive to many, that contains the Jeffersonian credo; and this part I want to return to later on, and not discredit it. Right away I can say that the tragedy of the leftist position is the uncritical fusion of these two parts, that discredits the whole. The fact is that society will not allow the university to be a locus of social agitation. Period. This has been the lesson since the Free Speech Movement at Berkeley and, more strikingly, at Columbia and at the State Colleges in California. The university is immersed in the larger context of a powerful, basically conservative, increasingly anxious and frightened society. That society, and its elected demagogues, will not allow the university to topple it.

The ambition to make the university the center of social revolution is ridiculous in its unreality; it would have elicited at most a strained expression in Marx, a shrug in Lenin, a derisive hiss in Stalin, an impatient flick of the hand in Mao. And yet the new revolutionaries, who claim a few of these men as their tradition, think themselves at the height of reality and in the center of cold clarity. Why look, didn't one of them smash the glass door of an administration building, and "claim it for the people"? The most that this kind of infantilism will accomplish is to have the university closed by the power structure, or kept open by them at reduced levels of functioning. Which means, basically, a fascist university— rigidly policed, with carefully screened enrollment, and with complete control by a dictatorial administration over a passive and compliant faculty. The monster is already stirring in the deep, and protruding part of its head.

These comments, of course, are not new or surprising, either to the general reader or to many of the leftists themselves. They are already learning the lesson that a true revolutionary needs more cold clarity than warm idealism; many of them are feeling a bit silly, or much disillusioned. Yet the most important negative thing to be said against their program remains to be faced, and it may be the most disillusioning of all. I mean, of course, the major lesson of the 20th century about revolutions: that even when they succeed, they fail in their major aim and justification—to liberate the spirit of man, to open the world to the unknown energies of each new generation. We know that the new revolutionary societies attempt to banish prostitution, racism, child exploitation, hunger, inequality of opportunity. There is plenty of room to argue the pros and cons of violent revolution on these things alone. But what we are talking about here is the *new quality of evolutionary life*, the spirit of man, in post-revolutionary society.

Specifically, we are talking about the university as the guardian and shaper of that spirit; and here there is no room for argument: the free university is invariably destroyed or emasculated in post-revolutionary society. If it is allowed to exist, it is tolerated only as the rubber stamp of the official state bureaucracy and its ideology. There is no need to review the case of Russia and China, or to remind ourselves of how casually Poland recently banished those professors and intellectual and spiritual leaders of whom it had been most proud: Adam Schaff, Leszek Kolakowski, and the rest. As soon as they came up against the ideology of the bureaucrats, there was no professorial or student power that could save them. The lesson is a paradigm, too, for those young idealists who would claim that "their revolution" would keep alive and introduce new qualities in the post-revolutionary society that would protect university freedom. What country was more jealous of freedom than Poland? And where is the intellectual-spiritual power going to come from that will oppose the bureaucrats, unless that power was protected in and during the revolution itself? In sum, this means that the lesson of the 20th century is that the university itself has to be protected against the revolution.

## *The Liberal Conception of the University*

This idea is not new either, but it brings us logically to the second antagonist in the present struggle—the liberal, the one who speaks for the massive "silent center." It is he who is above all dedicated to protecting the university against the passions of the larger social-political scene; he sees himself as the guardian of the tradition of knowledge, of free inquiry, who must somehow keep it safe from the extremists of left and right. He is the man of patience, of long vision, and of memory into the past, who sees his task as inherited from the Greeks; he is the man of quiet hope and faith in the future: if free inquiry can be protected, mankind will somehow meet its problems of adaptation and survival.

This is the positive side of the liberal aim, his passionate, dedicated task; he conceives it so augustly that he is prepared to use any amount of legal force against those who would destroy or impair the functioning of the university. After all, the whole meaning of the Western tradition is at stake. The accumulated knowledge must be preserved, added to, and passed on, even to the extent of housing university libraries in atom-bombproof shelters so that in the post-holocaust world man's best knowledge would not be destroyed.

This brings us directly to the negative side of the liberal position, and the reason that rebellious youth chafes against the university system of knowledge. It wants only to preserve, accumulate, and pass on, even in a world fallen into atomic ruins. It does not conceive of its task as directly changing that world, as directly altering the form and quality of the social and political life so that atomic war might be prevented. In a word, the liberal—for all the idealism of his historical burden—has delivered over the university to the manager-bureaucrats, to the standard social version of pragmatic truth. And he has made this delivery by rendering and keeping the university in a state of limbo, a state of neutrality *vis-à-vis* the momentous problems of the modern world.

To detail how he does this would take a full-blown critique of the university as it now stands; but for shorthand purposes, it is all centered in the central shibboleths of the modern university: the three-hour credit course; the scientific disciplines; the grade-point system. I call these shibboleths—and they are increasingly coming to be recognized as such—because they bear no direct relationship to teaching, learning, or to the problem of our time. Even more perversely, they bear little or no relationship to the central, substantive problems of science itself.[3] The disciplines in the humanities

[3] I am speaking only of the humanities and social sciences, upon which the basic humanistic and liberating image of the university rests. My remarks do not apply to the natural and pure sciences—physical and mathematics—or to the "service" disciplines like law, medicine, business. For an elaborative historical critique of the scientific disciplines see my book: *The Structure of Evil: An Essay on the Unification of the Science of Man*. New York: Geo. Braziller, 1968.

and social sciences proliferate their own special and artificial problems, and they are becoming hopelessly trivial and inverted. In undergraduate teaching their main aim is to recruit students for graduate specialization, not to open the minds and curiosities of undergraduates—much less to put together an intelligent picture of the world. What the youth needs and wants to know, is: What are the major problems of ourselves and our world, and what does the tradition of Western thought tell us about these problems so that we can open ourselves up and intelligently apply our energies to our world? This is the last thing the disciplinarian wants to impart, or is able to impart. Robert Hutchins and Jacques Barzun, among others, have in recent times eloquently told this sad story, so there is no point in dwelling on it here.

Yet even more sad is that this basic failure is concealed and justified by the grading system and the three-hour credit course. These two things fetishize the failure of the university to offer substantive knowledge, *by making it seem* that something exact, measurable, and meaningful is going on. If you tally up enough three-hour courses, why then you have the requisites for graduation; which means that you have *had* an education. If you get an A instead of a C, it "means" that you are bright, have done well, and have understood and mastered the *knowledge* that was presented to you. In short, you have the visible proofs, finely calibrated, and on important pieces of paper housed in the Registrar's Office, duly paid for with hard money. You are "educated." Besides, you have left so much sweat and anxiety in the process of being so educated; you have so twisted and turned and shrunk your soul to try to give sense and excitement to inane and teasing bits of knowledge, that you feel that something important and genuine *must have* taken place. And if it did not, then you are the guilty one after all. You suffered more because you were more inadequate.

Can anyone honestly deny that this sums up his own college experience? The university fails and disguises its failure with fetishes dutifully fed into IBM machines, detailed, and neatly filed. No wonder the professors will not abandon the grading system, the three-hour course, the entrance exams, or the endless quizzes. This is their elaborate mask, and if you pull it down, behind it there is at best wistfulness—but no general education. But this is not only a disguise for the failure of the professors, it is fundamentally and primarily a mask over the real function of the university itself: the university as a rubber stamp for the national manager-bureaucrats.

After all, if the university fails to produce liberated youths at the height of the problems of their society and their time, then it simply delivers youths over to the agreed social program for action. It takes obedient and uncritical high school graduates and turns them into obedient and uncritical college graduates. The "purpose" of the university has been fulfilled: it has not been allowed to tamper with the national ideology. The liberals have done their job, and cannot understand why the most courageous, idealistic, and aspiringly free students despise them so. The liberals could have done their job as serenely in Moscow or Peking; they could have put in the same eight-hour day keeping the show going in an unruffled way for the bureaucrat-bosses. Only they would not have been able to don the mask of the rhetoric of the "free world," they would not have been able so attractively to package the same produce.

## The Rightist Conception of the University

Let us consider, finally, the rightist conception of the university; it follows naturally upon the liberal conception, since it exaggerates whatever is bad in the liberal view. Here the university is seen to be frankly an instrument of social control, of public order. It is not a disguised instrument—it serves the status quo because that is its task: the university as a super-service institution.

Yet there is a positive side in the rightist view, a side which liberals miss, and a side which leads rightists and leftists to find themselves often agreeing in their criticisms of the way things are. The rightists want a super-service institution, but are not satisfied with the one the liberals protect. The rightists want the university to be not only a rubber stamp of the going bureaucratic game, but they want to call the game back to more traditional and patriotic values. They want to give the game depth, ideal values, and the aura of heroism. They object to value-freedom in the social sciences and humanities; they want values taught and separated out, with a view to upholding the *best* values, the traditional values, the old virtues of the forefathers, the republic, the early entrepreneurs. The university is anything but neutral, and it should declare itself; it should stop spoiling the youth with an aimless pluralism, a pointless relativism. Youth needs identity, and identity can only be grounded in personal values, in an identification with a tradition housing those values, with ancestors embodying them, with prescriptions for right action that applies them.

All of this taken together allows youth the possibility of manhood, dedication, self-transcendence, heroism. If youths had this possibility they would not rebel, but would find their natural growing place in the land of their birth; they would not dissipate, but would apply their energies in a common task of making their nation richer and grander; they would discover the natural fusion of their life-energies with the career of evolution itself: the unfolding of freedom, individuality, and well-being. They would dedicate their lives to promote and protect the values that assured these things, so they would know their place in creation itself, and be known and respected among their fellows. Only in this way can we have healthy persons in a healthy society; and the university today finds itself immersed in a sick society precisely because it has failed to turn out citizens dedicated to self-transcending values, citizens who understand their place in creation and in history, citizens who know right from wrong, citizens with dignity and courage, citizens able to sacrifice for higher ends, citizens who know the issues and the *one best* answer to the main problems of their time and their world.

So we may conclude our survey of the three antagonists in the present struggle around the university. In each we have been able to see a negative side: a side which is stupid or unreal, which causes needless suffering and tragedy, and for no good purpose—as in the leftist view that the university should be the locus of social revolution and militant agitation. Or, in the liberal position, a negative side literally delivers the university over to the bland mediocrity of modern bureaucracy, without giving the students a chance to creatively change their world, or to find their personal identity and dignity in it. In the rightist position, as we have said, this conception of the university as a service institution upholding public order and patriotism is even exaggerated, and unashamedly put forth as an ideal.

Yet in all three positions I hope that I have been able to make clear and compelling that there is a distinct positive side, a side that must be kept and separated out of the stridency of the claims, of the repulsion we may feel in reacting to the total package offered by each side, of the din of confusion and obscurity surrounding the battle. The leftist position has the positive virtues of Jeffersonianism: the need for autonomy, local governance, and self control, the need to use and expand the creative energies of each new generation—*now*, while the youths are growing and testing their adaptations against the problems they will confront as adults; not when they are already adults, and have been co-opted into a fixed system and are no longer free to question or to act. The power that the students want is the power of democracy itself: people controlling the forces which shape them, people influencing the events in which they are immersed, people making the decisions that will affect their lives.

The student demand for power in the university is not a threat to democracy, it is a threat to bureaucracy and habit, it is a threat to statism. It will certainly shake up the bureaucrats, but it will not bring the world tumbling down; rather, it will prop it up, prop it on the shoulders of persons, of responsible persons who know responsibility because they have been able to exercise it. Student meetings during the agitations at Berkeley were almost boringly held with the full rules of democratic process, of parliamentary procedure: everyone could speak his piece, and practically everyone did, and the final voting was long and tedious because all voices counted, and all positions had to be weighed and reviewed.

The liberal position of protecting the university at all costs against the passions and irrationality of the social world is a primary value. This value has grown out of the long groping toward the freedom and dignity of man since the contributions by the Greeks, and, in the East, the rise of the great universal religions that affirmed the human spirit. Without a free university, a locus of free inquiry and discussion, tyranny is inevitable; either by outright tyrants, or by cheerful bureaucrats and cold machines. Man might survive, but that survival would have no meaningful human quality. The university is thus as necessary to freedom in the present as it is to the creative advance of evolution itself. When the liberal expresses incredulous outrage against those who would destroy the university for political or personal reasons, he is defending a value which truly must be taken for granted.

The rightist idea that the university must answer the problem of value, of right action, of dedication, of youth's identity within a larger frame of things—this idea is basic to the real task of the university. And perhaps nowhere has the university failed as miserably as it has in the areas of giving youth a deep sense of heroism grounded in a vision of truth, a striving for ideal value with a secure sense of the ways to reach and judge that value. One question and one question alone is meaningful for youth, and for man everywhere—and it is this question above all to which the university should address itself: "What is my authentic talent, my true and unique contribution to world life? And how can I relate the two, so that I may feel that my existence is of consequence to creation?" The university is the one best place to seek an answer, to give its youth the excitement of awakening the question, the cognitive tools for approaching and exploring it. Yet today it fails. I do not mean to imply that the rightists are correct in their narrow, patriotic, and dogmatic formulation of this problem and the answers to it—far from it. But they are correct in their adumbration that this is the basic problem of education.

## Authentic Role of the University

We promised earlier that we would present a solution to the dilemma of the university, a reasonable and natural agreement among the three positions we have outlined. Such a solution would have to be a fusion that keeps the positive aspect of each antagonist's view, and that discards the negative aspects as I understand them.

### *The Creative Unity of These Three Positions*

We said that we could present such a solution with confidence, because it is the authentic solution proposed by the founders of modern democracy itself. It is, in fact, the only solution, and the best solution, at one and the same time. For such a happy unblocking of our bitter and tragic problems, we have only to thank the geniuses who ushered in our modern epoch: the thinkers of the Enlightenment, and some of the early theorists of our government. It was they who saw truly that the authentic role of the university would be to merge the things that go naturally together: science and politics, free inquiry and social action. And they saw how to do this in a peaceful, non-coercive way, a way which guaranteed to all parties their freedom and their own responsible decisions.

One would think that a solution of such elegance would be common knowledge today, with the ponderous volume of words and pages gushed out to try to make sense of the problems of our world. Or if not common knowledge, one might imagine that at least the academic intellectuals knew of this solution, nursed it among themselves, tried to publicize it among others. Yet none of this is true. We find ourselves in the astonishing position in which neither the public, nor the legislators, nor even the academics, know the really great liberating ideas of their own history. Little wonder that our fate is potentially so tragic. We are apparently not using the brain given to us by evolution.

Probably the most liberating idea of the modern epoch, an idea which is the key to our dilemmas, is one which sprang from the cataclysmic French Revolution. It is the real and continuing fruit of that Revolution. I mean the idea of a scientific society as proposed by Condorcet and others in France, and by the idealist philosophers in Germany. An idea also espoused in England by J. S. Mill and the English Comteans, introduced as the very basis of our republic by Thomas Jefferson, and kept alive as a program and hope all during the 19th and early 20th century. Only today is it a forgotten dream, or at best a visionary fantasy, utterly unrelated to our situation. This is how far the republic has come. Let us look more closely at this idea and its sad fate.

The idea of a scientific society had a twofold aspect. The first was strictly scientific. The aim was to present an organized structure of scientific knowledge, a coherent world picture gathered from the latest and best knowledge. This picture would be taught in the universities and presented to the public, as the best answer to the outstanding problems of human misery and human adaptation. All great and anguished questions about man's condition in the modern world would be referred to the scientific world picture. The hope of the European Enlightenment and the new democratic societies which grew out of it was, in the most direct way, to bring the best thought to bear on the moral problems of modern life. Nothing could be more logical or straightforward.

The second aspect of this program was political. That is, the new scientific world picture would be elaborated and taught in the universities, but it would be applied to the national parliamentary life—to the governing and lawmaking agencies—so that the leaders and lawmakers would be able to govern according to the latest, most humane, and most liberating and potentiating knowledge. It was in France, above all, that this experiment was tried by a group of social scientists known as the *idéologues*. They were members of the famous *Institut* which would elaborate the scientific world picture, and they were as well members of the parliament which would instrument it. Again, nothing could be more logical or straightforward. This was the experiment on which was founded the hope of a new scientific society, a society instrumented gradually and peacefully through democratic processes. It was a world-historical opportunity and vision. Unhappily, it was clear too to the most consummate statist of the time—Napoleon; and when he saw the threat that the *idéologues* posed to his own authoritarian centralization of power, he promptly closed down their section of the *Institut*. And that was that.

In Germany there was a similar hope, early in the 19th century, of relating scientific knowledge to the national political life in an intimate, critical way. But from 1848 on, and after Bismarck and the rise of militarism, this hope gradually slipped away. The famous *Verein für Sozialpolitik* slowly abandoned its aims of being a critical advisor to government, and became instead a learned professional body, inverted on its own problems and divorced from any power to alter the course of the national life.

The best that the English could do, for their part, was to keep alive the old tradition of having the universities elect their representatives to parliament. This did have the advantage of surely placing at least a few men of intellect regularly into the national political life—and at times it placed great ones like Newton, William Pitt, Palmerston, and Gladstone. Yet even this toehold was abandoned after World War II. The British never got started on the big visions of J. S. Mill and the English Comteans. All they could do was to keep the hope alive and write about it in a visionary way, hoping that someone would take the idea seriously and implement it. John Beattie-Crozier asked for a National Bible, a coherent scientific world picture that would serve as an infallible guide to the problems of the nation. H. G. Wells called for a "World Brain" that would be used by all nations, to best solve their problems in a peaceful, intelligent, evolutionary way. In the United States this idea was kept alive, after Jefferson, by a few thinkers, notably Lester Ward, Thomas Davidson, John Dewey, and Horace Kallen. Ward, like Condorcet and Jefferson before him, wanted a National University in Washington, so as to be right at the pulse-beat of the governing process. This wish was to no avail.

We can see how the political side of the hope for a new scientific society simply went bankrupt through disuse. But this bankruptcy was due partly to the fact that the scientists themselves failed their earlier hopes. They did not elaborate a coherent scientific world picture that anyone could use, even if they wanted it. The national scientific meetings of our day do not give opinions on urgent questions of social life and political policy; they are merely rituals of self-perpetuation, where people go to get and to offer jobs, to eat and drink and meet friends, and to wheel and deal for grant monies and power in the national scientific organization. When a budding, young, idealistic scientist gets up at such a meeting and asks that the organization make a public pronouncement out of its particular expertise, on an urgent national question, he is voted down in shock and anger. "How untidy, and unseemly, this young man; how did he get into the coveted councils of science? Someone must have slipped up along the way of his university career." When a legislator of the stature of a Fulbright laments the failure of the specialists and the university, this is what he means. Even if parliament were to turn to science for advice on how to make the world better, how to avoid national disasters, the scientists themselves would slip away like sand.

The terrible fact is that the scientists have no coherent world picture, nor are they working on one. They abandoned that quest—almost cheerfully it seems—in the latter part of the 19th century, when they launched themselves on the paths of separate scientific disciplines. Now we have armsful of disciplines and hordes of specialists, but we do not have any science we can use to answer moral and social questions. With the rise and flourishing of the scientific disciplines, fact and value came apart in the modern world.[4] The universities themselves became bureaucratized. There is now no place to get knowledge "at the height of the times"—to use Ortega's apt expression. Nor is there any way to apply this knowledge to the governing process: the bureaucrats, the successors to Napoleon, do not want to be ruffled any more than he did. It is no longer absolute power which the critical vision of scientists might threaten, but the peaceful eight-hour bureaucratic day. And given the ingrained nature of primate habit, the grip of bureaucratic routine is as jealous and steady as an iron fist.

## Solving the Problem of Role

So much then, for the briefest sketch of the great seminal idea of modern democracy, and its fate. Just to sketch this idea must quicken the pulse of all but the most cynical; all but those who have an inflexible vested interest in maintaining things the way they are; or all but the most extreme, those who must have their way without giving in to compromise or to more compelling reason. For the fact is that it is easy to see how the modern democratic idea solves easily and naturally the problem of the university today, how it would keep the best in the positions of each antagonist. If we elevate the university to a dominant role in the formation of the national consciousness, we make the nation dependent upon its best knowledge, upon the quality of its thought. Without this quality the ship of state flounders and errs as Jefferson knew it would. The liberal, then, need have no fears for the continuance of his favorite institution.

[4] For a fuller elaboration of the whole problem that I am merely sketching here, see the two papers cited in Footnote One, and my books: *The Structure of Evil: An Essay on the Unification of the Science of Man* and *Beyond Alienation: A Philosophy of Education for the Crisis of Democracy*.

The fact is that since we have failed to make the university a central and dominant critical influence in the national life, it is the university itself that is threatened by the irrationality of an insane society. The logic is ineluctable. The State of California this past year congratulated itself on the 100th anniversary of its service to the people of the state, via the University of California. Yet on this very anniversary the elected representatives of the people proved that it was the university itself that they most feared and hated. In other words, the university, for a century, had failed to influence critically the quality of life around it, and was suffering a just retribution. The liberal feared for a university whose fate he himself had helped seal, by keeping that university in a state of impotence to influence critically the quality of political life. By insisting on making the university a mere rubber stamp of the going game of the society at large, the university became in fact a pawn to the fears and anxieties of that society. It was a stamp the people themselves felt they should use. Biblical justice, it would seem, still unfolds in the modern world. The conclusion is ineluctable, too: if the liberal would protect and keep his university he must transform it into the original Jeffersonian vision.

What does this transformation of the university entail? I have written about it at length elsewhere, so there is no need to elaborate here.[5] Let us just mention the major thing that would have to be done. We have said that the university fails because it does not give what it promised to give to the citizens of democracy at the beginning of the modern epoch: namely, a coherent, scientific world picture that would be an authoritative guide to moral and social problems. It would be a picture that would address itself to the dominant issues in the student's social world, and the dominant problems of his own life and freedom. It would give the student knowledge "at the height of the times" and so put him at the center of his powers, give him a footing in his world. He would then be able to take his place in the university as a real adult, knowing the best that man has fashioned about himself and his problems, and be able to fulfill the role of a citizen of a rational democracy. The major thing that would have to be broken down in order to get this result is the present disciplinary approach to undergraduate teaching, the impotent and scatterbrained fragmentation that we now practice. This has been known for a long time, and at least every

[5] See: *Beyond Alienation: A Philosophy of Education for the Crisis of Democracy*. New York: George Braziller, Inc., 1967.

few decades there is a great clamor for a revival of "general education" away from special education, so that the major task of the university can be fulfilled. Yet aside from a lot of published papers, books, speeches, commencement talks, and symposiums, nothing comes of it.

The disciplinarians continue to thrive and to extend their domain. It has gotten to the point where "anything goes" in a discipline, as far as specialization is concerned: the most inverted problems are encouraged; the disciplines are becoming arcane societies which nourish conundrums for their own sake. In an anthropology department in which I taught, it was proposed to hire one man at a very high rank, who was doing work in mathematical analysis that only he understood. And this was the reason given for hiring him: that no one else could understand what he was doing, but it looked so imposingly scientific, and he was so involved in it, that it *must* have been really outstanding. The example will surprise no one—any university student could add ten of his own. Students no longer take courses in areas of knowledge; they take, for the most part, courses in the pet specializations of their professors. These specializations can be, and usually are, unrelated to the main body of disciplinary work, and to the major problems of the discipline itself.

I believe that we have arrived at a point where the teaching that represents the discipline is even narrower than the discipline itself! This is terrifying. And this process is all protected and legitimated by the grading system and the three-hour course. If you get a D in Professor Jones' course on the classification of jokes and riddles in the Malay archipelago, then you are less educated than someone who gets an A. It is quite clear. Professor Jones' pet pastime is given three hours' worth of credit, which "means" that it represents a three-hour portion of knowledge. If you add up enough three-hour portions of the pet preoccupations of an assortment of people who may themselves be scientifically irrelevant to the main problems of their field—if you do this, why you have what it takes to get a diploma and certify that you are educated. This is disgusting.

I admit that none of this is very new either; the situation was fully reviewed and argued during the 19th century, when the elective system, much to the alarm of many, gradually came to prevail in our universities. A recognizable body of agreed-upon basic knowledge was no longer necessary to get a diploma, and the specialists were in effect given a mandate to trivialize the student's mind. The problem for us is to stop talking about the situation, and to start stopping it. If we could get started on supplanting the disciplinary approach to teaching, we would almost automatically make the universities relevant to our lives. We would get at the basic knowledge that science possesses, we would teach such knowledge and debate it, we would show its linkages among its various branches, and its direct outleadings to our world and its problems. Most of all we would get back to the point where the universities once were: the place where really substantive, central problems were examined and debated, and where answers were sought to them. It is these *substantive, central* issues that have been obscured, sidestepped, and buried by the disciplinary pursuit of special, segmental problems. I once asked a social psychologist what the central problem of social psychology was, and he said there was none! Imagine it! When I pressed him that each science begins with a central problem, and only truly progresses by continually reforming theory around that central problem—he accused me of being a troublemaker.

There was a time when the universities were the seats of great discussions and great debates, about really important things. At the end of the past century the University of California at Berkeley could group a national conference on the "Problem of God," and present men like Howison, Royce, and Le Conte to give the latest and best knowledge on the question. And the student could feel secure that he had, for a while to come, the latest and best on that issue. The universities talked about the "Economic Question," the "Social Question," the "Question of the Soul." It was all remarkably correct and beautiful, as far as natural curiosity and the growth of knowledge were concerned. There was a time, too, when students went to a university because the leading minds were there, and these minds talked about the most important problems. When Schelling gave his lectures at the University of Berlin in the 1830's, it was no accident that Kierkegaard, Marx, Federbach, and other leading young thinkers found themselves in the same classroom. Were they all filling in a three-hour credit? Obviously not: they were there to get the latest and best by the greatest, on the most important and vital. Then they could go on from there with confidence.

Contrast the situation today: each petty expert protects his colleague, by claiming that all knowledge is equal, and all professors are doing important work. No one, they claim, is truly outstanding, no one is doing really overshadowing work; there is no one who is at the "height of the times." The student can only choose "what" he wants to study, and "where" he likes to live. It never occurs to these experts that the student does not want to study a "what"—he wants the best knowledge available on the leading problems; and he usually does not care where he lives in order to get it.

All this leads us back to the positive side of what the "leftist" students especially want; in this their intuition and their idealism are unerring: they want the university to be a major influence on the social question, they want it to house the national conscience, to put them on top of their times and their world so that they can understand that world and refashion its moral failings. I think we are in a position to see that there is indeed immense room for university reform, and an intimate place for student action and agitation centering around that reform.

## Constructive Student Agitation

If we agree on where the failure of the university centers, perhaps we may be ready to do what is necessary to remedy that failure. If we are ready, then, we can mount an entirely new critique of the status quo, a critique that the students themselves can instrument, a critique confined *within* the university itself. In other words, the students have a whole program for idealistic protest, without bringing down the wrath of the society around them. Furthermore, it is the only truly constructive protest available to them, the only action grounded in reality, the only action they can undertake which actually will bring about deep-seated changes, and begin the serious transformation of their world. If the students could bring about the demise of the disciplinary approach to learning, on the undergraduate level, they would fashion nothing less than a rebirth of the university in the original democratic vision. Having fashioned this—as we shall shortly see—they can bring about the transformation of society itself. As far as I can see there is no other way that this can be done, while at the same time keeping a guarantee of human freedom.

From all we have said, it is obvious that the main failing of the university is in the scientific disciplinary approach to teaching. The major agents of that failing, then, are the professors themselves, as far as their tasks are now construed. It is hard to say this plainly, without running the risk of being misunderstood in one's intent and basic allegiances, but the fact is that the professors are the main obstacle to a meaningful college education. Many of their habits, preferences, and prerogatives would have to be shaken up if the university is to be saved.

The major concern of student protest, then, would have to be the professors themselves, and the fetishes the professors use to cover up their failure. Except in the natural sciences and the "service" disciplines, the idea of letter and percentage grades will have to be completely abolished.[6] *Completely,* not merely replaced by euphemistic words that mean the same things: "High pass," "pass with honors," etc. Simply: "Pass" or "no pass." Along with this change, class attendance must be made entirely voluntary. These two related things alone could revolutionize the present system of knowledge, since they will oblige the professors to aim for relevance, or suffer the consequences of a natural boycott of their classes. They will have no more artificial coercion over their students, but must instead depend on the natural coercion of the attractiveness of the ideas they represent, as well as their skill in presenting them.

Furthermore, chronically poor professors, those who have no talent for teaching ideas or commanding attention, those who mumble irrelevancies into their beards day after day and year after year—these professors should be the object not only of poor ratings in student evaluations, but of an actual boycott by students. If the professors try to protect such incompetent teachers by making their courses "required" in a sequence, then the students should station one stenographer in each large lecture class, to take notes for all concerned. Student funds can be set aside for this, and for the duplication of the notes to make them available to all students taking the course. It is questionable how long the professor could lecture to one student.

Along with this, students should have a voice in the retention

[6] I make this distinction between the natural sciences and the social sciences and humanities, not because I think such a distinction ought to be absolutely made, but because a better case can be made out by those disciplines for keeping the grading system, since they do want to keep it. There are large bodies of technical data that students must master in the natural sciences, before they can move on to more advanced work. In effect, these disciplines prepare specialists, and not generalists; and in true specialism finer distinctions regarding mastery of the subject may be more easily justified. The social sciences and humanities, on the other hand, are generalist, critical disciplines. Their major aim and justification is the change and growth, and *general* mastery, that they awaken in the student. It is this growth that cannot be accurately measured and, indeed, should not. It is the *student's private business* how much he grows and changes.

and hiring of gifted teachers—something they have wanted for years, only to be continually put down with the most casual and cynical disregard of their wishes and their torments. It is obvious that the professors are protecting themselves. The Ph.D. degree, as we have long known, is a fraudulent degree as far as teaching talent is concerned. There is no recruitment among Ph.D. candidates for those gifted in teaching, there are no standards for teaching ability that have to be met. All one has to do to earn a Ph.D. is to do some specialized research. Then, when he gets it, it "certifies" him as a university teacher—the highest teacher in the land! This is fraud, based on false pretenses. It is as though we were to give medical degrees to those who did research in medical sciences, and then certify them to do surgery immediately upon completion of their library studies in parasitology, for example. Such a practice would be insane, but so is the Ph.D. certificate of qualified teaching. Teaching, mind you: the art of awakening the imagination, developing the human spirit, leading youth on to vistas of self-discovery and the revelation of the wonders of their world. No holier task, as has been known since shamanistic times; yet a task that we treat with a casualness close to scorn. And we know that doctors can be sued for malpractice, while professors cannot. The flesh is then more sacred than the soul.

The problem of the failure of teaching derives not only from irrelevant standards of recruitment and training, it is intimately connected with the professionalism of the disciplines. The fact is that the high and mighty disciplinary careerists, for the most part, could not care less for undergraduate teaching. This is considered "beneath" them. At a department meeting of sociologists at Berkeley, it was actually proposed to "phase out" undergraduate teaching, and to confine their work to graduates only. One professor protested that this might work against them, because they recruit their graduate students from the undergraduates. But the others quickly pooh-poohed that. "We don't get our graduates from Berkeley, we get them nationally." In other words, we don't need the undergraduate students here at Berkeley. Imagine this: Here is a group of professors paid by the angry and frustrated taxpayers of California to teach their young—paid almost $30,000 a year, some of them. Some of them, too, are asked to teach only one or two courses a year. The prestige of having such "great" men live and work at Berkeley is more than enough to warrant such salaries and such exemptions from teaching. But look what these men do: they take the taxpayers' money, spend it by jetting around the world to national and international meetings and giving papers furthering their own prestige and careers. They aim to recruit graduate students from other universities, and think nothing of cutting their obligation to teach undergraduates at Berkeley. In other words, they are using Berkeley as a personal sinecure for their own national careerist operations, and as a nesting place for their recruitment of protégés from other states. Do we wonder that student protest began at Berkeley—at the place where the "most successful" careerist professors had settled? The disciplinarians, when they succeed, fulfill almost none of the obligations of a university teacher. The higher the standing of the university, the more the large bodies of undergraduate students are orphaned. It is entirely perverse.

Student meddling in these matters, then, is justified because these matters concern them, and no one else seems to want to do anything about them. Student meddling in their own affairs would come next, and be even more an area for the exercise of self-governance and autonomous decision. The little control that the students have over their own affairs in the university today is nothing short of disgraceful. They are treated literally like children. They should control their own activities, their own organizations, their own funds, even optimally, their own discipline. How else make them responsible? We have been astonished at the recent student violence, yet who is really to blame? If you close off to your child any channel whereby he may approach you with his grievances, in a responsible way—why, you invite a temper tantrum. It is the only behavior that he has left.

There is no reason to fear student protest and meddling in the university; the problem of irresponsible action is a two-sided one. In order to be responsible (response-able), one has to be *able* to *respond*. And this the students have not been allowed to do. We want them to conform to democratic, parliamentary rules of courtesy and free give-and-take. But we do not treat their claims as valid; we ignore their legitimate grievances. In order for "fair-play" rules to hold, there is an obligation on those in power to give dissident claims a rightful status. All of which means, simply, that *if* we want students to demonstrate according to rules, we must provide them a channel for honestly responding to their claims. Anything short of this is hypocrisy or self-delusion. The experience at Berkeley shows that if the students had been given the status of democratic equality they would not have been driven to irresponsible (non-respondable) channels of agitation.

Furthermore, if you systematically eliminate from the student body all the students who annoy you with their constant demands to discuss principles and initiate reforms, what do you have left? You have students who will no longer approach you to discuss reforms, but who will find other ways to make their energies felt. The Heyns administration at Berkeley systematically eliminated students of the caliber and clear idealism of Mario Savio, Frank Bardacke, and Susan Stein, among others. They were eliminated for minor infractions of the rules, like passing out leaflets, refusing to report weekly to a dean because of a minor rule violation, etc. Recently one student dean complained that the students no longer came to talk to him. People like Savio and the others would not even have set a match to a cigarette, but today buildings are burning. Now that these idealists have been eliminated for the comfort of the administration, and all agitation on matters of principle has been curtailed, less idealistic and more bitter students are finding new ways to express their temper tantrums. It is really apodictic. When the students at Berkeley voted that the graduate students should be members of the student union, Heyns promptly took the control of student funds away from them, as punishment for such egregious autonomy. When the students wanted to name their new auditorium the "Martin Luther King" auditorium, this was not allowed by the administration. It was named dutifully "Zellerbach Hall," because Zellerbach put up a million dollars to complete it; the students had put up only six million. When students in the most orderly way possible drew up petitions of thousands of signatures to keep favored professors, their orderly pleas were ignored. All this is to catalogue the guilt of the university, a guilt that need not be expiated, but that simply needs to be avoided in the future by placing students' desires and students' affairs more squarely within their own hands.

Power, alas, is not something one gives up with alacrity, and bureaucrats perhaps less than anyone. The students want autonomy, but the administrators almost pleadingly reiterate that they will give the students anything they want—but that. The whole dispute over Black Studies curricula centers around this. The administrators are perfectly willing to give the blacks their own courses—after all, what difference do more courses make in the already impotent pluralism of the elective system? No danger here. But the students want autonomy, and this is a new and total threat to the present distribution of power. What if it catches on with the white students? Who will control the university then? The students will have a share in running it, a say in hiring, a say in admissions. The thing is frightening to the entrenched bureaucrats, and anyone in their place would be equally anxious. In order to accommodate to the wishes of the students they would have to do what primates hate and fear most, namely, change deep-seated habits and procedures, relinquish control and power over daily events. It is almost too much to ask of fragile *Homo sapiens*.

But is it so terrible? The blacks want "unlimited" admission to those who want to learn. Who would suffer under an influx of masses of students? We know that the whole psychological testing system, as well as the present grading system, is largely show and sham. Why should the students not decide among themselves which of their juniors will be admitted from the high schools? If the present grading system is largely a dodge for the professors, who would be harmed by ignoring it? If the social sciences and humanities exist to further the inner growth, change, and general mastery of each student, why cannot ordinary or poor students expose themselves to this growth? Do the students exist for the disciplines and the professors, or vice versa? How can we have a society of mass-elitism, a society in which the general level of *everyone* is raised at least a little bit up to the height of the time, if we do not open the universities to the people?

I have given this matter considerable thought, and as far as I can see the only area of real pain in such rearrangements would be the area that now is most in need of reform: the undergraduate lecture system. And the reform here, though broad and new, does not threaten any of the basic values of the university, or the integrity of disciplinary knowledge itself. It is truly astonishing how much we could accomplish, and how easily. For one thing, a sharp distinction would have to be made between undergraduate and graduate levels. The undergraduate level would be devoted to general education, with specialization only by the most advanced students capable of independent work, and desiring to go on to graduate school. All the esotericism of science would be preserved, and specialization would be encouraged in graduate school. This would free the undergraduate curriculum for a true general education.

This would do several things at one swoop: it would permit the university to use a "pass-no pass" grading system on the undergraduate levels, while reserving special honors programs for those who intend to go on to graduate school. No one would be threatened. The graduate programs could retain the grading system for their specialized bodies of knowledge.

It would pull all the specialist teachers and researchers up to the graduate levels of teaching, where they want to be anyway. And it would allow gifted generalist teachers to convey the undergraduate programs. It would take researchers and inverted specialists away from the undergraduates, where they only succeed in stifling natural curiosity. It would confine them to seminars and special guided research programs, where they are most comfortable and perform better, usually. Everyone would benefit.

The large influx of undergraduate students would necessitate a whole new approach to classroom teaching. We can no longer split the university up into smaller and smaller special programs, with more and more "intimate" contact with the professors, smaller classes, etc. This whole trend would have to be reversed, since it flies in the face of the problem of mass education. Let it be said once and for all that the idea of the small class and the intimate contact with the "great" professor is a fetish, pure and simple. This idea is meant to cover up the failure of the professors to present relevant, exciting knowledge on large, basic questions. They plead that the reason they do not "communicate" is because of the large halls, the large number of students, the vast distance that separates them. And the student believes it. He cannot imagine that the reason he seems to be getting nothing out of the "great" Professor Smith is that Smith is really giving nothing broad and vital, but only Smith's pet research project. Besides, if Smith is a poor teacher in the large lecture hall, he will usually not be miraculously transformed in the small room. How many students have not discovered this to their dismay? The small room merely draws them closer to nothingness. Great teachers can give great thoughts to thousands at a time, even to millions over TV. Who has not found himself stimulated and delighted by a face speaking so far away its features could not even be made out? And who has not been heartbroken by a face so close that its breath could be smelled? Well, enough concreteness, surely; but the point, it seems to me, is indisputable.

If the general education communicates broad vistas and exciting perspectives, deals with basic issues and great questions, then it can be stimulating to the largest audiences. This is what we will not admit, and what "small classroom" philosophy tries to disguise. We have, for the most part, abandoned these vistas and these substantive questions in our universities. At Berkeley I saw how exciting and gifted teachers could lecture to a thousand students, with no complaint by the students. Far from it: they themselves often organized voluntarily into smaller discussion groups, because they had ideas to discuss. They chose their own leaders for these groups, did their own further work; or, the groups were led by qualified teaching assistants of the same age roughly as the students. So there was intimate close contact, full discussion and give-and-take, as well as the possibility of mass education; both intimately combined and feeding each other.

The students can literally educate themselves if someone excites them with the basic ideas and opens their imaginations. This is the revolution promised by general education, a revolution in the substantive content and the scope of knowledge imparted. It harmonizes fully with the real capabilities of the students, and it answers fully and perfectly the question of finances for a continually costlier higher education budget. One of the major reasons that university budgets are shooting up is that the specialist professors teach less, and to smaller classes. Since this is all calculated on a three-hour basis, the influx of more students sends costs rocketing. Yet this is all unnecessary, even wrong. One gifted professor can handle 2,000 students at one-hundredth of the cost of 100 poor professors mishandling 20 students each. Again, let us look at the ineluctable logic of empirical fact. The taxpayers would save a fortune if the universities reorganized some of their useless, ingrained professional habits, and settled down to the job of teaching and awakening the youth.

Finally, since the failure of the disciplines is so abject, and since the goal of a general education would solve most of the outstanding problems of *quality, volume,* and *cost* of teaching, we can see that the program for constructive student agitation must also include pushing for curriculum reform, for the *quality* of what is taught to undergraduates. The student protests against the universities' involvement in war activities are a reflection of what is wrong, and what the students' intuition tells them is wrong. The whole idea of the value-neutrality of knowledge must be revised. It is this that has made the university a rubber stamp of the official immorality of the larger society, and completely subverted the original democratic promise of a university towering above society, giving it direction and moral quality. Perhaps the outstanding characteristic of our times, in the field of knowledge, will be the complete revision of the fallacious idea that science is value-neutral. We have learned to our alarm and regret that science must be subservient to truly human goals, to truly moral aims; otherwise it becomes a Frankenstein's monster that defeats our best hopes and aims.

Students should continually move for undergraduate curriculum reform that makes the knowledge of the social sciences and humanities relevant to today's world. One senior professor of sociology at Berkeley recently warned that no graduate students would be admitted to their program who brought values into sociology. It is this kind of asinine and morally callous position that the students must help attack, since the professors have proved that they are quite willing to go along with such a position. It is, of course, all part of the bureaucratization of science, that keeps science tied to the smooth continuation of the way things are, protects vested interests and the status quo. There is a very lot at stake in the separation of science from urgent moral questions, but this separation must finally be exposed for what it is. Nor are the natural sciences exempt here: the uncritical and anti-humanistic role played by the bureaucrats in biology and other natural sciences must also be exposed and denounced as anti-scientific. The idea that the university should contract for biological and other kinds of scientific warfare is a blasphemy against the human spirit, an utter corruption of the ideal of the university and the goal of knowledge since the time of the Greeks. That the liberals can continue to defend this posture is their most damaging self-accusation of irrelevance and amorality in today's world.

Once the idea that all facts are neutral comes under attack, it will bring with it a thoroughgoing reevaluation of the nature of facts. It can then more easily be seen that all facts are not of equal value, all questions are not of the same urgency, all researches are not inquiries into substantive matters. This notion of the total equality of all research questions, the sameness of all fact, is a fiction that the scientists perpetuate in order to prevent the exposure of incompetence among themselves. The thing they hate most is confrontation, debate, the exposure of fallacious positions, the negation of areas of inconsequential facts. Did we once imagine that this was what science was really about? It was, but the bureaucrat scientists have long since changed the game, and with it the whole meaning and dignity of human dialogue and discourse. The great ages of human creativity, as Huizinga somewhere points out, were ages of sharp debate, block confrontation between opposing intellectual positions, acrimonious struggles around ideological positions; and where the debate was most creative, as Saint-Simon already remarked, it was viciously passionate and ad hominem.

The thing that stifles human advance is automatic agreement based on obsequious respect for authority, so that all monolithic versions of truth have to be attacked, as well as the authorities that represent them. When we get beyond smug agreement, and the concrete persons that embody that agreement, the human spirit takes a new life. Do we wonder that our epoch is one of the most sterile in terms of liberating ideas, critical perspectives? The scientists have made a tacit convention among themselves not to argue, not to show each other up, not to confront opposing views. If science itself is cheated by this convention, in its creative advance, we can imagine how the youth is cheated. The university is no longer a real forum, the life has gone out of it; it is bloodless, passionless, a dry mumbling that rolls on day after day, covering a thousand thoughts, ten thousand researches, hundreds of subjects. Nowhere can the student penetrate to the quick of significance, nowhere does he step up on a commanding height.

The task is clear: the student must press for debate around continuing, substantive issues, in the history of thought, morality, and social action. What we need is a confrontation of the leading points of view, around the most vital issues. What is the best way to remedy the economic problem? The socialist way, or the tradition from Adam Smith? In what ways was primitive society superior to civilized society? Is state centralization or decentralization the best way to guarantee social prosperity and human freedom? What does psychology tell us about the problem of human freedom? Sociology? Anthropology? What does evolution tell us about the prospects of continued human advance? What does religion tell us about man's fate? How valid is it today? Has the search for absolute truth in the history of thought been a fruitful one or a failure? If fruitful, then what is truth; if a failure, then where does that leave *us*? What led to the demise of community and brotherhood in primitive and ancient society? How can we envision the return of these social forms and values?

These are some of the questions that would be covered by a general undergraduate curriculum, and that would be made exciting and intellectually manageable by gifted teachers. But even beyond that, the reintroduction of substantive, moral debate in the university would have repercussions on science itself. It would help remedy that great shame of the national scientific organizations and their annual meetings: I mean the shame of keeping absolutely quiet about the relationship of their best knowledge to the crisis of the modern world. We could once again see the national scientific councils in their original hope and meaning: that of authoritative forums mediating answers to our urgent questions. We would see science speaking out on social issues, with all the prestige of science, with all the carefulness of its researched facts, with all of its impartiality to vested interests, to social fears and passions. Only one value would it cherish, a value that all could agree on: the advancement, liberation, and elevation of the human spirit. People would take its findings seriously, or at least respect them coldly from a distance; they would act on them, or at least be forced to ignore them with discomfort.

At the very least, people would know that scientists *have* relevant knowledge, *have* informed opinions, *have* carefully elaborated answers to vital social issues. People would know that if we wanted to try to use this knowledge, we would at least know where to turn. They would know that after we had exhausted our demagogues, after our repressions and our police force had failed to give us safety, after our war machines had failed to guarantee peace, after all the tired opinions of our "old pro" politicians have been tried and failed—after all this, there would yet be a continuing body of men who recruit the best talents of each new generation, and who cultivate the best answers to the problems of our world. People would know that these men have worked in the universities and scientific councils, and have had no power to implement their views among us; yet such men have at least made our youth bright and questioning for a time, before they were again co-opted into our habitual system. Perhaps we might even learn to lay aside our fears, eschew the easy, quick, surface response; and, instead, try to work with the universities and scientists on the broad and deep-going reconstruction of our world.

So might the public reason one day, if the scientists and professors were to make themselves visible on questions of human concern. We say "might," because we have known since Plato that the public does not reason so, and neither do its leaders. From the Tyrant of Syracuse, through Napoleon and Bismarck, on up to the pint-sized demagogues of our day, the story remains the same. The men in power scorn the intellectuals who would radically change their world, rearrange its power relations, cut swaths into its cherished habits and traditions. As Plato so unmistakably taught us, and as he lamented with sorrow and disillusionment, the politicians are sick, along with their societies, but they will not turn to the "philosopher-doctors" to diagnose and cure their illness.

Our idealistic youths are surely not able to lament with the long-dead Plato; they will surely be impatient even with the vision of a morally-conscious university, if that university cannot bring its power directly to bear on social issues. It seems like a continuation of the liberal compromise, on a more sophisticated level of tragic awareness. What good is a "National Brain" housed in the universities and councils of science, if it cannot make its weight felt on the tired old politics of the nation? Is it enough to give vision and the promise of freedom to undergraduates for a few years, only to disgorge them back into the iron grip of the institutions of an irrational society? Even if we throw the university open to the larger masses of students, and elevate the critical awareness of these masses, how will they make their actual weight felt against the encrusted powers? Even if the masses of students grow and develop themselves with a superior critical education, how will this quality be translated into the actual functioning of the national life? When? Is not revolution of some kind inevitable?

## Active Role of the New University

So might well reason our impatient youth. The answer to the question of the desirability of revolution is still negative; it is not inevitable or desirable. What we need instead is an institutionalized way of making critical and moral weight felt on the national life. We need a way of influencing the quality of life that depends not only on the long-run development of masses of persons, but on the short-run meddling into political and social affairs. Only this meddling, as we said, cannot come in the form of political agitation in the community by the university: the present political powers will simply not allow it, and will not hesitate to sacrifice the university in order to stop it. We concluded this at the very beginning of our discussion. What we need is a democratic alternative role for the intelligence that the university represents; or rather, should represent, if it underwent the needed self-reform: it would be the locus of the critical "counter-vision" of the ills of society. But how to make the weight of this counter-vision effective on the momentous problems of the present?

The answer to this question was given by the British sociologist Victor Branford over 70 years ago, and, like the authentic vision of the university held by the founding fathers, it has gone unheeded. Branford presented the great seminal idea for healing the rupture between scientific knowledge and social life, for making the university the bridge between science and politics. He said that the first thing that had to be done was to make the social scientists themselves conscious of their heritage, the early promise of their science. This would be conceived as their *trust*, the trust of a tradition that stressed healing the ills of society with the best knowledge available. This trust we would bring to active consciousness, if we transformed the university as we have here outlined. The next step, and the crucial one, is for the social scientists and humanitarians to group themselves into *an active, oppositional political party;* to enter the arena of national life *with the scientific counter-vision,* and to try to win allegiance and following for it; to try to elect candidates to office who would themselves try to apply the scientific solutions to the social problems.

In this way, as we can recall from the early part of our discussion, we would try to recapture the scientific lobby on the legislative process, envisioned by Condorcet, Jefferson, Comte, Mill, Albion Small, Beattie-Crozier, H. G. Wells, Karl Mannheim, and many others. We said that this lobby failed because of active repression by dictatorial leaders; or because the political powers were simply unwilling to use the knowledge available in the national scientific institutes; or because science itself became bureaucratized, and lost its original consciousness of its historical trust and mission. The only way to reinstate this active lobby on the governing process may well be the best way: the way of a self-conscious oppositional party working with democratic forms.

We would then have not only a token 12-seat representation by the universities, such as the British parliament tolerated until 1948; we would have the chance of actually having a party in power, or at least a really strong public dissenting voice in opposition. We would have what some of the Marxists from East European countries recently called for: an oppositional party to counter the inevitable bureaucracy and dogmatism of the single-party Communist countries; but we would have such a party within an open democratic framework, based on the leading scientific thought, and working not against political oligarchies who might change laws at will, but against other political parties beholden to democratic processes.

The vision is simply breathtaking. The only ones who may not be pleased by it are the most radical extremists of left and right, those who cannot delay gratification one day, but must see their utopia tomorrow, or see it begun to be built on ashes. There is simply no way for them to have their wishes: the left cannot have its "social justice" all at once; the right cannot have its block "social order and dedication." In the real world there are no such things, and the extremists should begin to entertain the idea that *they too* may be surrounded by the tragic limitations of the human condition.

Yet, our scientific-political conception of the university must give the idealistic and activist youths of both left and right what they want: a chance to be at the center of things, to feel the growth of their powers in intellectual and political activity. This makes the university a locus of real events, real activities, the promise of real moral power; it relates the best of tradition to one's deepest identity, as the right wants; it makes youth the self-conscious representative of an unmistakable history, a trust of freedom and the best human aspiration.

In a word, it gives the university a mission, and youth an identity within that mission. As far as I can see, this is the best and only way out of the crisis of the university, and indeed of the crisis of our time.

## Prospect for Survival

I say "only way out" advisedly, because I fear that most readers will find the above pages unreal or utopian. Yet I believe that we must put all our energies into working for nothing less than the program contained herein. This is true, not only because it so well harmonizes with the basic promise of democracy, not only because the leading minds of each generation have kept alive the promise, but because our survival, and the quality of evolution itself, seem to depend on this course of action. The evolutionary crisis appears to be an ontological one. It is reflected in the tension between the unknown, erupting new energies that spring from human organisms, and the structures that contain and channel those energies. Bergson gave the sharpest conceptualization of this ontological crisis by viewing it as a struggle between the *élan vital* and the forms of social habit. In the second half of our century this struggle seems to be coming to a head, which is precisely the meaning of our crisis.

All over the world this struggle is erupting: masses of youths demonstrating for greater voice, greater recognition, new forms of things to meet new adaptations and to give birth to new energies. And against them moves the monolithic structure of social institutions, protected by the carapace of habit, and propelled by the anxieties and fears of the masses of men. The outcome seems already to be taking shape, too: either there will be daring and intelligent new inventions of ways of life, ways of absorbing the unknown energies of youth; or there will be massive solidification, repression, authoritarianism. We will either have a new human image, or we will have a face of man that will not be pretty to behold. If there is a balance struck between the two, it will be the balance of continued wars, struggles, social disorder, chaos; a time of waiting, a time of the distillation of the image of man in his own blood, and over his own body.

I draw this lurid picture because I think it is the correct one, but also because I want to make an appeal for real daring, real inventiveness, real openness in the present crisis. There is simply no room for the old solutions, for trimming, hedging, getting by, "business as usual." Least of all is there any room for tightening up, looking backward, making appeal to traditional virtues. Of all the antagonists in the present crisis, it seems to me that the extreme leftist revolutionaries and the extreme rightist traditionalists are the most unrealistic, the most sure to defeat a truly human alternative. Even the "intelligent" rightists, at least as represented by the writings in the *National Review*, are chilling in their insistence on Absolute Right and Absolute Truth. It is as though we were still in Biblical times, or in the Middle Ages; as though men like Diderot, Kant, Mill, James, Dewey, and countless others almost as great and representative of the main development of thought—it is almost as though they had never lived. There can be no reasonable forward momentum when large segments of people in power today ignore the best that mankind has written and thought. These rightists, for all the vested interests that they may represent, have no more at stake in a reasonable solution, and a hopeful future, than anyone else; yet they are surely blocking such a solution with their intransigence and simpleminded insistence on absolutes.

One reflects sadly, in this age of Freud, on the basic reasons that large segments of people cannot find their way to new adaptations to crisis. It is simply that they cannot relax, cannot open themselves to the world and the newness in it. We have learned that it is not minds that think, but minds in bodies; and the particular thoughts you have depend on what your body is: on its fears, anxieties, tightness, closedness, its terror of stepping into the new and unknown. I do not give this observation with the flair of psychoanalytic pronunciamento, in the hope of simply psychologizing an opposition unsavory to me. I give it as a sad and scientific reflection on man's condition.

When the organism finds itself in a particularly anxious situation in relation to an uncertain world, its mind works feverishly to allay and justify its anxiety. And so the rightists have fabricated a "domestic domino theory" to apply to the crisis of the university. If you give the students an inch, they claim, the students will take a mile, and soon they will want control of the whole university, and then of society itself; and all our hard-won and hard-earned world will topple over upon us. This is the reason the right gives for not negotiating with the black students, for example. But the domestic domino theory applied to the university makes about as much sense as the international domino theory applied to Vietnam. Yet, come to think of it, we *are* negotiating on Vietnam, after all. As of this writing, very few have tried to negotiate with the black students; very few have tested to see whether their demands are really "nonnegotiable" as they claim. I think they are tractable, as every realist must be. I think they claim the demands are not negotiable because they want to underscore their seriousness, and the fact that they will not allow the demands to be ignored, or whittled away in negotiations in which the blacks cannot bring to bear any real power. I think the more we refuse to negotiate with the students, on a level of equality, the more we bring to the forefront the extremist fringe among them, the more we push into the background the voices of reason and balance.

Do we imagine that the students will want to hire all the professors themselves? Make all the curriculum themselves? Judge all student admissions themselves? The things are impossible. They must depend on the accumulated knowledge that only the professors possess; they must conform to realistic criteria of selection, in order to have a workable university life. These things, if they do not already know them, they will soon learn. I think the most the students want today is *equality of representation* in all university matters that pertain to them: on hiring committees, on curriculum committees, etc. And this, after all, is a basic democratic idea, however hostile it may appear to the bureaucrats. If the bureaucrats cannot function with the basic democratic process, then let them go to some other country where they will be comfortable with totalitarian operations. (This is turning around the old taunt usually directed at radical reformers!)

Is equality of representation a threat to the university? Is equal voice an impossible thing to negotiate? Let us test the students; let us see if they want more than this, if they themselves are the cryptototalitarians who, hiding behind their agitation for a voice, really want more than a voice, really want total control. This is easy to test: let us just lay aside the domestic domino theory, approach them as human beings, and see how much they are willing to negotiate. If they are truly totalitarians, then there is time enough to club them on the head to protect ourselves. But let us make sure what we are protecting; let us give something before we protest that they want to take everything; let us draw a firm line according to democratic principles; let us draw a line at equal representation; let us draw a line based on openness to dialogue; let us draw a line based on empirical facts, not on fearful theories or absolute ideas.

Above all, let us be empiricists, for this alone is the test of the fitness to survive in evolution. This, too, finally, is the basic meaning of experimental democracy: that it reflects the need for a continual working adaptation to a new environment. As Dewey so well said, we can understand the anxiety of the conservative, because once we start thinking there is no telling where we will come out. That is why democracy is progressive, and not conservative, because it accepts to live with the anxiety of an unknown new world. It knows that absolute certainty is impossible, that one must change with the events, adapt to the context. Above all, experimental democracy means a full consciousness that people are transcended by the context of events. They can have no sure control over social outcomes. This is our tragedy, that we must work within our limitations, and cannot use even our best energies to bring about absolutely the kind of world we might want: we will always be transcended, surprised, disappointed, frustrated, in some ways. The dignity of democratic man is that he accepts to live with this uncertainty of outcomes.

A truly democratic alternative, a truly experimental approach to an anguished problem, is likely to please no one—neither right, nor left, nor center—because it caters to no one's guaranteed comfort; it calls everyone to the sense of tragedy, and to the dignity to accept the tragedy. The solution to the crisis of the university is just such an experiment in democracy. The question is whether the efforts we make can help us to survive, to move beyond the problem; not whether it settles the problem to anyone's satisfaction. Let us have the courage to begin to refashion a new university for a new political context, for an unknown future.

# 12

# Special Education: A Microcosm of Bureaucracy

### Ann D. Clark

In ATTEMPTING to examine bureaucratic control and systems in special education, one sees several relevant factors. Some of these factors are the following: (a) a system of categorization which has evolved from, and expanded upon, disability labels; (b) provision of important and efficient administrative procedures for evaluation, programming, placement, and resource allocation; (c) an important but relatively ineffectual concern for the perceived dangers in the rigidity of such a system; (d) mounting evidence of minority group discrimination and concomitant denial of service to children for whom the system was designed; (e) lack of demonstrated efficacy in a substantial number of programs as well as a seeming disregard for this evidence; (f) possible damage to large numbers of children through failure to provide appropriate educational experiences as well as damage to self and group concepts; (g) an immediate service and manpower crisis; and, finally, (h) the growth of a powerful supportive constituency among parents and professionals.

Each of these factors will be examined in turn in an attempt to delineate the relationship of freedom and bureaucracy in the public schools. Special education is the vehicle by which this examination is conducted because it provides a unique microcosm of the emergence of an educational subsystem with inherent and forceful bureaucratic controls that were present from its inception. This chapter will attempt to trace the development of these controls, and to show the problems within such a system and the potential inadvisability and impossibility of the continuation of the system in its present form.

Special education, for purposes of this paper, is defined as special classes and/or supplementary instruction services beyond the regular school program. This instruction is provided for children who deviate intellectually, physically, socially, and/or emotionally, so markedly as to be unable to profit significantly from regular programs. In the field these children are referred to as "exceptional."

Doll (1965), Hungerford (1964), Wallin (1958), and others have summarized the historical beginnings of special education, particularly in relation to the mentally retarded, which is similar to education for children with other handicapping conditions. Generally, the early field, prior to the 1900's, was characterized by individual efforts. J. M. G. Itard, noted for his work in attempting to teach language and social skills to a mentally retarded boy; Edouard Seguin, who formalized Itard's methods and was a significant force in the early institutional movement; G. Stanley Hall, in his investigation of the psychology of children and adolescents; and Montessori and W. E. Fernald, who extended and added to Seguin's efforts in educational practice, are only a few individuals active during this period. Widespread formalization of programs occurred in the first decade of the 20th century.

In the United States, Providence, Rhode Island, is credited with the establishment of the first special class for the mentally deficient in 1896, while St. Louis in 1914 was the first public school system to adopt definite eligibility standards for admission to ungraded classes and special schools (Wallin, 1958). After these first efforts began to extend legal sanctions to special programs, enrollment in special schools and classes increased by 83 percent in the years between 1948 and 1953 (Hill, 1956). By 1956, 48 states had special classes for at least one type of exceptional children (Lord, 1956).

## "Single Disability"

The development of these programs followed the concept of "single disability"; that is, a child was classified in terms of the most obvious handicap, such as blindness, deafness, or mental deficiency. Some states developed as many as eight distinct types (Lord, 1956). While this provided a valuable and efficient system for identifying and serving the handicapped individual, it also established a convenient system and justification for the allocation of funds and resources at the local, state, and federal level. This single disability concept clearly established what were later to become bureaucratic categories for the diagnosis, education, and institutionalization of exceptional children.

Because there was a relative consensus centering around the concept of classification of children in terms of overt handicaps, a built-in screening system was provided. For example, children who were examined for visual impairments were, in turn, classified by the results; the blind child was then tracked or placed in classes for the visually impaired. Such classification provides several positive functions and is relatively efficient when used to identify physical or severe mental handicaps. However, when classification was extended to include less clear-cut disabilities, often related to sociocultural background, it no longer functioned adequately, but instead relied on subjective value judgments which prepared the way for a subtle kind of segregation. Further, the application of legal definitions and sanctions to established practices continued to solidify these categorizations.

Legal and educational definitions of disabilities and types of children eligible for special classes specifically excluded children with other disabilities, such as in the limitation of a class for the physically handicapped to children of ". . . sound minds" (Hill, 1956). The single disability approach has been further perpetuated through the categorical aid system used in federal funding programs and in most state systems. Money is allocated to specific disability programs and, especially in the case of state funding programs, for the numbers of children who can be identified in each disability area. The category system provided an efficient procedure for determination of resource allocation.

In perspective, then, the recognition of problems of handicapping conditions resulted in individual scientists and educators taking actions to improve the situation of exceptional children and adults. This very recognition led to the classification of such persons in terms of a foremost single problem, with a legally sanctioned bureaucratic organization supporting this concept.

Yet as the barriers of specificity were being erected, some professionals were arguing for more flexibility in placement, testing, and mobility between regular and special tracks. Because IQ testing was the basis for much of the classification system, this argument was supported by the reaction against the concept of intelligence as a fixed quantum. Even Alfred Binet, the so-called father of intelligence testing, disputed this concept of intelligence and emphasized the importance of instruction in improving a child's mind (Hunt, 1961). In addition, intelligence tests themselves were criticized as being culturally biased, unreliable, limited in scope and type, and not predictive of future success.[1] Unfortunately, the battle lines of the debate were overly simplistic, and arguments were generally limited to advocating or annihilating special education (Sullivan, 1964; Hunt, 1957; Newland, 1957; Magnifico, 1958; Mullen and Itken, 1961).

However, this controversy seemed merely a smoke screen, in that most special educators recognized the value of special classes for many children, but knew that many children were and are misidentified as exceptional on the basis of sociocultural experience and intelligence testing. Based on statistics alone, Hurley (1969) states that New Jersey schools, especially in the heavily urbanized areas, contain up to a 50 percent ratio of children who could be considered mentally retarded. The first racial analysis of California's 65,000 mentally retarded schoolchildren found that children with Spanish surnames constitute 15.22 percent of the school population but represent 28.34 percent of the enrollment in classes for the educable mentally retarded. Black children comprise 8.85 percent of the total public school enrollment in California but 25.5 percent of the enrollment in special classes for the educable mentally retarded (Leary, 1970). It is ironic that the Civil Rights Act of 1964, which provided protection against discrimination by race, also may have prevented the collection of data on minority group children in special education. While states have begun, as in the case of California, to do this, no nationwide data on this point are currently available (Heller, 1970). One estimate by a leader in special education places the figure for minority group and low status children enrolled in classes for the retarded at between 60 and 80 percent of the total (Dunn, 1968).

Thus, social and legal definitions led to misplacement of children within special tracks. Programs themselves, however, seemed to provide evidence of further inequities. Dunn (1968) summarized such inequities when he questioned the use of special classes with the educable mentally retarded, or children whose measured intelligence falls within the range of 50-85. Citing evidence from several

[1] Several critical reviews of these biases have been written. For a more complete consideration, the reader is referred to: J. McVicker Hunt. *Intelligence and Experience.* New York: The Ronald Press Company, 1961; Allison Davis and Kenneth Eells. "Davis-Eells Test of General Intelligence or Problem-Solving Ability." New York, 1958; and Richard L. Masland, Seymour S. Sarason, and Thomas Gladwin. *Mental Subnormality.* New York: Basic Books, Inc., Publishers, 1959.

sources (Kirk, 1964; Hoelke, 1966; Smith and Kennedy, 1967; Johnson, 1962; Rubin, Senison, and Betwee, 1966), Dunn suggests that these children, as well as the emotionally handicapped, do as well in regular classes as in special.

## The Case of Diana

Not only are the real educational needs distorted, but the labeling which is inherent in special placement has been found to be destructive to individuals' feelings about themselves (Meyerowitz, 1965, 1967; Goffman, 1963). To force labels on children in direct contradiction to the best judgment of researchers, teachers, and educational psychologists regarding limitations of educational assessment is indeed tragic. Clearly, the questioning of such tracking and special class placement is appropriate, and perhaps required by law as indicated in the J. Skelley Wright decision concerning tracking as a violation of the Fifth Amendment to the Constitution. In another case, *Diana et al.* versus *State Board of Education,* California, it was established that Mexican American children may have been misplaced in classes for the mentally retarded, and must be reexamined with individual intelligence tests given both in English and "... in the primary language used in [their] home."

In juxtaposition to the failures and limitations in the special education picture is the record of success which it has enjoyed. In spite of the bureaucracy with which it is encumbered, the area of special education functions. The U.S. Office of Education reports that special education served thousands of children in the past year, while reports of the positive effects of special education can be found in journals, from parents, teachers, and students themselves. Is it contradictory, therefore, to condemn the bureaucracy which has shown itself to be so effective? Yet it is perhaps this effectiveness which has caused the bureaucracy to become its own victim. That is, the efficiency with which children can be categorized and treated, with which funds can be allocated, is exactly what allows the inequities to exist. The case of *Diana* (Leary, 1970) perhaps best exemplifies how the very efficiency of the system has served to work against the purposes for which it was intended.

Diana, an eight-year-old Spanish American child, was tested at her school with the Stanford-Binet Intelligence Test, given in English. Her score was 30, well within the limits of intelligence cutoffs established for the placement of children in special education classes for the educable mentally retarded. Upon retesting in Spanish, Diana scored 49 points higher, well above the cutoff score used to remove her from the regular class originally. Diana was one of eight other children in this situation. What of the total population of 65,000 mentally retarded schoolchildren in the state of California? What are some similar situations and to what extent do they occur across the country?

The bureaucratic manner in which children are categorized, tested, and placed in special education seems more than apparent. What may be further apparent is that it is the bureaucracy which is being served, rather than the children for whom the system was intended. The possible misplacement of thousands of California children in special classes, the discrimination against minority and racial groups on the basis of language and test biases, the recognition of the lack of efficacy and service by those persons who administer programs and lead in the field provide some substantiation. At issue, then, is whether truly handicapped children will receive the appropriate special education services, or whether children who should not be defined as handicapped and do not need these services will continue to occupy the available places.

If the latter continues, then the obvious concomitant leaves handicapped children inappropriately placed in regular classes and perhaps excluded from school. That this situation exists and will continue to exist is evident in the data regarding manpower crises.

The number of children needing or receiving special services is almost impossible to substantiate. Elliott (1960) suggested that special education would be required to serve 5 million to 6 million children and youth, and was short at least 125,000 teachers and other personnel in 1959. The Western Interstate Commission for Higher Education estimated that less than half of its exceptional children were being provided for through public day and residential schools, and identified a concurrent need for one-third more special teachers (Sprague and Dunn, 1961). The study further demonstrated the impossibility of meeting the demands under the current employment practices.

It is interesting that the annual demand for teachers of the educable mentally retarded was almost as large as the demand for all other specialists combined. Yet this is the area in which the least efficacy has been presented and at which the most criticism has been aimed. Obviously, the bureaucratic response has not been appropriate to the evidence presented: it has ignored the number of reputable studies that indicate that the educable mentally retarded or emotionally handicapped child does as well in regular as in special classes. Perhaps the bureaucratic response is a self-serving administrative convenience that overlooks the needs of schoolchildren.

## Programs and Personnel

Too late, says Garrison, have we become aware of the school's narrowing concept of normalcy. The concept of "average" has replaced the view of "normal." That is, many behaviors falling well within acceptable ranges of normal behavior have been singled out as deviant from the "average" and therefore abnormal, or requiring special teachers, therapists, and/or a host of special services. By failing to recognize the broadness of the range of normal behavior, we create a population which is impossible to serve (in sheer numbers alone), and we remove from the "regular" teachers and the school any responsibility for children who are "abnormal."

The excuse that special programs and specially trained personnel are not available can become a rationalization for not serving children. It is widely recognized that special education has been a common "dumping ground" for "problem" children; it can now be seen that a significant proportion of the public school population which general education chooses not to serve is being misplaced in special education categories. The bureaucracy will continue to classify, but it will be increasingly unable to cover up the fact that *general* education, not special education, should be serving minority children. The bureaucracy will be unable to obscure the fact that the schoolroom deficiencies of minority group children result from the social rather than the educational system. The classification system used by the bureaucracy makes it appear that special education is needed when, in fact, it may not be. In doing so, the system has disregarded much of what special education research has reported to date.

In examining any bureaucratic system, one must also examine the supporters of it. In the past the plight of the exceptional individual was considered only when it was of scientific or humanitarian interest to do so, as exemplified in the work of Itard and Seguin respectively. As problems reached the attention of the public, officials and administrators, in contrast to the individual efforts of earlier years, were called upon to develop programs and take action, and the largest constituency for support was parents. That parents have provided the impetus and support for such action in special education has long been recognized. The upsurge of special education programs in 1951 is due, says Wallin (1958), to the ". . . embattled fight of the entrenched parent groups." In a nationwide survey of classes in learning disabilities, over half the states having such programs named parental pressure as being the basic impetus for program implementation (Richards and Clark, 1968). Only one program listed the needs of the child as the basic impetus.

The importance of parents could be further documented, but it is most interesting to note that in a similar survey with responses from 48 states (Frank, 1969), concerned with programs in parent counseling, only ten state directors of special education indicated that their states provided what they considered as adequate programs of parent counseling. It is parents who have played a major role in the formation of school programs in special education. Parents and their children are the most directly affected by these programs, and yet evidence is mounting that both the parents and children seem to be receiving less than adequate service, and in some cases, disservice, as exemplified in the case of *Diana*.

Perhaps the reason that needs of parents are not adequately met lies in the role of parents within the bureaucratic system. Parents have been considered as a unified constituency, but a closer examination renders such a conclusion dubious. In fact, parents can be separated into two groups—those who are satisfied with special education and those who are dissatisfied. The satisfied are parents whose children are receiving adequate service, especially in disabilities with overt characteristics such as blindness or orthopedic disabilities; such parents, understandably, actively support the system of special education. Dissatisfied parents are exemplified by the case of *Diana*. In other words, minority group parents are upset because their children are labeled in a derogatory and determining manner. Their complaint is against the subjective bureaucratic confusion of social and educational disability.

## Need for Change

Historically, attempts to change the behavior of deviant groups and individuals have not been uncommon or unacceptable. The development of group norms and standards is well documented in a variety of contexts. In relating these attempts to handicapped or exceptional individuals, we have provided a confused picture of humanitarian and scientific interest, and a tenuous balance between true interest in individual welfare and administrative expediency. Under the best of systems seeking to provide help for deviant groups, some bureaucracy develops. The positive benefits of this cannot be overlooked. The fact that the system has continued to function well in providing service, in spite of all the inappropriate demands placed upon it, is important to recognize.

The following conditions strongly indicate that changes must be considered and acted upon immediately: (a) there is evidence that funding and support have become dependent upon the bureaucracy itself and not the needs of the individuals to be served; (b) special education may now be used for racial and minority group segregation; (c) certain types of programs are not efficacious and in some cases are detrimental; and (d) a portion of the constituency defined as supporting the system is actually in serious opposition to it. Special educators have for several years outlined plans for change (Dunn, 1968). Certainly the self-serving trends indicated even in this paper can no longer be tolerated. However, the difficulties in attempting to modify or change the direction of such movements must not be underestimated.

The plans and modifications which have been presented may not have been actually implemented because of the failure of initiators to recognize the bureaucratic structure which supports existing systems. It would seem that an understanding of the system is critical before it can be confronted. To wait for courts, parents, and manpower shortages to revise or possibly eliminate the system is irresponsible and unnecessary. In attempting to institute change, certain basic considerations should be given to the modification and alteration of institutional structure rather than to single parts. Such considerations include the following:

1. Whom is the system attempting to serve? If indeed it is only the children requiring special education, then others must be removed from that realm, most obviously the children whose sociocultural background has caused them to be defined as "deviant."

2. Who are the decision makers in the existing system, and what is its constituency? If indeed the constituency is defined as parents and professionals, then the resistance to change should not be severe, according to previous actions taken by these groups for change. One must therefore delve deeper into the bureaucratic system for consideration of the vested and self-serving interests which may have become institutionalized and which may have maintained the parents and professionals as constituency rather than as decision makers.

3. The role of institutions, especially the university with its

training functions and governmental agents with their funding policies, must be carefully evaluated. Recognition of the bureaucratic systems-within-systems should be carefully analyzed before strategies for change can be implemented.

4. Finally, a reconsideration of the scientific and empirical evidence relating to the field of special education must be undertaken. When evidence is persuasive, findings must be accepted and acted upon within the total system. To do less places the responsible individual or profession in a posture of hypocrisy that is incompatible with the humanitarian concerns of special education. Perhaps Dunn (1968) has best summarized this point as follows:

In my best judgment, our honor, integrity, and honesty should no longer be subverted and rationalized by what we hope and may believe we are doing for these children—hopes and beliefs which have little basis in reality.

## References

Jack I. Bardon and Stanley I. Alprin. "An Approach to the Educational Classification of Mentally Retarded Children." *Exceptional Children* 27 (5): 235-38; January 1961.

Eugene E. Doll. "Trends and Problems in the Education of the Mentally Retarded: 1800-1940." *Historical Review of Mental Retardation*. Symposium, 1965.

Lloyd M. Dunn. "Special Education for the Mildly Retarded—Is Much of It Justifiable?" *Exceptional Children* 35 (1): 5-22; September 1968.

Carl Elliott. "New Horizons for Special Education." *Exceptional Children* 26 (8): 433-35; April 1960.

Rochelle Reiser Frank. "An Evaluation of Parent Education for Parents of Children with Neurologic Dysfunction." Unpublished master's thesis, University of Wisconsin, May 1969.

Ivan K. Garrison. "A Broader Concept of Normalcy." *Journal of Education*, March 1954.

Erving Goffman. *Stigma: Notes on the Management of Spoiled Identity*. Englewood Cliffs, New Jersey: Prentice-Hall, Inc., 1963.

Herbert Goldstein. "Mentally Retarded Children in Special Programs." *Journal of Education* 147 (1): 95-100; October 1964.

J. P. Guilford. *The Nature of Human Intelligence*. New York: McGraw-Hill Book Company, 1967.

Harold W. Heller. U.S. Office of Education, Bureau of Education for the Handicapped. Personal Communication, September 1970.

Arthur S. Hill. "A Critical Glance at Special Education." *Exceptional Children* 22 (8): 315-17, 344; May 1956.

G. M. Hoelke. *Effectiveness of Special Class Placement for Educable Mentally Retarded Children.* Lincoln: University of Nebraska, 1966.

Richard H. Hungerford. "The Schooling of the Mentally Retarded— A History and Philosophy of Occupational Education." *Journal of Education* 147 (1): 5-16; October 1964.

J. McVicker Hunt. *Intelligence and Experience.* New York: The Ronald Press Company, 1961.

J. T. Hunt. "Special Education: Segregation." *Education* 77 (8): 475-79; April 1957.

Rodger L. Hurley. *Poverty and Mental Retardation—A Causal Relationship.* New York: Random House, Inc., 1969.

G. Orville Johnson. "Special Education for the Mentally Handicapped— A Paradox." *Exceptional Children* 29 (2): 62-66; October 1962.

S. A. Kirk. "Research in Education." In: H. A. Stevens and R. Heber, editors. *Mental Retardation.* Chicago: University of Chicago Press, 1964.

S. A. Kirk. *The Diagnosis and Remediation of Psycholinguistic Disabilities.* Urbana: University of Illinois Press, 1966.

Mary Ellen Leary. "Children Who Are Tested in an Alien Language: Mentally Retarded?" *The New Republic* 162 (2892): 17-18; May 30, 1970.

F. E. Lord. "A Realistic Look at Special Classes." *Exceptional Children* 22 (8): 321-25, 342; May 1956.

Bertha M. Luckey. "The Contributions of Psychology to the Problems of Mental Retardation with Some Implications for the Future." *Historical Review of Mental Retardation.* Symposium, 1965.

L. X. Magnifico. "The Retarded Need Special Classes." *School Board Journal,* August 1958. p. 33.

J. H. Meyerowitz. "Family Background of Educable Mentally Retarded Children." In: H. Goldstein, J. W. Moss, and L. J. Jordan. *The Efficacy of Special Education Training in the Development of Mentally Retarded Children.* Urbana: University of Illinois Institute for Research on Exceptional Children, 1965. pp. 152-82.

J. H. Meyerowitz. "Peer Groups and Special Classes." *Mental Retardation* 5: 23-26; 1967.

Frances A. Mullen and William Itken. "The Value of Special Classes for the Mentally Handicapped." *Education Digest* 27 (2): 46-49; October 1961.

T. Ernest Newland. "Why Special Education?" *Education* 77 (8): 455-59; April 1957.

Judge Robert E. Peckham. *Diana et al. Plaintiffs* v. *State Board of Education.* C-7037 RFT Stipulation and Order, U.S. District Court, Northern District of California (Filed February 5, 1970).

Charlotte J. Richards and Ann D. Clark. "Learning Disabilities—A Nationwide Survey of Existing Public School Programs." *Journal of Special Education* 2 (2); Winter 1968.

E. Z. Rubin, C. B. Senison, and M. C. Betwee. *Emotionally Handicapped Children in the Elementary School.* Detroit: Wayne State University Press, 1966.

H. W. Smith and W. A. Kennedy. "Effects of Three Educational Programs on Mentally Retarded Children." *Perceptual and Motor Skills* 24: 174; 1967.

Hall Sprague and Lloyd Dunn. "Special Education for the West." *Exceptional Children* 27 (8): 415-21; April 1961.

Helen B. Sullivan. "Mentally Retarded Children in Regular Programs." *Journal of Education* 147 (1): 101-104; October 1964.

T. G. Thurstone. *Learning To Think Series.* Chicago: Science Research Associates, 1948.

J. E. Wallace Wallin. "To Set the Historical Record Straight." *Exceptional Children* 25 (4): 175-76; December 1958.

Judge J. S. Wright. *Hobson v. Hansen: U.S. Court of Appeals Decision on the District of Columbia's Track System.* Civil Action No. 82-66. Washington, D.C.: U.S. Court of Appeals, 1967.

# Part Three

## *Perspectives: A Look to the Future*

THE final section of this work includes three chapters and my own summary of the Yearbook. These perspectives on the future are not as reassuring as one might hope, for indeed the monsters of bureaucracy and standardization are upon us—not something we can simply ignore or wish away.

Two of the chapters deal with the federal government and its role in education, for it is in this area of concern that many feel the essential challenge of the next ten years will be located. Thomas A. Billings, a former director of a federal program, Upward Bound, states a succinct case for a federal system of schools. Reviewing the major arguments for the adoption of such a system, Billings feels that sheer equity demands a federalized system of schools and that those who oppose such a move are persons who wish to maintain the status quo and status privileges.

J. Myron Atkin, Dean of the College of Education at the University of Illinois, offers a disquieting analysis of the impact of federal intervention up to this time. His major criticisms center on the notion of programistic aid as opposed to general aid. He develops the link between the world of the behavioral scientist and the input-output specialist from government and industry, and indicates its general *inapplicability* to the field of schooling. Clearly he views the increased federal support in the fifties and sixties as "a mixed blessing." Imposed guidelines, the "fickle quality of funding," and the impossibility of long-range planning are but some of the issues Atkin observes. He concludes with a review of a national model of change—that of Great Britain. He indicates that "dramatic local initiatives may not be taken until a new breed of local educational leaders begins to emerge, leaders that command attention to their independent ideas because of the quality of their thought and the forcefulness of their advocacy."

In his chapter, James B. Macdonald takes the reader on an ideological journey which details some of the contradictory forces in schools and society. The contradictions between ideal and reality take several forms: the professed ideal of individual interaction vs. the reality of groupings and mass instruction; the ideal of creative endeavor vs. the reality of stultifying procedures; and the ideal of an informed rational citizenry vs. the reality of a lack of problem solving in schools. The list goes on and on.

Macdonald then presents his reader with the "four faces of schooling" and indicates the structural and philosophical problems in making up these faces. Macdonald is not at all optimistic for the future. He sees a "widening gulf between our democratic ideals and individual human fulfillment," and the schools as essentially subservient to a monolithic technological system.

I have taken the liberty to review many of the persistent bureaucratizing elements in the society, to indicate the positive and negative features of schooling patterns, and finally to suggest possible courses open to educators.

The grip of a large national bureaucratic state is upon us and the task for educators is not always clear. What is imperative is a realization of the problem before understanding and action can take place. These chapters have attempted to do just that, and it is with a sense of hope that they are presented to ASCD and to the publics of this nation.—V. F. H.

# 13

# The School as a Double Agent

## James B. Macdonald

THE reality of American education reminds old-timers of a radio program starring "The Shadow," who, listeners were reminded each week, was "in reality Lamont Cranston." Or, less charitably and from a more radical point of view, perhaps "Mata Hari" would do. In either case, American schools tend to be two-faced and ridden with unspoken assumptions, more often than not determining operational procedures, which are in conflict with the rhetoric and idealism of American school values.

The conflict will be no surprise to any interested observer of American culture. It has counterparts in other areas. Anthropologists have noted for many years that we display a fairly extensive set of important cultural conflicts. For example, we treat adolescents as adults for consumer purposes, but delay their entrance into the productive system. What may come as a shock to some is the pervasive and paralyzing extent of cultural conflict in the schools.

It is also a charitable gesture to call the school a "double" agent, for it is clear by now that "quadruple agent" would be more accurate. We shall return later to this assertion.

The American school system has been predicated upon the development of the democratic ideal. Realization of this ideal entailed an education dedicated to rational processes of problem solving with the concomitant ethical principles. It also entails honoring attitudes and values which facilitate the fulfillment of justice, equality, and liberty for all. Central to this doctrine is faith in the dignity and integrity of each human being and the resultant prizing of the necessary actions which facilitate the development of individual uniqueness and potential. The schools should serve the youth of our society by helping them become better democratic citizens and better individuals. According to this doctrine there is no separation of the individual and society, for society's wants demand the development of individuals committed to and capable of functioning as members of a society which in turn creates the very conditions which best allow individuals to flourish. Thus, the acts of facilitating the development of individual human potential and the functional participation of persons in democratic social processes are mutually supportive.

One would be hard pressed to find evidence that the above description is in fact an accurate portrayal of goals which determine the realities of schooling. But if this seems a bit harsh let us say that *no one* who looks at schooling with a critical eye would allege that the democratic ideal and individual development are the primary determiners of programs and practices in any but a very small minority of cases.

Evidence for this conclusion is relatively easy to come by. A recent study of primary school classrooms across the land published by Goodlad, Klein, and associates (5), for example, reports very little evidence of individualization of instruction in classrooms; this in spite of 70 years of child development research, the progressive education movement, the content and orientation of most teacher education programs, and the greatly increased activity and materials production over the past 15 years to develop increasing individualization in programs at the primary school level.

Jules Henry's (8) case studies of high schools are further documentation of the failure of schools to live up to the above general ideal, as is Edgar Friedenberg's (2) work. The more limited but equally disconcerting study of Jackson and Getzels (9) on the response of the school to creative children is another case in point.

And the list goes on, to a point where one begins to wonder even where our ideals came from or if they have any influence on American social behavior at all.

The fact of the matter is that schools have not produced an informed citizenry, and there is very little evidence that rational processes of problem solving are ever learned and/or practiced by students in schools, or that they are utilized in society. Concomitantly the aura of justice, equality, and liberty which hangs over the schools (and society) is reflective of the lack of value placed in these ideals. Certainly, for example, liberty and lack of choice or freedom, justice and lack of equal opportunity, and equality and the myriad categorizing procedures in schools are not resolvable in terms of ideals.

The vast majority of schools, teachers, and other concerned persons do not trust students. The basic assumption of the schools' orientation to students is that students will do the wrong thing (what you do not want them to do) unless you make them do the right thing. If this were not so, most school policies and classroom disciplinary procedures would not be justified. Surely, faith in the worth, dignity, and integrity of individuals is not in evidence.

Institutional facilitation of the individual's uniqueness and potential is easily refuted when we examine curricula and teaching practices. By and large, curricula are standard, vary little from locale to locale, and are monitored by virtually identical quality control test devices. Further, teaching methods are predominantly group procedures, characterized by discussion procedures or assignments which discourage individuality and expect the same "right" answers of all students.

The interpersonal conditions of living in schools are perhaps the final blow to our ideal of schooling. Though there is some evidence that most teachers are well-meaning and generally have positive predispositions toward the young, an authoritarian administrative structure is infused throughout. Opportunities to learn about democracy and to build the necessary understanding of the democratic process through the living of a democratic life are almost totally absent.

To paraphrase Friedenberg (3), there is no difficulty in understanding why, under these conditions, a federal judge who, when he was in school, had needed a hall pass to go to the toilet until he was 17 would not hesitate to refuse the issuance of a passport to an American citizen who was a member of the Communist Party.

There are at least two directions in which one might go to explain the gap between ideals and realities. One might assert, as many social reformers have, that American society is characterized by the same general conflict between ideals and administrative "necessities" and that the school merely reflects the general culture. This is a strong and difficult argument to refute. Still, the school is a rather special sort of institution, and there is much that could be done within the schools themselves to bridge the gap if we would attend to contradictions built into the structure of schooling. In this spirit of optimism let us turn to the contradictions which may be conceptualized and, hopefully, improved.

## Major Contradictions: The Four Faces of Schooling

The "quadruple agent" referred to earlier may be described as four faces or orientations which only sometimes act in concert when program and practice decisions are made. We may describe them as conflicting ideas of the role of the school, although in many instances the "role" must be inferred from observation.

The first role has already been described under the guise of the "democratic ideal." The double agent aspect of schooling comes in a schizophrenic sort of activity which might be called the "four faces of schooling." The "other" aspect or agency has three personalities which we may call: (a) school as the preparation of new teachers (or discipline specialists); (b) school as preparation for the occupational structure; and (c) school as a place of work with its attention focused on status, role, and maintaining the system.

### School as Preparation for School

It is one of the well recognized truths about schooling that success in school is most closely related as a predictor variable to further success in school. No other prediction may be made with anywhere near the certainty of this. Thus, Taylor (13) was able to show that even creative research scientists, a breed of highly trained academics, do not attribute much of their success on the job (out of school) to those variables (intellectual attributes) that are high predictors of school achievement. It seems highly reasonable that we may explain many practical decisions most easily if we assume that one face of schooling represents it as an agent for the parent disciplines that provide the major substance of the traditional curriculum.

How else, for example, do we explain instruction in the division of fractions found in many sixth grade mathematics books? How else can one explain the placement of much material at grade levels in terms of a logical sequence of difficulty? How else does one readily explain the almost fanatic urge on the part of most teachers to cover the curriculum in order that students will be "ready" for the next step? Surely, these and many other behaviors and activities that can be observed are remotely connected to development of human potential, preparation for occupation (other than academician), and even bureaucratic needs of the school system. It is foolish to suggest that these practices cannot be rationalized in these terms, but the simple idea that often school practices and programs are justified in and of themselves as good because they lead to further success in schooling is a much more reasonable explanation.

We live in an era when one might argue that a highly technological society is developing a form of tyranny best called the tyranny of knowledge. It may be true that no knowledge is disastrous and that "a little knowledge is a dangerous thing," but for a culture to be dominated by knowledge is a form of tyranny. We live in such a dictatorship today. We are not speaking of knowledge in its broad anthropological meaning, as culture. Surely, all cultures through their customs and mores restrict individual choices and provide constraints upon behavior. But when a culture enshrines specialized knowledge as its fundamental "good," then tyranny as it is meant here sets in. Knowledge of this sort may free "man" from physical limitations, but it enslaves "men" in the process. We, in other words, are being subjugated by the very process which is intended to free us.

This tyranny may be seen in a number of ways in schools; priorities of the standard curriculum are hard to explain without it. Areas such as the arts and humanities are slighted because they do not represent "hard knowledge," the real stuff of the curriculum. Concepts of prerequisites and other forms of sequencing are imposed and shape experiences for the sake of knowledge. The school curriculum over the years looks like a series of separately strung beads with no attempt to relate them to each other, and the consequent experience of students is of several varied and disconnected experiences which are often forgotten shortly after they are encountered.

The educational technician is partner to this tyranny, as illustrated by the behavioral objectives movement. We often justify the procedures of schooling in terms of the knowledge (or skill) ends in the process. No one is quite clear where all this knowledge will lead to in the end; but if we sequence the whole curriculum on this basis we can be sure that it will lead to the next step, and this appears to be a satisfactory outcome for many. Thus, the technician often simply accepts the knowledge goals of experts and proceeds to develop a set of procedures and conditions which will lead to the efficient achievement of these goals. The greater the realization of their intentions, the more securely tightened is the screw which holds the life of the young to the tyranny of knowledge.

## School as Preparation for Occupation

In some ways the heading of this section is somewhat misleading, for only a small part of this face of schooling is truly related to what is known as vocational education in its curricular sense. On the other hand, many school practices and programs reflect the essential commitment to the idea that a school is a degree factory, a credential provider, or a certifier that it is necessary for people to experience before they enter into the real occupational world.

It does not seem to matter whether or not there is any direct connection between credentials and later functioning, inasmuch as the social uses of schooling are apparently convenient ways of making occupational hiring decisions which provide an access to social mobility and affluence for members of our society. Paul Goodman (7), for example, has quoted work by Ivar Berg of Columbia which Goodman contends shows that dropouts do as well as high school graduates in less pretentious jobs in our society.

Some critics have also noted that war is one of our major occupations. Thus, the schools are directly serving the military-industrial complex in our social system. A careful examination of this allegation suggests that it is overly simple, yet how can many of our reporting, grading, and testing practices, our authoritarian relationships, and our prizing of docility, punctuality, and attendance be more readily explained?

Our evaluation procedures *in toto* tell us a great deal about this. It is not so much the processes themselves, though many objections may be made to these, but the usage of results which provides the important clues. The social consequences of testing are rarely given a careful examination. Tests have become so useful that the question of whether or not they should be administered at all has been replaced by "what would you use instead?"

Teachers may often claim that test results help provide them with evidence which helps them to redesign their methodology and goals to facilitate learning. Educational psychologists will be quick to note that "feedback" is essential to reinforcement. Yet neither position justifies the social uses of testing, for the use society makes of grades and test scores transcends the learning situation. No student's slate is ever wiped clean, there is no forgiveness in schooling. Instead students are both taught their abilities by continuous evaluation and allotted social slots on the basis of their cumulative performance. This provides a useful way for society to deal with the young as they emerge into the work force, for we can be assured that their predictive success (in terms of tests) has been set (psychologically and socially) as early as fourth or fifth grade.[1]

It is interesting to note further that the education industry is now one of the largest in the country. Under these circumstances, it is of considerable importance to keep as many people in school for as long as possible. This may be an accidental development, but the nature of our economic arrangements would certainly lead to a societal reinforcement of the need for schooling as the collection of more and more advanced credentials. Thus, the social use of schooling becomes an integral part of the structure of our society. The school as a consumer of goods is an important part of this economic complex, and the demands of the economy are increasingly becoming part of the role of the school as a double agent.

## School as a Place of Work: The Face of Self-Serving Bureaucracy

Every school, school system, or, for that matter, every classroom is a place of work. People spend significant portions of their lives as members of a work force which by necessity has some form of structural relatedness. An organizational structure becomes necessary to coordinate the different functions and roles that inevitably arise. When the concerns for maintaining the organization become more important than the stated goals of student learning and development, a form of self-serving bureaucracy results.[2] More often than not, the policies and practices of schools are more reasonably explained by this phenomenon than as rational decisions and arrangements for facilitating their stated goals.

Maintaining a complex organization is surely not an easy task, although decentralizing large school systems might improve the situation. Yet one would be hard pressed to argue that many school policies, schedules, organizational formats, communication networks, and status-role relationships are the only way a school (or system) can be maintained. There is instead such a large degree of blatant hypocrisy involved in the justification of dress codes, hall passes, schedules, and teacher and student freedom of choice and movement that we must look elsewhere for explanations. Perhaps the simple

---

[1] See: Benjamin S. Bloom. *Stability and Change in Human Characteristics.* New York: John Wiley & Sons, Inc., 1964.

[2] See, for example: Amitai Etzioni. *Modern Organizations.* Englewood Cliffs, New Jersey: Prentice-Hall, Inc., 1964. This volume gives a generalized statement as to how bureaucracies become more concerned about their own incumbents than about the clients they serve.

idea of inertia is a better explanation. Whatever the primary causes are, they are not justifiable in terms of the democratic ideal and individual development.

An enlightening and frightening view of the epitome of this process in American society has been provided by Goffman (4) in regard to total institutions such as prisons and mental institutions. His description of the privilege system, for example, found in total institutions has a familiar ring to observers of schools.

According to Goffman, there are three basic elements in the privilege system: (a) "House rules" or a formal set of prescriptions and proscriptions that sets the requirements of inmate conduct; (b) a small number of clearly defined rewards or privileges held out in exchange for obedience; and (c) punishments designed for occurrences of rule violations. Schools, in other words, operate in many ways like total institutions, and certainly to greater degrees than other social institutions in our society.

Perhaps the most crushing blow has been a more recent realization, as dramatically highlighted by the New York City teachers strike in the Brownsville case,[3] that teachers are not only potential classroom bureaucrats, but that teachers organizations are in a major struggle for control of the total bureaucracy. The attempts to control on the part of teachers are not what is at issue here. The dawning realization that does hurt is that we are seeing the rise of another essentially self-serving force whose major concerns and efforts have up to this date had little to do with bringing about the realization of the American ideals for education. We appear to be witnessing a struggle between those who would run the system for their own benefit. It is, in other words, the conditions of work that motivate most of the activity and concern.

Again we must hasten to add that the need to be concerned about conditions of work is not being criticized, but that the phenomena of how all this is taking place appear to show that teachers are tuned into the heart of the question—the control of the bureaucracy. It is the fact that this is the jugular vein that is cause for alarm. The classroom as a place of work comes in for its own share of bureaucratic self-serving. The nature of the composition of teaching staffs and the behavior of teachers in classrooms cannot easily be explained without granting their duplicity and perhaps open-armed welcoming of the self-serving ethic.

[3] See, for example: Martin Mayer. *Teacher's Strike: New York*. New York: Harper & Row, Publishers, Inc., 1968.

According to Charters (1), the career patterns of female teachers can be described rather accurately as "in and out," whereas the male patterns are more nearly "up or out." In either case the classroom teacher today appears to have primary personal allegiances to something which his occupation gives him/her that is not inherent in the activity of teaching itself. As a career, elementary or secondary teaching is not highly prized by the education profession when compared to the role of supervisor, administrator, or college professor. Further, the persons who choose teaching as a career are primarily individuals who are upwardly mobile in the class structure (upper-lower to middle), or persons opting for teaching in order to preserve a middle class status while unable or unsure enough to pursue this through other avenues.

As a consequence, teachers tend to be security oriented and essentially conservative in many of their social attitudes. They represent, as someone remarked, a sort of "clerk" mentality in our culture, and as such fit beautifully into a bureaucratic setting.

The schools are full of a "they won't let me" syndrome on the part of teachers, and the risks that are taken for the sake of ideals are at a premium. It is difficult to see how teachers who acquiesce to the authoritarian and self-serving milieu of the system could provide conditions other than those same ones in their own classrooms. In fact, this is what one often finds.

Teachers teach from textbooks, manuals, and, if possible, commercial lesson plans. Teachers teach groups of children because it is easier to do so, and have often acquiesced to "homogeneous" grouping in schools primarily because they feel it is easier to teach this way. Teachers often avoid controversial issues, deny the erotic aspects of the nature of human beings, and avoid the discussion of anything which is not planned ahead of time. Many teachers are consumed by the fear that they will lose control, that some situation will present itself in which they must operate as a responsive human being rather than a status symbol of authority. Under these sorts of circumstances, it pays to get things "organized" and to develop managerial techniques whose primary goal is the maintenance of control.

## The Double Agent Revisited

In the end, the various faces of schooling lead to the fundamental schism in our society—the widening gulf between our democratic ideals and the individual human fulfillment possible through our social structure as influenced by the pressures and strictures of an industrial nation.[4] In oversimplified but rather direct terms, we must ask whether school activity essentially reflects service to democratic ideals and individuals, or service to a monolithic technological social system with all its attendant specialization, depersonalization, and self-serving forces.

McLuhan (10) has a section in one of his latest communications entitled "Education as War." To him the answer to the above question is clear. The educators (including schools) are aggressors who "simply impose upon them [youngsters] the patterns that we find convenient to ourselves and consistent with the available technologies." As a result, we are creating, maintaining, and communicating an environment in schools which is past-oriented and not a meaningful part of the new media environment as the young come to experience it.

In order to impose this we cannot afford to let rational democratic processes operate in schools or allow the unique growth and capacities of individuals to develop. The "generation gap" is more than an age gap, it is essentially a cultural gap.

Roszak (12) characterizes this situation as a compulsion proceeding from the assumption that the young must be made to learn, "as if in truth education were *contra naturam* and required clever strategies." But why this compulsion? Because, he says, the society we live in fears that its culture is not interesting or important to the young. Thus, we must compel the young to learn what we wish them to learn in order to perpetuate the status quo.

That this compulsion goes far beyond the imposition of certain courses and areas of content is clearly revealed by a recent ASCD publication on *The Unstudied Curriculum* (11). The nexus of the effect of teacher expectations on pupil learning, the impact of school philosophy and practice on human development, the secondary consequences of schooling, the socializing function for the middle class, and what is learned about authority and authority relationship is cogently described. It is not difficult to conclude that these are powerful social reinforcers of the compulsion noted earlier.

What we may have to do eventually is to take seriously the position frequently presented by Goodman (6). Goodman not only agrees that the school is a double agent, but it is Goodman's contention that the schools have no real alternative to being repressive

---

[4] See, for example: Hendrick M. Ruitenbeck. *The Individual and the Crowd: A Study of Identity in America.* New York: A Mentor Book, The New American Library, 1964.

and acting out the compulsion to make students learn. The very nature of compulsory education dooms the system. Goodman feels that the total social environment is far more educative than the schools. He is convinced that with the exception of perhaps 15 percent of the young who would choose to attend, the others are being definitely harmed by attending high school and college.

Further, he feels that the attendance of all (or large numbers in college) actually destroys the legitimate functions of schooling, which are the development of a community of scholars and the commitment to the pursuit of academic activities.

The social task of education, he feels, is to make the total environment more educative and responsive to the young rather than to incarcerate the total adolescent population in one location or institution and attempt to "educate" them with an essentially single track curriculum.

Thus, the contention that the school is a double agent and that this duplicity is negative and destructive to the young is agreed upon by many critics and concerned observers of the educational scene. Accepting this perception, the question remains whether the reformation of schooling can best proceed from within the institution itself or by enlarging the domain to the broader society. McLuhan and Goodman, for example, would surely take the latter course; whereas many persons involved with the educational establishment can see myriad possibilities of radical improvement from within. One of the interesting aspects of it all is that in the opinion of almost all of these concerned persons the issue is no longer whether or not the traditional school can be adequate, but whether or not schools as we have known them can exist at all as places for productive fulfillment of human potential.

## References

1. W. W. Charters, Jr. "The Social Background of Teaching." *Handbook of Research on Teaching*. Chicago: Rand McNally & Company, 1963. pp. 715-813.

2. Edgar Friedenberg. *Coming of Age in America*. New York: Random House, Inc., 1963.

3. Edgar Friedenberg. *The Dignity of Youth and Other Atavisms*. Boston: Beacon Press, 1965.

4. Erving Goffman. *Asylums*. New York: Anchor Books, Doubleday & Company, Inc., 1961.

5. John Goodlad, Frances M. Klein, and associates. *Behind the Classroom Door*. Worthington, Ohio: Charles A. Jones Publishing Co., 1970.

6. Paul Goodman. *Compulsory Miseducation and the Community of Scholars.* New York: Vintage Books, Random House, Inc., 1966.

7. Paul Goodman. "High School Is Too Much." *Psychology Today* 4 (5): 25ff.; October 1970.

8. Jules Henry. *Culture Against Man.* New York: Random House, Inc., 1963.

9. Philip Jackson and Jacob Getzels. *Creativity and Intelligence.* New York: John Wiley & Sons, Inc., 1962.

10. Marshall McLuhan and Quentin Fiore. *War and Peace in the Global Village.* New York: Bantam Books, 1968.

11. Norman V. Overly, editor. *The Unstudied Curriculum: Its Impact on Children.* Washington, D.C.: Association for Supervision and Curriculum Development, 1970.

12. Theodore Roszak. "Educating *Contra Naturam.*" In: Robert R. Leeper, editor. *A Man for Tomorrow's World.* Washington, D.C.: Association for Supervision and Curriculum Development, 1970. pp. 12-27.

13. Calvin W. Taylor. "A Tentative Description of the Creative Individual." In: Walter Waetjen, editor. *Human Variability and Learning.* Washington, D.C.: Association for Supervision and Curriculum Development, 1961. pp. 62-79.

# 14

## *Alternatives and Innovations*

### THOMAS A. BILLINGS

WEBSTER defines a maelstrom as "a powerful, often violent, whirlpool sucking in objects within a given radius," literally, "a grinding stream." The criticism of the American school system during the past two decades has created a domestic maelstrom which threatens to carry the American schools and much of America's promise to an untimely and tragic grave.

Attacks on the schools come off the press at an alarming rate, increasingly negative, irrational, and strident. Gone is the sense of reason and balance which characterized earlier criticisms—for example, Paul Woodring's *Let's Talk Sense About Our Schools* and James Conant's *The American High School Today*. Polemics and rage, now fashionable—and marketable—have replaced the restrained, concerned, and moderate voices of the past: *Up the Down Staircase, Compulsory Miseducation, The Student as Nigger, The Architecture of Educational Chaos, The Vanishing Adolescent,* and finally *Growing Up Absurd*. In each case, I think, the attacks are readable, marketable, and irresponsible.

Since such attacks have become fashionable, they add still another current to the maelstrom. Certainly the American schools are not all, or even close to what they could or should be, but relentless, negative criticism accompanied by passionate, irrational confrontations threatens to put an end to what is, warts and all, "the last best hope of mankind."

It has been axiomatic among American statesmen and schoolmen—from Thomas Jefferson to John Gardner—that the success of the American experiment in living depends largely on the excellence and vitality and imagination of the nation's educational enterprise. If the schools fail, the society ultimately fails.

## Three Observations

Rather than add to the violent criticism of our schools, or develop a button-bag of educational gimmicks which singly or together would not add up to anything more than a button-bag full of pedagogical tricks, I want to formulate three observations which occurred to me repeatedly as I directed the national Upward Bound program in the Office of Economic Opportunity. Those observations are the following:

1. If the nation's schools are alarmingly inadequate, it may be because we have no "nation's schools," no cohesive and comprehensive federal educational system. Not infrequently our schools are an erratic, willy-nilly, catch-as-catch-can attempt to educate the youth of the nation. The lack of a consistent, cohesive, and comprehensive system of federally supported schools probably results in millions of youthful casualties each year. On the one hand, many of our schools are simply inadequate; on the other hand, many are irrelevant. Youngsters graduating from inadequate schools are undereducated; those graduating from irrelevant schools are miseducated.

2. A system of federally supported schools—kindergarten through the graduate school—would be just as tenable, certainly as fruitful, as the system of superhighways which now connects all parts of the nation in one vast network of well-planned, well-constructed, well-maintained thoroughfares. The nation needs a system of high quality schools as much as it needs a system of high quality roads; our immediate and future needs require a comprehensive system of schools in which quality control can be maintained from region to region, state to state, community to community, so that a child entering school in Shreveport or Birmingham or Little Rock or Sacramento or Seattle or Minneapolis or New York or Armpit, Nevada, will have education of high quality immediately available to him and, upon moving, be quickly reenrolled in schools of equal excellence. In such schools, initiated and financed by the federal government, quality control would be the joint responsibility of the state school officers and the U.S. Commissioner of Education.

3. Most of us would agree that the nation's superhighways give testimony to the genius of the American people. They are one of the most artful and functional products of American technology, industry, and labor as well as a great national asset. The initiative

for their development came from two segments of the private sector: the automotive and oil industries. Whatever the motive (probably at worst enlightened self-interest), the product of their initiative is of enormous value to the nation. A system of federal schools could be a comparable addition to the nation's wealth and strength. Many gnawing domestic problems might immediately be relieved and finally resolved if such a system of schools were made available.

## Basic Questions

Obviously the three observations give rise to several serious questions. These questions are of two orders: (a) political questions regarding the historic relationship of the federal and state governments concerning the function of each in the education of American youth; and ancillary questions regarding the curriculum, staffing, and quality control of the schools once they are in place; (b) a second order of questions concerning the logistical and fiscal requirements of a comprehensive system of schools, in terms of both initial outlay and sustained operating costs calculated on the basis of a dozen ever-changing economic and social factors. Responses to the second order of questions would be a demographer's delight, more amenable to hard, statistical conjecture and projection than are questions of the first order. (This is not to suggest that the science of demography has reached a level of precision equal to astrophysics, but that it has sufficient sophistication of method to grapple with questions of national educational need with something approaching competence.)[1]

The political questions embedded in a plan for a federal system of schools are tough and durable, more easily identified than resolved. First among such questions is one of jurisdiction. The question is usually: What about the historic (perhaps Constitutional) jurisdiction of the states in educational matters? Has it not been the American tradition to leave the education of the young to the several states, with little or no federal involvement?

Of course, the answer to that is "Yes, the education of the young has been left to the states." Not because the Constitution

[1] For example, the National Assessment of Education, as conceived by Ralph W. Tyler and others with Carnegie support. This program is aimed at determining, comparatively, the levels of achievement region by region, class by class, and age group by age group throughout the United States.

assigned the task to the states, but because the Constitution was strangely silent about the matter. Hence, education became the states' jurisdiction.

Yet an ambiguous principle of jurisdiction should not be sustained if the principle, in effect, results in a staggering number of youthful casualties each year. Highway construction was left to the states until the need for a comprehensive system of highways which would serve all the states and all the citizens became acute and clear. Hopefully, a new and viable principle of federal-state relationships could be formulated which would permit the development of the federal system of schools while safeguarding desirable local and state educational priorities and pluralisms. In the best sense, this new principle might be called "creative federalism." Designing the elements of this new relationship would necessarily involve educators, political scientists, jurists, political and civic leaders.

A second major question would be the nature and purpose of the curriculum. I am confident that the creation of a federal system of schools would trigger bitter criticism from those who suffer a chronic fear of any consolidation and centralization. These durable educational anarchists would see in a national school system an insidious conspiracy in support of a "political" curriculum and an escalation of "political control" of education. That education has been under the political control of the states for the past 100 years does not alarm them; it is "federal control" they fear. Horace Mann spent much of his time as the nation's first superintendent of public instruction fighting this general war against educational and social anarchy. Horace Mann won the battle for public education at the local and state level, but I am confident that much the same war must be fought for a federal system of public schools.

A third major question will be one of preparing faculties and staffing a system of super-schools. That we are in no way equipped for such a task is painfully clear. A markedly streamlined and upgraded program for the preparation of teachers would be necessary as we begin to build the kind of comprehensive system the nation needs. And, of course, the nature and purposes of the federal schools would in large measure determine the elements of the professional preparation of our teachers. About this matter I have a serious tangential comment: the American secondary school has traditionally suffered from an ambiguous mission—whether to prepare youth for college, for skilled employment, for service employment, for the great society, or for what? In the ambiguity of their mission many if not most of the nation's high schools have failed to serve any of their possible purposes well. Or, if they concentrated on one set of objectives, it was usually at the expense of half to three quarters of the students in attendance.

In a federal system of schools, the curricular purposes and programs should be sufficiently diverse to reflect and accommodate the technical, occupational, and professional needs of the nation as well as the interests of the youngsters. That is, in addition to the academically and professionally oriented programs, there should be comprehensive, technical training programs of high quality available as alternatives within the federal system. The campuses need not be separate, but the purposes and thrust of the alternative programs do require a simple and straightforward separation. The mushy mission of the American high school requires immediate and straightforward clarification; a system of federally supported high schools should be built upon a radical redefinition and refinement of this mission.

A fourth major question would be: After we have the physical system in place, the curriculum developed, the faculties prepared, how could we maintain quality and mission control in this comprehensive network of schools?

As a former director of a national education program for disadvantaged youth, responsible for the quality control of federally sponsored programs in each of the 50 states and the territories, I do not view the problem of quality control as hopeless. In a sense, the national Upward Bound program is a microcosm of a comprehensive system of federal schools. Each of the 300 programs was funded on an 80/20 basis by the federal government and the host institutions, most of which were state colleges and universities. Each institution, within the parameters of the national Upward Bound guidelines, was free to develop its own academic program, its own staffing arrangements, its own set of regional priorities, its own style. The clearly stated purpose of the national poverty program was to get high school age youngsters out of poverty via higher education. The host institution could serve this purpose in any way it saw fit.

Quality control was maintained in the program by the recruitment and training of a cadre of site-visitors and monitors who visited each of the federally supported programs periodically for the express purpose of assessing the quality and vitality of each of the 300 projects. Recruitment of monitors was done on a regional basis; educators from the Deep South were prepared to monitor programs in the Deep South; educators from the northeast were prepared to review programs in the northeast; black, Indian, and

Chicano site-visitors generally monitored programs which were predominately of their race or ethnic group. Deliberate efforts were made to attend the deep regional, cultural, and racial pluralisms which characterize the nation in the recruitment of monitors for this federal program. A site-visitor from Boston is often insensitive to the racial and cultural nuances of rural Louisiana and frequently misinterprets a rich and vital approach to human problems of which he sees only the surface. A site-visitor raised in Shreveport may be equally insensitive to the life style characteristic of Boston. Hence, uncommon care was taken in the recruitment and assignment of federal monitors in the Upward Bound program. Sensitivity about this matter paid enormous dividends in good will.

It seems to me that a similar strategy, refined and amplified, could serve as a model for quality control in a system of federal schools. Southerners might well be more receptive to federal schools and federal monitors if they could be certain the monitors were selected from among their own and that they would not be at the mercy of "hot shots from the North," or "bureaucrats" out of Washington. Since most modern nations have extensive quality control programs in operation, the mobilization of a federal task force to observe and analyze such programs would be an early priority in the development of a federal system of schools.

I believe that the nation is sufficiently mature, that there is sufficient cohesion in the American ethos, to permit the development of a school system which will see us into the 21st century with something approaching greatness. If our willy-nilly, catch-as-catch-can approach to this problem continues, the nation runs the very real risk of being swept into the vortex of the social and political maelstrom and sunk into a watery grave. Surely the development of a federal system of schools is as sound an investment in the nation's future as the development of a multi-billion dollar ABM system. My hunch is, if we survive as a nation into the 21st century, our schools will play a larger and more productive part in our survival than will our everywhere-pervasive, staggeringly expensive, singularly negative "defense system." The nation's final defense is a well trained, well educated, and humane people.

## The Advantages in a Federal System of Schools

1. A federal system of schools, once in place, would permit the nation to provide education of high quality and consequently equality of access and opportunity to every American youngster.

Since the fates have arranged profound differences of talent and ability, a federal system of schools could not overcome the mysterious outcomes of these ancient inequities. Yet such a system of schools could overcome all those inequities which are not the product of fate but are the product of human greed, ignorance, apathy, and racism. Equality of educational opportunity is the necessary first step toward equality of opportunity in the social, economic, and political life of the nation for all of our people.

2. In his inaugural address as the 37th President of the United States, Mr. Nixon chose as the theme of his administration a plea that he had seen on a sign during the campaign. The sign read—"Bring Us Together." The President pledged his administration to an attempt to take us "forward together." My experiences suggest to me that there is no more powerful or productive way to unite and revitalize a people than by uniting and revitalizing their schools. A sustained and comprehensive attempt to modernize, streamline, and revitalize the nation's educational enterprise is one of the best ways—indeed, perhaps the only way—Mr. Nixon can take us "forward together."

The brilliant record of Terry Sanford as governor of North Carolina is remarkable because he gave the state's educational enterprise top priority during his tenure as governor. A comprehensive plan for educational excellence was developed and the Governor marshaled the political and economic will of the people in support of it. As a result, North Carolina's schools were greatly improved. Is there any reason that the chief executive officer of the nation could not achieve a similar success on a national scale? Could not a comprehensive plan for a federal system of schools be developed and the national will marshaled in support of it? In the absence of some such plan, and in the feeble light of past and present federal leadership, our schools and perhaps the nation drift along toward the great domestic maelstrom.

3. A federal system of schools would permit the continuous, efficient upgrading and deployment of the nation's educational resources. The already established, federally supported Regional Educational Laboratories, now generally irrelevant in the educational jungle, might, in a comprehensive federal system of schools, come into their own. The regional laboratories would become the regional switching stations, generators of revitalization, experimentation, and reform, the cloverleaves of the nation's educational enterprise.

The directors of the regional laboratories would become, if not by title at least by function, assistant commissioners of education, responsible for the effective management of the region's educational life, responsible for identifying, articulating, and safeguarding the necessary and desirable pluralisms embedded in the region. In a federal system of schools, regional laboratories would be responsible for the education-employment interface; for the development and coordination of teacher preparation programs; for the effective deployment and utilization of educational technology; for demographic projections to be used as a basis for congressional priorities and appropriations; for sustained experiments in how best to solve regional and national educational problems.

4. A federal system of schools would facilitate an equitable distribution of the costs of education on a national basis. The current paradox in which areas of greatest educational need are least able to meet those needs would be relieved by the federal system; an unhealthy regional economic base would not result in inadequate schools and crippled life options for youngsters as is currently the case. Although there are several factors involved in Mississippi's inadequate educational enterprise, the state's economic plight at present may be responsible for most of the educational—and perhaps social and racial—problems of the area. Until such economic plight is relieved, we can expect a dreary repetition of social and racial tragedies. Only sustained federal involvement can relieve the situation. Those who wait on American industry for relief are "whistling Dixie." Industry will be attracted to the South, perhaps, but only after a highly skilled, educated work force is made available. A federal system of schools would accomplish just that; and one of America's more durable woes would vanish.

5. If there is a connection between education and employment and lack of education and unemployment, between skill and affluence, ignorance and poverty, then a comprehensive system of federal schools would eventually put an end to poverty. The millions currently unemployed in the nation are, for the most part, unemployed because they are unemployable; they are adrift in America's industrial society, without skill, without training, without hope. The decade of the sixties is, in some respects, the decade of the disadvantaged, a savage and explosive period, a sustained and forlorn and ominous cry from the human slag heap which has developed at the margin of our affluence and our apathy. No sooner were voices raised in protest than they were silenced by rifle fire, first in

New York, then in Dallas, then in Los Angeles, finally in Memphis: Malcolm X, John Kennedy, Robert Kennedy, and Martin Luther King.

6. A federal system of schools would create a markedly expanded reservoir of trained manpower for the nation's expanding technical, vocational, and professional workforce. As we confront our staggering ecological problems, as we attempt to restore the broken balances of nature, as we attempt to reclaim our rivers, our air, our lakes, our oceans, our cities, and each other, we will have need of all our human resources of body, mind, and spirit. In a recent address, President Nixon, discussing the urgency of our domestic problems, announced flatly: "It is now or never." Who would argue with that? It is always now or never. But in the great chain of human history, it may have fallen to this generation—and to this generation of Americans—to take a giant step for mankind. Federalizing our schools will not save us from all evils, foreign and domestic, but it may well help make us worth saving.

Briefly then, the reasons for federalizing our schools are:

1. To provide relief from persistent geographical inequities
2. To allow for mobility without inequity
3. To facilitate the free flow of ideas
4. To expand and equalize the tax base
5. To effect economies in building, purchasing, etc.
6. To remove curriculum from narrow parochialism without destroying useful pluralism
7. To accommodate the range of student abilities and interests by broadening the base and diversifying the mission of our schools.

## Arguments Against a Federal System of Schools

Probably one argument against such a system would be that federalizing our schools will centralize policy and programs, making them more remote and insensitive to local and regional concerns. This argument is valid only if the federal plan neglects strategies to ensure against federal insensitivity, or fails to develop local safeguards to protect against overcentralization. Media technology alone is an ever-present safeguard against federal remoteness. Given the capabilities of modern communication media, there is little reason to believe that federal school officers would be less sensitive to local and regional concerns than present state and local school officers and boards of education.

It could be argued that the local officers, under present circumstances, are in no position to be sensitive to the needs of youngsters; for the most part, they lack the information that sensitivity to those needs requires. In an increasingly mobile society, sensitivity to the needs of youngsters involves sensitivity to forces and changes in the life of the nation. Local school officials operating in the current anarchy are commonly crippled in their efforts to develop comprehensive and relevant programs simply because they lack the information out of which relevant and forward-looking programs must grow. Two major components in the federal system are structural safeguards against remoteness and insensitivity: (a) the regional laboratories; and (b) the cadre of site-visitors and monitors. Keeping the federal system sensitive to local and regional concerns would be among the central functions of both the laboratory staff and the federal monitors. Federal officers would be only as remote as the nearest telephone.

A second argument against federalizing our schools might be that such a move would add more administrators to an educational system already top-heavy with them. This argument is valid only if the federal system failed to revise, modify, and streamline present state and local school jurisdictions. A comprehensive federal system would require a general consolidation of current overlapping jurisdictions; consolidation of districts would greatly reduce present duplication of effort and thus greatly reduce the number of administrative officers. Present duplication of effort accounts for a school system top-heavy with administrators; a consolidation of these efforts should greatly reduce administrative costs.

A third argument against a federal system is that it would center curriculum control in bureaucracies, experts, and others, rather than in the people's elected representatives (that is, school boards). Yet is there any reason to believe that elected boards of education would cease to function in a federal system of schools? Using the national Upward Bound program as an example of a federal system, each local program was required as a matter of policy to have a functioning Community Advisory Council (a school board) for the express purpose of providing the local and national program officers with a continuous sense of local priorities and purposes. Upward Bound Community Advisory Councils were, by policy, to be involved in all dimensions of the program operation—from initial planning to daily management. These local councils, free of the responsibility of generating financial support for the programs, could turn their attention to matters of genuine educational significance. Would not federalizing our schools permit local boards of education to attend the educational needs of youngsters by freeing them of major financial responsibilities which presently have them engaged on a full-time basis? Relieved of the pressure of the annual budget election, local boards of education might well come into their own as policy makers. My hunch is that a federal system of schools would markedly increase the role of the local school board.

An additional argument against federal schools is that it will require more money than is now spent because, to achieve its purposes, the federal program must expand opportunities through new programs and facilities. There is validity, of course, in this argument. Providing high quality education for all American youngsters would require an increase of funds. Yet the American people have, over the past 15 years, committed themselves to that end. At this juncture, the nation is deeply confused about how to reach that end. If a federal system of schools is the best way to achieve our objectives, I am relatively confident that the nation will commit itself to the necessary costs. The concern is about means, not about ends or costs.

A final argument against federal schools may be that this is part of the pie-in-the-sky approach to human problems and assumes that through centralization and more money the schools can get rid of poverty and other conditions produced by numerous factors other than schooling and its quality. A plan for a federal system of schools does assume a close correlation between level of education and economic circumstance. This is the chief assumption underlying the American educational enterprise. It is the Cardinal Principle of the American middle class, and the economic mobility—via education—of the American middle class comes close to a proof of the validity of the principle.

As the nation confronts its serious domestic problems, schoolmen should guard against nostalgia for an agrarian past in which the "little red schoolhouse" was generally adequate in meeting the educational needs of the time. Looking backward to a simpler time is a common human failing when the future seems threatening and uncertain and overwhelmingly complex. Yet a wistful recall of "the little red schoolhouse" is roughly analogous to donning a sturdy pair of walking shoes when our 747 flight is suffering a temporary delay. Nostalgia keeps us from articulating the needs of youth in the last quarter of the century, keeps us from developing a system of schools within which American youth could find themselves, their nation, and their promise, a system of schools equal to the complexity which surrounds them. Those who propose 19th century responses to 20th century problems are irresponsible.

# 15

## Federal, Local, and In-Between

### J. Myron Atkin

EDUCATION of the young is a responsibility of the individual states. The U.S. Constitution makes no provision for explicit involvement by the federal government in educational policy formulation or in running schools for children. Until recently Washington agencies concerned with education (primarily but not exclusively the U.S. Office of Education) restricted themselves largely to surveys of the status of various characteristics of the educational enterprise, such as the number of children in schools at different grade levels and the amount of money spent for education in the separate states. To the extent that such studies influenced educational policy or practice at all, the influence was indirect.

To be sure, there was gradual expansion of the federal role to meet some specific problems. In 1917, the Congress began to provide federal support for the improvement of vocational education. During World War II there had been legislation to aid communities that experienced large influxes of population related to defense activities. In certain selected fields, the federal influence was central—in the education of many Indians, for example, and in the education of children of personnel in the armed forces overseas. But the dimensions of federal involvement in American education are considered in this chapter only insofar as such involvement has affected the thousands of local education authorities within the 50 states— the overwhelming majority of American schools.

Certain aspects of the recent story of federal involvement in educational matters are by now familiar. In the late 1950's, as a direct result of the conclusion by Congressmen that the United States was lagging behind the Soviet Union in its defense posture, legislation was adopted to bolster and expand the teaching of science, mathematics, and foreign language in American elementary and secondary schools. At the same time, increased appropriations were provided for the National Science Foundation, an agency established a few years earlier, to encourage the development of courses in science and mathematics in order to help formulate a curriculum for the more effective education of greater numbers of scientists and engineers. It was clear that the Congress was providing these funds because the members saw schools as crucial in developing the educated personnel needed to support our defense system at an appropriately sophisticated level. The Soviet Union had launched the first artificial space satellite in 1957; we had to catch up. It was also clear that Congressmen did not then see the schools as performing adequately the function of educating scientific and technical personnel.

## Federal Involvement—with Strings Attached

The National Defense Education Act of 1958 made funds available to the states, through the U.S. Office of Education, for the improvement of facilities for science, mathematics, and foreign language instruction. It also provided some funds for teacher education. The National Science Foundation authorizations enabled that organization to support course content improvement projects involving scientists, mathematicians, and teachers in the development of course materials, at both elementary and secondary school levels, that reflected a view of the subject fields more in consonance with the perspectives of professional scientists. Grants were usually made by the National Science Foundation to university scientists who assumed leadership for development of new courses.

While there were restrictions on the use of federal funds at the local level, there was still considerable latitude. While a school district had to use NDEA money for the purchase of materials in selected subject matter fields, there was still a considerable range of choice within those fields. With respect to the new science and mathematics courses developed with the support of the National Science Foundation, the appeal was even more indirect. The prestige and assumed worth of the new courses were expected to provide sufficient impetus for their adoption locally. The federal government could not and did not try to mandate adoption of new curricula.

By the mid-1960's, however, it was no longer as clear to the Congress as it had seemed to be seven years earlier that the primary ailment of American education was the inadequate preparation of future scientists and engineers. By this time American concerns were turning more to problems of poverty and race. Perhaps it was no longer as apparent to the American public that our defense system was in jeopardy. Or it was no longer as clear that the resolution of our defense problems lay so strongly in reorienting elementary and secondary education. Or other priorities seemed more deserving. In any event, the major education legislation of the 1960's, the Elementary and Secondary Education Act of 1965, focused in large measure on improvement of education in urban slums. In fact, it was attentive to the plight of the poor generally. Americans had become appalled by the fact that so many of their children, particularly from poor and black families, were not learning to read or to compute. Their time in school seemed to be wasted—and during a period in our history when we could ill afford to be negligent about poverty or racism. It was decided that federal funds would be used to remedy this situation.

As the 1960's drew to a close, problems of our threatened physical environment began to compete for the attention of the American public with problems of race and poverty. One could detect the beginnings of a strong federal emphasis to improve education in such a manner as to reduce pollution and thereby increase the probability of continued healthy inhabitability of the planet.

Thus for the 15-year period beginning about 1956, federal involvement in elementary and secondary education was a response to crisis, or at least a response to what was perceived as crisis by the Congress. There seems little reason to question the fact that members of Congress were taking the public pulse accurately.

Assuming that our description to this point is reasonably accurate, at least two further inferences might be made. First, the members of Congress may not have felt that the local education authorities, if left to act independently, had the wit to respond to pressing social problems identified by the Congress. Additionally or alternatively, the local authorities did not have the funds to react appropriately.

The latter point, to the extent that it is valid, represents an acknowledgment of the tenuous tax base of American public schools and marks a major development in federal/state relationships. Local education authorities are heavily dependent on the property tax for the support of education beyond the foundational base provided by the individual state governments. As the state governors (and others) point out repeatedly, the federal government takes the lion's share of the American tax dollar. However, the American taxpayer can most readily express his resistance to increased taxes by action at the local level. He often rejects school bond referenda and increased tax rates for local services. How can the schools mount dramatic new efforts in response to emerging social problems if the tax base to continue even existing operations is in jeopardy?

When the distribution of the American tax dollar is reorganized, it is probably inevitable to look toward the federal government for the support needed to meet educational problems. But what are some of the difficulties in relying on Washington?

The style of federal support has been to provide funds for particular programs, rather than to increase the general support level for American schools with the increased funds to be used at the discretion of the local education authorities. The presumption is that the federal government is in the best position to identify problem areas in education, at least national problems, and that local education authorities, to benefit from the new sources of support, must subscribe to the same view of educational priorities. The embattled schools, indeed, have attempted overwhelmingly to make themselves eligible for the new federal money. Perhaps their assessment of educational need corresponds closely to the assessment in the federal government. Or perhaps they are in such strained financial straits that any new dollar is welcomed. Or perhaps there is prestige locally in securing large federal grants. However, if either of the latter two factors is true, there are questions raised about the independence of the local education authorities in asserting their view of educational needs.

## "Inputs" and "Outputs"—and Schools

Problems associated with independence and local initiative are accented by the styles of management that began to permeate the federal government in the 1960's. The Secretary of Defense in the early 1960's, Robert McNamara, introduced certain new managerial techniques in an attempt to rationalize expenditure of the federal dollar, techniques that were based on high-order quantification and detailed description of "inputs" and "outputs." Exactly what investment is being made for what program? And what, precisely, are the results?

The system as applied to the Department of Defense seemed so attractive to President Lyndon Johnson that he decreed in 1965 that systems analysis, planning-programming-budgeting, operations analysis, and similar techniques be utilized in all agencies of the federal government. It became crucial for each agency to describe in concrete terms the objectives for each of its programs, the anticipated results, and the exact cost. Thus, in responding to each newly perceived crisis, objectives for new federally-supported programs had to be identified in unambiguous terms, in a highly operational form, in order for federal authorities, at least in the executive branch, to make a judgment about the desirability of the requested investment.

General support for a reading program became impossible under the new management system. It became essential to identify exactly what the reading program was intended to "produce." Indeed the managerial model implemented in the late 1960's and refined in the Department of Defense was drawn from the business world and the world of the factory. An attempt was made to apply the same types of perspectives to social needs such as the alleviation of poverty and the effective education of young children. It became natural in such a system to embellish the analogy between school and factory, and in such a managerial system the child came to be seen even more as "product" of the educational system.

The characteristics of the "product" came to be described in performance terms. Performance specifications had been utilized in factories that designed automobiles or airplanes. Why not in schools? Exactly what could the child do as a result of his educational experience? In fact, the precise terminology, "performance specifications," began to be used in the planning of educational programs! One began to hear about "performance criteria" or "behavioral objectives," on the apparent assumption that anything a school might do could be described in such short-term operational language.

## Designs for "Accountability"

The model for educational planning was a model drawn from engineering, electronics, and business. Efficiency, "accountability," and "feedback" were guiding principles.

Models for curriculum design that are most compatible with this particular conceptualization of the educational change process were identified and elaborated 15 years ago. Ralph Tyler 20 years earlier had articulated such a model. (His work, in turn, was based strongly on the ideas of J. F. Bobbitt and others.) Tyler suggested that the first step in curriculum development is the identification of the objectives in as strong an operational framework as possible. Then the program is developed to meet the objectives. Finally, one evaluates the curriculum based on how well it meets the objectives, just as one evaluates any engineering process by how well the final product meets the initial specifications.

The model was refined intensively in the 1950's and 1960's, usually by task-analytic psychologists who had explicated various theories of behaviorism and their applications in agencies such as the Air Force, wherein they had developed efficient and effective programs for the training of technicians. They did not see the problem of training a radar operator as essentially different from that of teaching science to children. What behaviors are expected of the child after he finishes the program? How can we engineer the learning sequences to inculcate these behaviors?

With current demands for "accountability" in the schools, this approach was particularly attractive to many school people because the evaluation problem is so straightforward, at least by comparison with the evaluation task utilizing any other model in which goals are not defined so explicitly. One need only look at the elaborately detailed pre-specifications for the curriculum and assess how well the final product meets the initial aim. And since the specifications for the final product, the initial "behavioral objectives," are detailed so clearly, the evaluator knows exactly what he needs to attend to in his final assessment. In this production-line model of education, the emphasis is on the replicable and the highly quantifiable, the readily describable and the unambiguous.

It is possible and even plausible to claim that the managerial techniques imposed throughout the federal structure starting in the mid-1960's are appropriate for managing large enterprises if the public is to exercise policy control. In addition, it might be claimed that the level of talent required to apply these techniques with discernment and intelligence exceeded the level of talent of the individuals typically attracted to a governmental agency such as the Office of Education. It is in fact the case that the Office of Education was a minor agency until the late 1950's and that relatively few outstanding professionals were apparently attracted to employment there. With dramatic increases in funding through the Office of Education that began in the late 1950's, the agency had to grow exponentially at top policy levels, managerial levels, and below. It is quite likely that the McNamara-fostered techniques were applied mechanically and without sensitivity by individuals who were not equal to the task.

Whatever the case, it is possible to view federal support of American education between 1958 and 1970 as a mixed blessing.

Because of weak local tax bases, schools could not always obtain funds needed for new enterprises, and the federal dollar was welcomed.

On the other hand, the restrictive use of federal money may have exerted a long-term debilitating effect on the schools in accenting uniformity and depersonalization.

Not the least of the problems associated with federal support in the form that evolved during the 1960's is, as suggested earlier, the fickle quality of the funding. The American people do not tend to focus upon a single crisis for a long period of time. Therefore, the federal perception of social need tends to fluctuate rapidly. During one Congress, new funds are provided for elitist educational programs. During a succeeding Congress, funds for that program are phased out and a new program for the "disadvantaged" is identified. Such a funding procedure makes long-term planning at the local level impossible.

In our system of government, there is the recurring question of our ability to plan for the long term. Presidents are elected for four years, representatives for two, senators for six. Historically, it has often been the senators who have tried to take the longest view of the future. However, in a dynamic period, one in which social values are shifting rapidly, long-term planning becomes difficult in any social sphere at the federal level, and education is no exception.

While change is needed in our various social policies, including educational policies, predictability and stability are needed as well. Perhaps an educational system in which planning consists primarily of crisis management on a short-term basis is a system doomed never to meet adequately any crucial social issue.

The problems of federal/state relations in education reflect some of the crucial issues in the American form of government wherein education, by law, is primarily a responsibility of the individual states. For example, it may be seen legitimately as a federal problem that identifiable segments of the population are penalized by certain features of the organization of local educational systems. As in the U.S. Supreme Court decision of 1954, it may be recognized that racial isolation in and of itself leads to unequal treatment of the races.

The federal government may decree racial mixing. But when policy formulation goes beyond protection of individual rights, federal authority is less clear and there is considerable room for discovery of the appropriate relationship between federal and state agencies.

## Impetus for Change

Observers of schools abroad are sometimes struck by the fact that the decentralization of educational authority in the United States has not resulted in much greater diversity than one finds in the highly centralized educational system of countries like Sweden and Norway. It is usually a shock to Europeans to learn that one can have, legally, a highly decentralized system with 50 major responsible authorities and thousands of smaller authorities in a huge country, and yet have a high degree of uniformity. The reasons are not apparent, and they certainly are not all attributable to a heavy federal hand, which, after all, is fairly recent and still of limited impact. Are the schools in the United States so similar because we as a people largely share the same kinds of educational aspirations? Perhaps. Is it because our models of success are limited? Perhaps. Is it because our educational administrators see themselves largely as managers rather than innovative leaders? Perhaps. Are we somehow a more conforming people than others, so that we tend to construct identical social structures in communities that differ widely geographically and socially? Perhaps.

Possibly it is futile to plan for federal/state relationships that foster independence, but there is evidence that such relationships are possible, at least in some countries abroad. Many observers are impressed with the decentralization and the independence to be found, for example, in the United Kingdom. At present, in Britain, there is something of a revolution in primary education, with strong moves toward "openness" and flexibility. About one-third of the infant schools (schools for children five to seven years old) reflect this trend. Another third are still quite formal. The responsibility for change rests on the local level, and on the various headmasters.

There are some pressures for change fostered by the central government through the Department of Education and Science. And Her Majesty's Inspectors are an influential group. These influences, however, are relatively soft and indirect. Hundreds of schools in Britain are unaffected by the movement. The local administrators are firmly independent, by tradition if not clearly by law, of external pressures of all kinds. They are even relatively independent of chief education officers and of parents.

Perhaps it is possible in the United States to build a federal role that capitalizes on local initiative, one that may even recognize the primacy of the individual teacher. Perhaps the American public is coming more to value individual assertiveness and expression and so will tolerate such local independence. It may be possible to build a style of federal and state relationships that places high priority on working cooperatively with individuals in local education rather than around them. It has often been the federal posture, usually implied but sometimes explicit, that administrators at the local level are of limited capability, and it is necessary to affirm greater federal wisdom. Yet it is unlikely that significant change ever takes place in the public schools that is not based on recognition of the values held at the local level by the school principal and the classroom teachers.

Dramatic local initiatives may not be taken until a new breed of local educational leaders begins to emerge, leaders that command attention to their independent ideas because of the quality of their thought and the forcefulness of their advocacy.

It seems probable that U.S. "linear" models of educational change, models which largely have been utilized by the federal government, are faulty. Such models assume that change patterns are designed by some group and then "disseminated" and "diffused" through the local education authorities. These models insufficiently capitalize upon the insights of those in closest contact with the children, the teachers and the local administrators. The United Kingdom offers an example of locally initiated innovation, with central governmental agencies serving partly to improve the network for exchange of ideas among talented and inventive individuals who are trying to adapt the local educational system to meet local educational problems. Central government figures inject their own ideas for consideration by teachers and headmasters, but mandate practically nothing.

The entire question of educational change and how it takes place has been examined only minimally in any country. There are few models that are so clear with respect to their worth that they demand adoption. This is a field in which considerable study is still required, both to examine existing patterns in educational systems around the world and also to underscore some of the assumptions underlying each pattern.

The local-versus-central impetus-for-change question has been a recurring theme in the history of the United States. Sometimes legislation is required to produce change. Sometimes new and respected norms are established without legislation. Education is an expression of social policy. As such the politicians as well as professionals have a role in the determination of educational policy and practice in this complex arena. But to use the authority and power in a fashion that enhances rather than limits the options open to the individual requires that the nation be vigilant to counteract pressures for uniformity and indoctrination. It is not at all clear that our traditions will be sufficient to enable us to be so vigilant.

# 16

## Does the Common School Have a Chance?

### Vernon F. Haubrich

THE reality of today's schools beclouds the hopes, aspirations, and dreams of many students and parents, and those of thousands of teachers and administrators who are searching for "a better way." It seems that the goal of the American Common School embracing ideals of an enlightened citizenry, "preventing poverty," [1] offering social mobility, and affording intellectual curiosity is in grave danger. While the holding power of the school has increased dramatically over the past 50 years,[2] it is apparent that this achievement of custodial care of the young has been a mixed blessing. While universal schooling for 12 years may seem to be the ultimate in achievement, the business of grade advancement has not necessarily been associated with equally dramatic advances in literacy, competencies, or self-esteem.[3]

---

[1] Horace Mann's comment on education as preventing poverty and being "the balance wheel of the social machinery" is contained in his Twelfth Annual Report (1848) to the State Board of Education of the State of Massachusetts.

[2] Robert A. Dentler. "Dropouts, Automation, and the Cities." *Teachers College Record* 65 (6): 475-83; March 1964. Dentler notes "a pattern of eight decades of increasing levels of school retention, with a dramatic shift from a likelihood of .80 withdrawal from high school to a likelihood of .80 of graduation." He estimates a "more or less permanent dropout rate" at about .15 percent by 1975.

[3] Because students are held in school does not mean they progress in reading. See, for example: Eleanor B. Sheldon and Raymond A. Glazier. *Pupils and Schools in New York City*. New York: Russell Sage Foundation, 1965. In fact, what happens is that some fall progressively further behind.

Many critics [4] of today's schools feel that the state of dependency engendered by the institutionalization of education is one of the chief drawbacks to compulsory schooling. They hold that this institution should be abolished in favor of alternatives arrived at through local initiative emphasizing education and learning. One critic of the schools suggests, in the face of more than a century of efforts for the establishment of compulsory schooling, a bill of rights for children which would include "the state shall make no law with respect to the establishment of education." [5]

For those who have long fought to make class lines less restrictive, who have progressed up the socioeconomic ladder, who have found the school a place where intellectual activity and basic skills were taught and practiced, the words of the so-called "new romantics" seem to indicate a betrayal of one's own history.

## Why the Impasse?

What then are the circumstances by which we came to such an impasse over teaching, schooling, curriculum, and administration? What are the constraints which have operated and are operating in schools either to retard or to block reform? What are the chances for the survival of the Common School now beleaguered by critics on all sides?

How did we come to where we are? This question has been documented by historians of the Common School,[6] by scholars of secondary school development,[7] and by critical observers [8] of the con-

---

[4] See the works of some of the new critics: Ivan Illich; Paul Lauter and Florence Howe; Edgar Z. Friedenberg; Jonathon Kozol; and Paul Goodman. Illich is especially critical of compulsory schooling in his article: "Why We Must Abolish Schooling." *New York Review of Books,* May 1970.

[5] Ivan Illich, *ibid.,* p. 11.

[6] See, for example: Lawrence A. Cremin. *The American Common School, an Historic Conception.* New York: Bureau of Publications, Teachers College, Columbia University, 1951.

[7] Edward Krug. *The Shaping of the American High School.* New York: Harper & Row, Publishers, 1964. This is the leading work in the field.

[8] Kenneth B. Clark. *Dark Ghetto.* New York: Harper & Row, 1965—documents the issue of social class and race in an urban ghetto. Patricia Cayo Sexton. *Education and Income.* New York: Viking Press, 1961—remains one of the best documents linking the quality of schooling with family income. Jules Henry. *Culture Against Man.* New York: Random House, 1963—presents a general critique from an anthropological standpoint. See also: Thomas Szasz. *The Myth of Mental Illness.* New York: Harper & Row, 1961—reviews aspects of mental health applicable to the ideology of schooling.

temporary scene. What we can do here is to indicate some critical factors in the growth of large scale school systems and the increasing depersonalization of schooling. Among the first factors which must be taken into account is the tendency on the part of educators toward a middle class view of behavior, criteria of success, and perceptions of social differences.[9]

The social origins of the teacher have grown increasingly heterogeneous, since the profession has remained one of the relatively easy roads to professional status open to daughters and some sons of the working class. These social origins have, in the past, largely conditioned the outlook, the demeanor, and the expectations of those who teach, administer, and control the system of schooling. This is *not* to disparage such an outlook or disposition, but only to record that teachers do not come to the classroom as neutral agents, open to all suggestions, languages, behaviors, and values. Teachers are part of a larger culture in which survival in school is heavily dependent upon the ability to gain acceptance within the culture of the teachers and administrators, which emphasizes certain basic outlooks and dispositions.[10]

A recitation of these dispositions has been documented by others,[11] but let us note here some of the more salient of these factors. First, a basic commitment to the competitive ethic dominates much of what teachers believe and the way in which schools are organized.

Second, the teacher has learned to plan for the future and to prize the concept of time ("Time is money!"). Concomitantly, tests and testing reinforce the notion of tomorrow's planning; once time is *lost* we can never regain it.

Third, the value of work is emphasized by teachers as a good unto itself. "Work makes lift sweet," goes a European adage, and so it is in many classrooms.

Fourth, the teacher has learned the system of success, for he is part of the group that has survived dropouts, push outs, or those who choose not to become involved at all. This system of success operates inexorably to maintain a system of grading, testing, mark-

[9] Robert J. Havighurst and Bernice L. Neugarten. *Society and Education.* New York: Allyn and Bacon, Inc., 1962. pp. 459-76.

[10] *Ibid.*

[11] See, for example: Robert S. Lynd and Helen M. Lynd. *Middletown.* New York: Harcourt, Brace & World, Inc., 1937. A more recent work: Joseph A. Kahl. *The American Class Structure.* New York: Harcourt, Brace & World, Inc., 1957.

ing, sorting, and classifying which still remains intact, alive, and healthy today.[12]

The reinforcement of these basic dispositions exists in the structure of the school system, in its administration, and in its control. Perhaps it is more accurate to indicate that the system of schooling, the basic structure of our industrial, technological society, and the values therein have shaped and molded the dispositions of the teachers and helped to socialize the teacher in his basic role. But the fact remains that the dispositions of teachers, the administrative pattern of schooling, the inductive process which socializes and retains only those teachers who conform, and the reward pattern in career advancement have caused the schools to be headed—skewed—in a particular direction.

## A National System?

In considering the nature of the educational system, some writers [13] have concluded that we have, *de facto,* a national system of education. The evidence which one can muster for this conclusion centers on four basic, though indirect, indices for a national system. These are:

1. There exists a national recruitment of teachers.
2. Students move from school system to school system with little difficulty.
3. Instructional materials enjoy a national market.
4. There is, in effect, a national examination system.[14]

What we are faced with at the start of our analysis is a loose confederation of 22,000 school districts with little difference among them in organization, teaching, curriculum, or means of separation and promotion. The existence of this large scale organization, serviced by supporting and ancillary systems,[15] indicates that the prospect of *local* attempts at innovation and change will suffer at the

---

[12] Paul Lauter and Florence Howe. "How the School System Is Rigged for Failure." *New York Review of Books,* June 1970. This is an excellent review of the tracking and channeling system used in schools.

[13] Sloan R. Wayland. "Structural Features of American Education as Basic Factors in Innovation." Reprinted with permission of the publisher from: Matthew B. Miles, editor. *Innovation in Education.* New York: Teachers College Press, 1964. pp. 587-613.

[14] *Ibid.,* pp. 599-602.

[15] *Ibid.,* pp. 595-96.

hands of a superbly functioning interlocking series of schools, the top of which is the graduate department of the modern university.

This last point is critical, for it is the final step in a hierarchical school system, with great power, influence, and decision making at the top. The selectivity, recruitment, and efficiency which are built into any bureaucratic structure are also part of the system of education in which the interests of the higher group of educators are serviced by those immediately below. Educators in public schools have had training in the college and, often, in the graduate department of a university. The interpenetration of staff, function, and, especially, control over entrance to the graduate departments of a university creates a self-contained and self-perpetuating system. The system is geared to a series of supportive structures which relate to the testing, the time, and the curriculum regularity in the system as a whole.

What we see in this brief analysis is a view of the school system which is clearly bureaucratic in the same sense as defined by Max Weber in 1922. Specialization of function, limited role definition, and an interdependence of various substructures characterize the system of schooling in the United States. One additional factor which causes both a difficulty and a direction should be noted. The enormous turnover of teachers [16] increases the regularity and the rigidity of curriculum, procedures, and induction techniques.

There is an additional finding regarding the "system" of education. The large city school systems seem to develop a sense of climate which is unique to each city.[17] Boston sets forth, based on a unique history and tradition, one kind of organizational climate, while New York City entertains another. A recent study of the New York City system [18]—and there is substantial evidence to adduce that this is not unique to New York City—indicates the enormous power wielded by the "corps of supervisory employees at the headquarters building." The crucial nature of the power was in the area of budget and curriculum, but included other areas of school operation as well.

Again, this study reinforces the point that school systems tend to generate their own bureaucracy, tend to limit the nature and rate of change within the system, tend to function with their ancillary

[16] Martin Haberman's comments in this Yearbook on the dropout rate of teachers confirm this extraordinarily high turnover rate.

[17] See the work of Alan Rosenthal, Rutgers University, on this point.

[18] Marilyn Gittell. *Participants and Participation: A Study of School Policy in New York City.* New York: The Center for Urban Education, 1967.

structures in a national system of education, and tend to create a uniformity of response so as to protect those within the system from those without.

## To Absorb Change

What we have then in this system of education is:

1. A hierarchical system with much power above the level of teaching, but centered most probably on the middle level functionaries

2. An interlock between levels of education, with the graduate school as the capstone of the system [19]

3. A bureaucratic system in which role definition and specialization of purpose tend to place the teacher in the role of functionary rather than autonomous professional

4. A *de facto* national system of education which is linked to several functions and which is supported by a formal system as well as complementary and independent ancillary structures related to testing, accreditation, and promotion to higher levels.

What emerges from this consideration of the system of education in the United States is *an enormous capacity to absorb change while not changing at all.*

The capacity of the system to adopt, modify, accommodate to, and make regularly hundreds of program changes indicates the enormous political power which this informal system can exert. It takes virtually anyone into camp and has, as a consequence, more camp followers than troops.

What has developed in the Common School has been a not-too-common philosophy or outlook. In fact, the interlock of the various bureaucratic components in the school system creates, for particular individuals, enormous obstacles which are often impossible to overcome. Sociologists, putting the matter in terms of cultures, subcultures, etc., have indicated, in many works over the past 25 years, that the schools are organized to promote the interests of those who control them.[20] This control is almost always centered

---

[19] Wayland, *op. cit.*, Chapter 23.

[20] From the earliest works (W. Lloyd Warner, Robert J. Havighurst, and Martin B. Loeb. *Who Shall Be Educated?* New York: Harper & Brothers, 1944.) to the more recent (Theodore Caplow. *The Sociology of Work*. New York: McGraw-Hill Book Company, 1964.), schools seem primarily to represent vehicles for the benefit of those who control their operation.

on middle-class school boards, administrators, and teachers. Such control is carried through by elaborate sorting and tracking devices, and results, for many individuals, in an unequal opportunity to utilize the benefits of schooling.

By itself, this is a powerful indictment of the discriminating power of schools. Yet when this discrimination in school is tied, as it is, to discrimination in the gaining of employment and one's occupational future, then the social role of the school becomes vastly more powerful than anyone ever thought possible.

The *reasons* for the continuing bureaucratization of schools, their resemblance to the factory system, and the ever-present cult of efficiency [21] are not difficult to discover. To do this, one needs only to observe the connection between schooling, status, occupational choices, privilege restrictions, limits in the size of colleges, and the *determination of those who have control to maintain control*. The unfortunate conclusion one must come to is that the Common School, once thought by many to have such a unifying and enlightening function for the entire body politic, has for a substantial period of time (perhaps even longer than we realize) been the handmaiden of power, privilege, and position.

The utter irony of the situation is that the poor actually finance (in proportion to income) the privileges of the well-to-do by tax structures, by regressive sales taxes, and by unequal opportunity for higher education.[22]

Let us grant from the beginning the tendency on the part of parents to want the best for their children. Let us also grant that the competitive ethic can be perverted so as to enhance the chances of one person or group of persons over others. Let us even grant the existence of selective factors when tracking, testing, and offering special classes give institutional support to those of privilege. Given all these incredible advantages, one might hope that those who have all these advantages would at least have the decency to pay for them!

What we are confronted with in this over-bureaucratized, over-specialized, over-polluted, over-administered, and over-debilitated system of schooling is that the circumstances which have led to the

[21] Raymond Callahan. *Education and the Cult of Efficiency*. Chicago: University of Chicago Press, 1962. This excellent work documents the rise of "efficiency" in factory and school in the early 20th century.

[22] Lee Hansen and Burton Weisbrod. *Benefits and Costs of Public Higher Education in California*. Chicago: Markham Publishing Company, 1969.

creation of an unequal school system have also created the barriers and constraints now threatening the very life of the public school.

## The Chances for Survival

Consequently, let me go immediately to my third question. What are the chances for survival of the Common School? If we will but admit one major point—the enormous contradictions between ideals and reality, between the claims of equal opportunity and the existence of inequality of opportunity—then, and only then, can the Common School survive. Survive is not a good word, for it implies that the school as it now exists is what we are all attempting to save. Rather, let us put the question in another way—what are the chances for *reform* of the Common School? For it is only in a reform of the basic purpose of schooling that educators will be able to reestablish those root lines to the source of their authority and commission—the community they serve. And this community is not organization, not bureaucracy, not testing services, not grand curriculum movements, not the federal state, not the pentagon of power,[23] but human beings who have been denied those elemental aspects of learning and schooling which enable man to survive, to expand, to grow, to develop, and to be what he best can become.

The reform of which I speak is the reform which acknowledges and affirms, provides and proclaims, that each child in this land is of inestimable worth to us all, that he has dignity and capacity and potential. That simple declaration of faith—for indeed it is the only faith which justifies the Common School at all—is the absolute beginning of a reform of public schooling. When we realize that schools are made for children and that the democratic ethic carries with it an equal claim on the school by each child, then we can finally understand that it just is not possible for a teacher or administrator to prefer the education of one child to that of another. Children of rich artistic potential, of scholarly bent, of craftsmanlike leanings, of earnest work, of poetic outline, of all the traits and qualities known to man can be beneficiaries of the curriculum of tomorrow. We need a curriculum fashioned by the things people can do—not what they can't; by the potential in their development—not by the inabilities in standardized tests. When we enable these and other qualities of teaching and learning to emerge, we can begin to

---

[23] See: *The New Yorker*, October 31, 1970. p. 98. This is now available in: Lewis Mumford. *The Pentagon of Power.* New York: Harcourt Brace Jovanovich, 1970.

realize that schools can promise warmth, succor, development, and a *gemeinschaft* (a community "based on shared intimacy and interdependence")[24] to children and youth.

Given this basic acknowledgment of inequality on the one hand and a profession dedicated to reform on the other, what are some of the more practical first steps which could be taken by those charged with the education of the young?

Because of the circularity of the problem, it seems wherever we start it is not enough. Indeed, we often act as if the problem were linear and that if we only correct one failure, all else would follow. However, there is another way to go about the problem, and that is to recommit human and material resources at all levels so that the problem is attacked—gestalt-like—as a puzzle which slowly takes form and texture, contour and design. Immediately, reforms suggest themselves on the basis of the analyses made in this volume:

1. A new educator must be prepared. While the schemes vary, new career programs in which the poor and disenfranchised are taken into the workings of the school are urgently in order.[25]

2. A new administrator, with skills centered on political negotiations, building community consensus, and acting in the interests of children (an advocate for children, if you please) can be found and prepared.[26] Sources of talent not usually developed by departments of educational administration must be uncovered in local communities.

3. Schools must be decentralized as quickly as possible. There is no panacea in such schemes except as they touch the need for community—the *mystique* which binds children, adults, and institutions into a place in time where values are caught, and where feelings of mutual cooperation and aid are the rule rather than the exception. In this ideal, the school serves the community by being *of* the

[24] Fred M. Newmann and Donald W. Oliver. "Education and Community." *Harvard Educational Review* 37 (1): 61-106; Winter 1967.

[25] See: Arthur A. Pearl and Frank Riessman. *New Careers for the Poor.* New York: The Free Press, 1965.

[26] An exciting new consortium of programs to prepare leaders in schooling, especially administrators, is being currently undertaken by nine universities with support from the Ford Foundation. These are Atlanta University; University of Chicago; Claremont Graduate School; University of Massachusetts; Ohio State University; University of Pennsylvania; Stanford University; Teachers College, Columbia University; and the University of Wisconsin.

community—not an alien force which imposes teachers, curriculum, and control from the larger technocratic society.

4. Diversity of schools, curriculum, teaching, and organization must become the guide to future development. We must distinguish between diversity of various plans and the lack of purpose in an increasingly bureaucratized society. Diversity of teaching styles and diversity of curriculum do not mean a lack of coherence and purpose; plans can coexist, share outlooks, be characteristic of the same society, and still retain the vital nature of pride in one's difference. Diversity looks to the ideal of Louis Adamic, Horace Kallen, and others, who saw in America not a bland melting pot in which one's identity was lost to the larger society but a nation in which the identity of individuals and groups would be encouraged and preserved for the benefit of all.

5. Equality of opportunity must be encouraged through legal, social, and educational programs which will guarantee to each child equal treatment *at least* in the economic sphere.[27] The vast inequalities between schools, teachers, and programs must be ended. While this is not a plea for sameness, it is a plea for substantial equality in the economic realm. The Association for Supervision and Curriculum Development, the National Education Association, the American Federation of Teachers, and all organizations concerned with the education of children should begin, forthwith, to aid in ending legal and economic barriers to equal opportunity in schools.

6. Schools must become advocates for children. Many children in our society are victims of much abuse, crowded housing, poor diet, inadequate medical care, and discrimination by public agencies. It is time that educators act as agents for children's rights rather than opposing or being "neutral" on the subject. We no longer can afford the luxury of a school system removed from the issues children must face daily.

It seems that the schools of America are vulnerable on all sides. The new critics indicate the "irrelevancy" of schooling, its stale curriculum and factory-like existence. The old critics wait in the wings for the cycle to come around, the pendulum to swing, to bring charges of "softness" and lack of academic rigor.[28] Legislatures

---

[27] The chapter in this Yearbook by Arthur E. Wise and Michael E. Manley-Casimir is instructive on this issue.

[28] Critics such as Arthur Bestor and Admiral Rickover—post Sputnik—can easily begin to renew *their* criticisms, given an appropriate ideological, international, or crisis development.

demand more for their dollars while parents want new programs to aid children or to provide for idiosyncratic desires; representatives of the federal government are in the act and make their own demands, which never seem to hold for more than two or three years, given the yearly nature of federal funding. Pressure seems to grow as the schools become more involved in the politics and economics of everyday life.

In the context of these pressures and demands, it is apparent that the public school as we know it will probably undergo changes of a rather dramatic nature. Implications and predictions are guesses at best, but given the situation today and the history of schools, let us try to piece together a conservative series of these guesses.

1. The pressure for decentralization in large urban areas will continue, and political accommodations will be essential by schoolmen, boards of education, and legislative bodies.

2. A less bureaucratized, smaller school unit seems to be in order. The school as factory and mass processor will not long remain as an agent for intellectual curiosity, social mobility, or self-improvement.

3. The custodial role of schooling must be modified; and more flexible time, curriculum, and work dimensions must be included in the program of schooling.

4. The sorting and tracking process must receive immediate attention from the best minds in the field.[29] Greater efforts to modify the grading system are clearly in order.

5. New teachers, new courses, new teacher aides, and new forms of community involvement are desperately needed by an over-credentialed and over-licensed profession. A far broader consensus than now exists must be built if the school is to survive the 20th century.

6. Agencies outside the control of the public school need to be carefully considered by legislative bodies as alternative means of educating children. These agencies, whether "storefront schools," "street academies," or "community-type schools," have the value of spontaneity, drive, and identity, while needing support and a sense

---

[29] See: Miriam Goldberg and others. *The Effects of Ability Grouping.* New York: Teachers College Press, 1966; and Walter Borg. *An Evaluation of Ability Grouping.* Salt Lake City: Utah State University, 1964. Such studies must be supplemented and extended.

of public responsibility. The melding of those two factors—enthusiasm and localism on the one hand, with a broad public commitment and responsibility on the other, will be the context of much discussion in the next decade. Constitutional questions, questions of tax-support, and the role of the present staff of the public schools will be the forum for the coming debate.

The Common School will survive only as it revises its base of support and extends its range of capabilities. Simply put, those who have not fully shared in the benefits of the Common School must now be included in the planning and the benefits or we all will face the end of the Common School.

# Notes About the Authors

DONALD ARNSTINE is currently Professor of Education at the University of California, Davis. He has taught Philosophy of Education at the University of Kansas City, University of Wisconsin, and Boston University. Dr. Arnstine has published widely in educational and philosophical journals and is the author of *Philosophy of Education* (New York: Harper & Row, Publishers, 1967).

J. MYRON ATKIN is Dean of the College of Education at the University of Illinois, Urbana. Before joining the faculty at Illinois, he was a science teacher and consultant in New York. His interests focus on the need for flexibility in educational practice and planning, and on the formulation of national policy for educational research and development activities.

ERNEST BECKER is Professor of Education at Simon Fraser University in Vancouver, British Columbia. He has taught at the State University of New York, Syracuse University, the University of California at Berkeley, and San Francisco State College. He is the author of several books including *Beyond Alienation: A Philosophy of Education for the Crisis of Democracy* (New York: George Braziller, Inc., 1967) and *The Lost Science of Man* (New York: George Braziller, Inc., 1971).

THOMAS A. BILLINGS is Professor of Education at Western Washington State College, Bellingham. He was a teacher and administrator in the Oregon public schools, and taught at Sacramento State College. On leave of absence from WWSC, he served as National Director of Upward Bound, a project of the U.S. Office of Economic Opportunity.

ANN D. CLARK is a Research Associate in the Center on Mental Retardation and Human Development of the University of Wisconsin, Madison. She has taught regular and special classes in public schools. Prior to joining the staff of the Department of Studies in Behavioral Disabilities, she was Director of Evaluation and Research for Title I in Wisconsin.

WILMER S. CODY is the Superintendent of Schools in Chapel Hill, North Carolina. He has been an elementary school teacher, has served as an elementary principal, and has taught on the faculties of Emory and Atlanta Universities.

LARRY CUBAN is former Director of Staff Development and presently team leader and teacher in the Washington, D.C., Public Schools. He is the author of *To Make a Difference: Teaching in the Inner City* (New York: The Free Press, 1970), *Promise of America*, and *Negro in America* (both Glenview, Illinois: Scott, Foresman and Company, 1970).

AMITAI ETZIONI is currently Professor of Sociology and Chairman of the Department, and is Director of the Center for Policy Research, at Columbia University. He is the author of numerous studies. His latest book is entitled *The Active Society: A Theory of Societal and Political Processes* (New York: The Free Press, 1968).

MARILYN GITTELL is Professor of Political Science and Director of the Institute for Community Studies at Queens College of the City University of New York. She also served as a consultant to the Ford Foundation on urban school problems and school decentralization and was a consultant to the Mayor's Panel on School Decentralization in New York. Among the books she has written is *Participants and Participation: A Study of School Policy in New York City* (New York: Frederick A. Praeger, Inc., 1969); and she is co-editor of *Confrontation at Ocean Hill-Brownsville* and *The Politics of Urban Education* (both New York: Frederick A. Praeger, Inc., 1969).

HARVEY GOLDMAN is Associate Professor in the Department of Educational Administration, Supervision, and Curriculum of the University of Maryland, College Park. His writings have focused on the nature of the principalship, the impact of personality variables on the teacher-administrator relationships, and on the problems of educating urban youth.

MARTIN HABERMAN is presently Professor of Education at the University of Wisconsin, Milwaukee. During the past decade he has been associated with efforts to equalize educational opportunity by preparing more effective teachers.

As a teacher educator, his extensive writing, consultation, and research have contributed to the development and evaluation of some of the more innovative programs. His most recent book, *The Art of Schoolmanship* (St. Louis: Warren H. Green, Inc., 1970), is an attempt to help urban pupils, teachers, and administrators utilize the large school system rather than be exploited by it.

VERNON F. HAUBRICH, the ASCD 1971 Yearbook Committee Chairman, is a Professor in the Department of Educational Policy Studies and a Senior Researcher with the Institute for Research on Poverty at the University of Wisconsin, Madison. Dr. Haubrich has taught in public schools in Wisconsin and Illinois and was a Director of Curriculum at Niles Township High School, Skokie, Illinois.

Dr. Haubrich's college teaching and research have included work at the University of Utah; Hunter College; Teachers College, Columbia University; and Western Washington State College.

HERBERT M. KLIEBARD is currently Professor of Curriculum and Instruction and Educational Policy Studies at the University of Wisconsin, Madison. His major interests are in curriculum and teaching theory, and he is a co-author of *The Language of the Classroom* (New York: Teachers College Press, 1965). Dr. Kliebard is currently pursuing research in metaphorical roots of curriculum theory.

JAMES B. MACDONALD is Chairman of the Department of Curriculum and Instruction and member of the Department of Social and Philosophical Foundations at the University of Wisconsin, Milwaukee. Dr. Macdonald has served on the faculties of the University of Texas at Austin, New York University, and the University of Wisconsin, Madison.

Formerly, he served as Chairman of both ASCD's Research Commission and Publications Committee and is presently a member of the Board of Directors. His writings have been published in a variety of professional journals and he has authored numerous research monographs.

MICHAEL E. MANLEY-CASIMIR is currently working toward a Ph.D. in Educational Administration at the University of Chicago. Before returning to graduate study, Mr. Manley-Casimir was a teacher and administrator in the secondary schools of British Columbia.

JOHN W. M. ROTHNEY is Professor of Counseling and Guidance at the University of Wisconsin, Madison. He has served as a consultant to many public schools, colleges, and organization research projects. Dr. Rothney has authored 12 books, over 80 articles, and many research reports. Most of the books and articles are reports of research.

ARTHUR E. WISE is Associate Dean of the Graduate School of Education, and is Assistant Chairman and Assistant Professor in the Department of Education, of the University of Chicago. Dr. Wise is the author of *Rich Schools, Poor Schools: The Promise of Equal Educational Opportunity* (Chicago: University of Chicago Press, 1968).

# ASCD 1971 Yearbook Committee Members

VERNON F. HAUBRICH, *Chairman and Editor;* Professor of Educational Policy Studies, School of Education, University of Wisconsin, Madison

VERNON E. ANDERSON, Professor of Education, College of Education, University of Maryland, College Park

WILMER S. CODY, Superintendent of Schools, Chapel Hill, North Carolina

HARVEY GOLDMAN, Associate Professor of Educational Administration, College of Education, University of Maryland, College Park

MARY ELLEN PERKINS, Associate Director of Teacher Education, Georgia State Department of Education, Atlanta

# ASCD Board of Directors
## As of November 1, 1970

### Executive Council, 1970-71

*President:* John D. Greene, Director of Instruction, Baton Rouge Public Schools, La.

*President-Elect:* Alvin D. Loving, Sr., Assistant Dean, School of Education, University of Michigan, Ann Arbor

*Immediate Past President:* Alexander Frazier, Professor of Education, The Ohio State University, Columbus

Joyce Cooper, Professor of Education, University of Florida, Gainesville

O. L. Davis, Jr., Professor of Curriculum and Instruction, The University of Texas at Austin

Delmo Della-Dora, Office of School Decentralization, Detroit Public Schools, Mich.

Ronald C. Doll, Professor of Education, Richmond College, The City University of New York, N.Y.

Minnie H. Fields, Consultant in Elementary Education, Florida State Department of Education, Tallahassee

Barbara Hartsig, Director of Elementary Education, California State College, Fullerton

Frances R. Link, Curriculum Development Associates, Washington, D.C. (on leave from Cheltenham Public Schools, Pa.)

John U. Michaelis, Professor of Education, University of California, Berkeley

Audrey Norris, Tomorrow's Educational Systems Today, Cincinnati, Ohio

Glenys G. Unruh, Assistant Superintendent for Curriculum and Instruction, University City Public Schools, Mo.

## Board Members Elected at Large

Mitsuo Adachi, Arizona State University, Tempe (1974); Paul M. Allen, University of Arizona, Tucson (1972); Robert H. Anderson, Harvard University, Cambridge, Mass. (1971); Louise M. Berman, University of Maryland, College Park (1974); O. L. Davis, Jr., University of Texas, Austin (1973); Marie Fielder, University of California, Berkeley (1974); Richard L. Foster, Berkeley Unified School District, Calif. (1974); Jack R. Frymier, The Ohio State University, Columbus (1972); Barbara Hartsig, California State College, Fullerton (1971); Dwayne Huebner, Columbia University, N.Y. (1972); Daisy M. Jones, Arizona State University, Tempe (1973); Frances R. Link, Curriculum Development Associates, Washington, D.C. (on leave from Cheltenham Public Schools, Pa.) (1973); James B. Macdonald, University of Wisconsin, Milwaukee (1974); John U. Michaelis, University of California, Berkeley (1972); Edward G. Ponder, New York University, N.Y. (1971); J. Richard Suchman, Palo Alto, Calif. (1971); Dwight Teel, Milwaukee Public Schools, Wis. (1973); Glenys G. Unruh, University City Public Schools, Mo. (1971); Jeff West, Dade County Public Schools, Miami Springs, Fla. (1973); Margaret S. Woods, Seattle Pacific College, Wash. (1972).

## Unit Representatives to the Board

(The Unit Presidents are listed first; others follow in alphabetical order.)

*Alabama:* Bernice Dilworth, Madison County Schools, Huntsville; Tessie O. Nixon, Bullock County Schools, Union Springs; Wilma M. Scrivner, Mobile.

*Arizona:* Mary T. Rill, Public Schools, Phoenix; Bruce Howard, University of Arizona, Tucson; James J. Jelinek, Arizona State University, Tempe.

*Arkansas:* Leon Hardin, Southern State College, Magnolia; Maurice Dunn, Public Schools, Hot Springs.

*California:* Ray Arveson, Hayward Unified School District, Hayward; Edward W. Beaubier, CESAA Project on Evaluation, Long Beach; Arthur Costa, Sacramento County Schools, Sacramento; John Huffman, San Diego County Schools, San Diego; Helen James, Los Angeles; Don Russell, Concord; Burton C. Tiffany, Chula Vista.

*Colorado:* S. J. Alioto, Aurora; Louise Corwin, Englewood; Doris Molbert, University of Denver, Denver.

*Delaware:* Charlotte Taylor, Newark School District, Newark; Melville F. Warren, Dover.

*District of Columbia:* Lorraine Whitlock, D.C. Public Schools; Bessie D. Etheridge, D.C. Public Schools; Octavia Webb, D.C. Public Schools.

*Florida:* Joseph W. Crenshaw, Department of Education, Tallahassee; Marian W. Black, Florida State University, Tallahassee; Charlie T. Council, Florida Atlantic University, Boca Raton; Pauline Hilliard, University of Florida, Gainesville; Glenn Thomas, Public Schools, Miami.

*Georgia:* Martha Sue Jordan, University of Georgia, Athens; Alice Arden, Chatham County Schools, Savannah; Emmett Lee, Clayton County Schools, Jonesboro; Susie Wheeler, Cartersville.

*Hawaii:* Elsie Hu, Leeward Oahu District, Waipahu; Robert Laird, The Church College of Hawaii, Laie; Oei Maehara, Honolulu District Office, Honolulu.

*Idaho:* Ray Reid, Cassia County Schools, Burley; Parker Richards, School District 25, Pocatello.

*Illinois:* Donald W. Nylin, Aurora West School District, Aurora; Margaret Carroll, Northern Illinois University, DeKalb; Reuben Conrad, Township High School District 214, Mt. Prospect; Lillian Davies, Illinois State University, Normal; Earl Dieken, Public Schools, Glen Ellyn; Raymond E. Hendee, Board of Education, District 41, Glen Ellyn; Eugene T. Swierczewski, Lake Park Community High School, Medinah.

*Indiana:* Ruth Hochstetler, Ball State University, Muncie; Charles L. Arvin, Crawfordsville; Jack Humphrey, Evansville; Otto Shipla, Indiana State University, Terre Haute.

*Iowa:* Mrs. Lucretia Story Craw, Ames; Horace Hoover, Dubuque; Elaine Merkeley, Ames.

*Kansas:* Barbara Keating, Public Schools, Wichita; Dean L. Oberhelman, Unified School District 379, Clay Center; Ed Sherraden, Public Schools, Salina.

*Kentucky:* Dorothy Dreisbach, Public Schools, Louisville; Edna Quarles, McCraken County Public Schools, Paducah; Pat Wear, Berea College, Berea.

*Louisiana:* Julianna L. Boudreaux, Public Schools, New Orleans; Edwin H. Friedrich, Public Schools, New Orleans; M. F. Rosenberg, Jr., Public Schools, New Orleans.

*Maryland:* Benjamin P. Ebersole, Baltimore County Board of Education, Towson; Morris McClure, University of Maryland, College Park; Elizabeth McMahon, Public Schools, Upper Marlboro; Richard F. Neville, University of Maryland, College Park.

*Michigan:* Morrel Clute, Wayne State University, Detroit; Barbara Bird, Grand Rapids; Gerald S. DeGrow, Public Schools, Port Huron; Phil Robinson, Public Schools, River Rouge; William F. Young, Board of Education, Dearborn.

*Minnesota:* Ben Rank, Roseville Public Schools, St. Paul; Stanley Gilbertson, Public Schools, Bloomington; Ray Henderson, District 241, Albert Lea.

*Mississippi:* Sale D. Randle, Public Schools, Greenville; R. B. Layton, Public Schools, Jackson.

*Missouri:* Wanda Gray, Public Schools, Springfield; Wilbur C. Elmore, Public Schools, Lebanon; W. Dean Grigsby, St. Charles.

*Montana:* Lyle Eggum, State Department of Education, Helena; Dan F. Sweeney, Public Schools, Butte.

*Nebraska:* Ron Witt, Millard; Gerald Bryant, Grand Island; Dale D. Rathe, Public Schools, Lincoln.

*Nevada:* Rose Bullis, Washoe County School District, Reno; Preston T. Bishop, Clark County School District, Las Vegas.

*New England:* Raymond Houghton, Rhode Island College, Providence; Annabelle Allen, Public Schools, New Canaan, Conn.; Edward G. Hunt, Public Schools, Warwick, R.I.; H. Stuart Pickard, State Department of Education, Concord, N.H.; Villa Quinn, State Department of Education, Augusta, Maine.

*New Jersey:* Sam Maggio, Public Schools, Ridgewood; Robert Chasnoff, Newark State College, Union; Mary Jane Diehl, Monmouth College, West Long Branch; Deborah Wolfe, Queens College, Flushing, N.Y.

*New Mexico:* Patricia Christman, Public Schools, Albuquerque; Wendell Henry, Public Schools, Alamogordo; Chon La Brier, Public Schools, Dulce.

*New York:* George K. McInerney, Public Schools, Jamaica; Lawrence S. Finkel, Public School 115, New York City; George C. Jeffers, State University College, Potsdam; David E. Manly, State University of New York, Geneseo; Milton Michener, Central High School District 1, Valley Stream; Mildred Whittaker, Public Schools, Lancaster.

*North Carolina:* Barbara Day, University of North Carolina, Chapel Hill; Doris Hutchinson, Public Schools, Greensboro; Douglas Jones, East Carolina College, Greenville.

*North Dakota:* Ron Torgeson, Upper Red River Valley Education Service Center, Grand Forks.

*Ohio:* Gary H. Deutschlander, Public Schools, Berea; Robert Boyd, Ohio University, Athens; Lloyd W. Dull, Public Schools, Akron; Anna Freeman, Franklin County Schools, Columbus; Alice Holt, Wood County Schools, Bowling Green; Hugh Morrison, Miami University, Oxford.

*Oklahoma:* Mervel S. Lunn, Public Schools, Oklahoma City; Otis Lawrence, Public Schools, Oklahoma City; Gene Shepherd, University of Oklahoma, Norman.

*Oregon:* Harry Boyd, Public Schools, Ontario; Charline Edwards, Public Schools, Corvallis; Robert E. McKee, Public Schools, Roseburg.

*Pennsylvania:* Frederick Haas, Public Schools, Glenolden; J. Ernest Harrison, Public Schools, Pittsburgh; Margaret McFeaters, Slippery Rock

State College, Slippery Rock; Gerald M. Newton, Public Schools, Beaver; Elwood Prestwood, Public Schools, Gladwyne; Claude P. Swartzbaugh, Jr., Public Schools, Hershey.

*Puerto Rico:* Lydia Diaz de Grana, University of Puerto Rico, Rio Piedras.

*South Carolina:* Lawrence Giles, University of South Carolina, Columbia; Olive C. Bennett, Public Schools, Cayce; Jack Boger, Winthrop College, Rock Hill.

*South Dakota:* Art F. Brooks, Public Schools, Brookings; Orville Pederson, Public Schools, Mitchell.

*Tennessee:* W. Elzie Danley, Memphis State University, Memphis; James Gaddis, Public Schools, Morristown.

*Texas:* Betty Menefee, Houston; Shelma Carlile, Public Schools, Texas City; Ted Edwards, Trinity University, San Antonio; Warren Green, Tyler.

*Utah:* Lee R. Cain, Public Schools, Ogden; Lynn F. Stoddard, Public Schools, Clearfield.

*Virginia:* William J. Hopkins, Public Schools, Sussex; Virginia Benson, Public Schools, Fairfax; Evelyn L. Berry, Public Schools, Petersburg; Gennette Nygard, Public Schools, Arlington.

*Washington:* D'Arcy de Juan, Public Schools, Spokane; Clifton A. Hussey, Public Schools, Spokane; Florence A. Orvik, Pacific Lutheran University, Tacoma.

*West Virginia:* Betty Livengood, Board of Education, Keyser; Lucille Heflebower, Jefferson County Schools, Charles Town; James L. Stone, Wyoming County Schools, Pineville.

*Wisconsin:* Willard J. Brandt, University of Wisconsin, Milwaukee; Harold Anderson, CESA, Madison; William Ernst, State Department of Education, Madison; Donald Tuler, Public Schools, Milwaukee.

*Wyoming:* Millard I. Meredith, Public Schools, Douglas; Laurence A. Walker, University of Wyoming, Laramie.

# ASCD Review Council
## As of November 1, 1970

HAROLD DRUMMOND, *Chairman;* College of Education, University of New Mexico, Albuquerque

WILLIAM M. ALEXANDER, College of Education, University of Florida, Gainesville

JACK R. FRYMIER, College of Education, The Ohio State University, Columbus

M. KARL OPENSHAW, Dean, School of Education, Sacramento State College, Sacramento

WILLIAM VAN TIL, Lotus D. Coffman Distinguished Professor in Education, Indiana State University, Terre Haute

# ASCD Headquarters Staff, 1971

*Executive Secretary*, Fred T. Wilhelms
*Deputy Executive Secretary*, Neil P. Atkins
*Associate Secretary; Editor, ASCD Publications*, Robert R. Leeper
*Associate Secretary*, Richard V. Brown
*Associate Secretary*, Ronald Stodghill
*Administrative Assistant*, Virginia O. Berthy

*Staff Assistants:*

| | |
|---|---|
| Sarah Arlington | Nancy Olson |
| Elizabeth A. Brooks | Mary Albert O'Neill |
| Martha M. Broomhall | Lana Pipes |
| Julita G. Cabel | Gloria Richardson |
| Barbara Collins | Alice H. Sidbery |
| Marie K. Haut | Barbara J. Sims |
| Teola T. Jones | Robert W. Stanley |
| Carvangeline B. Miller | Phyllis E. Stockman |
| Frances Mindel | Lyra M. Viegas |
| Barbara L. Nash | Alison Wells |

# ASCD Publications

(The NEA stock number appears in parentheses after each title.)

**Yearbooks** (clothbound)

| | |
|---|---|
| Balance in the Curriculum  (610-17274) | $4.00 |
| Evaluation as Feedback and Guide  (610-17700) | $6.50 |
| Fostering Mental Health in Our Schools  (610-17256) | $3.00 |
| Guidance in the Curriculum  (610-17266) | $3.75 |
| Individualizing Instruction  (610-17264) | $4.00 |
| Leadership for Improving Instruction (610-17454) | $3.75 |
| Learning and Mental Health in the School  (610-17674) | $5.00 |
| Learning and the Teacher  (610-17270) | $3.75 |
| Life Skills in School and Society  (610-17786) | $5.50 |
| New Insights and the Curriculum  (610-17548) | $5.00 |
| Perceiving, Behaving, Becoming: A New Focus for Education  (610-17278) | $4.50 |
| Research for Curriculum Improvement  (610-17268) | $4.00 |
| Role of Supervisor and Curriculum Director  (610-17624) | $4.50 |
| To Nurture Humaneness: Commitment for the '70's  (610-17810) | $5.75 |
| Youth Education: Problems, Perspectives, Promises  (610-17746) | $5.50 |

**Books and Booklets** (paperbound)

| | |
|---|---|
| Bases for World Understanding and Cooperation: Suggestions for Teaching the Young Child  (611-17834) | $1.00 |
| Better Than Rating  (611-17298) | $1.25 |
| The Changing Curriculum: Mathematics  (611-17724) | $2.00 |
| The Changing Curriculum: Modern Foreign Languages  (611-17764) | $2.00 |
| The Changing Curriculum: Science  (611-17704) | $1.50 |
| Changing Supervision for Changing Times  (611-17802) | $2.00 |
| Children's Social Learning  (611-17326) | $1.75 |
| Cooperative International Education  (611-17344) | $1.50 |
| Criteria for Theories of Instruction  (611-17756) | $2.00 |
| Curriculum Change: Direction and Process  (611-17698) | $2.00 |
| Curriculum Decisions ⟷ Social Realities  (611-17770) | $2.75 |
| A Curriculum for Children  (611-17790) | $2.75 |
| Curriculum Materials 1970  (611-17882) | $2.00 |
| Discipline for Today's Children and Youth  (611-17314) | $1.00 |
| Early Childhood Education Today (611-17766) | $2.00 |
| Educating the Children of the Poor (611-17762) | $2.00 |
| Educating the Young People of the World  (611-17506) | $2.50 |
| Elementary School Mathematics: A Guide to Current Research  (611-17752) | $2.75 |
| Elementary School Science: A Guide to Current Research  (611-17726) | $2.25 |
| Elementary School Social Studies: A Guide to Current Research  (611-17384) | $2.75 |
| The Elementary School We Need  (611-17636) | $1.25 |
| Ethnic Modification of the Curriculum  (611-17832) | $1.00 |
| Freeing Capacity To Learn  (611-17322) | $1.00 |
| Guidelines for Elementary Social Studies  (611-17738) | $1.50 |
| The High School We Need  (611-17312) | $ .50 |
| Human Variability and Learning  (611-17332) | $1.50 |
| The Humanities and the Curriculum  (611-17708) | $2.00 |
| Humanizing Education: The Person in the Process  (611-17722) | $2.25 |
| Humanizing the Secondary School  (611-17780) | $2.75 |
| Hunters Point Redeveloped—A Sixth-Grade Venture  (611-17348) | $2.00 |
| Improving Educational Assessment & An Inventory of Measures of Affective Behavior  (611-17804) | $3.00 |
| Improving Language Arts Instruction Through Research  (611-17560) | $2.75 |
| Influences in Curriculum Change  (611-17730) | $2.25 |
| Intellectual Development: Another Look  (611-17618) | $1.75 |
| The International Dimension of Education  (611-17816) | $2.25 |
| The Junior High School We Need  (611-17338) | $1.00 |
| The Junior High School We Saw  (611-17604) | $1.50 |
| Language and Meaning  (611-17696) | $2.75 |
| Learning More About Learning  (611-17310) | $1.00 |
| Linguistics and the Classroom Teacher  (611-17720) | $2.75 |
| A Man for Tomorrow's World (611-17838) | $2.25 |
| New Curriculum Developments (611-17664) | $1.75 |
| New Dimensions in Learning (611-17336) | $1.50 |
| The New Elementary School (611-17734) | $2.50 |
| Nurturing Individual Potential (611-17606) | $1.50 |
| Personalized Supervision  (611-17680) | $1.75 |
| Strategy for Curriculum Change  (611-17666) | $1.25 |
| Student Unrest: Threat or Promise?  (611-17818) | $2.75 |
| Supervision in Action  (611-17346) | $1.25 |
| Supervision: Emerging Profession  (611-17796) | $5.00 |
| Supervision: Perspectives and Propositions  (611-17732) | $2.00 |
| The Supervisor: Agent for Change in Teaching  (611-17702) | $3.25 |
| The Supervisor: New Demands, New Dimensions  (611-17782) | $2.50 |
| The Supervisor's Role in Negotiation  (611-17798) | $ .75 |
| Theories of Instruction  (611-17668) | $2.00 |
| Toward Professional Maturity  (611-17740) | $1.50 |
| The Unstudied Curriculum: Its Impact on Children  (611-17820) | $2.75 |
| What Are the Sources of the Curriculum?  (611-17522) | $1.50 |
| Child Growth Chart  (618-17442) | $ .25 |

Discounts on quantity orders of same title to single address: 2-9 copies, 10%; 10 or more copies, 20%. All orders must be prepaid except those on official purchase order forms. Shipping and handling charges will be added to billed orders. **The NEA stock number of each publication must be listed when ordering.**

Subscription to **Educational Leadership**—$6.50 a year. ASCD Membership dues: Regular (subscription and yearbook)—$20.00 a year; Comprehensive (includes subscription and yearbook plus other publications issued during period of the membership)—$30.00 a year.

Order from: **Association for Supervision and Curriculum Development, NEA
1201 Sixteenth Street, N.W.    Washington, D.C. 20036**